Handbook

Handbook for College Admissions

A Family Guide

THIRD EDITION

Thomas C. Hayden

**Director of Admissions at Oberlin College
and former Director of College Counseling
at Phillips Exeter Academy**

Peterson's Guides
Princeton, New Jersey

Library of Congress Cataloging-in-Publication Data

Hayden, Thomas C.
      Handbook for college admissions : a family guide / Thomas
C. Hayden. — 3rd ed.
          p.   cm.
      ISBN 0-87866-799-7
      1. Universities and colleges—United States—Admission.
I. Title.
LB2351.2.H38   1989
378.1'056'0973—dc20   89-8544
                                                         CIP

Composition and design by Peterson's Guides

Printed in the United States of America

10 9 8 7 6 5 4 3 2 1

To 4,000 or so Exies and their parents, who taught me as they learned about the college admissions process.

Contents

(continued)

Introduction

This is a book for high school juniors and seniors and their families. It is designed as a guide to the complicated journey called college admission. Although it cannot promise its readers they will gain admission to the college of their choice, it can and does pose the significant questions that families and students should ask themselves as they go through the process. It also offers suggestions for presenting special strengths to college admissions officers and provides many examples of dos and don'ts for applicants and their families. In addition, the book surveys the financial and educational factors to be considered by students when selecting the right college to attend from among those to which they have been admitted. Finally the important topic of making the crucial adjustment to college life is discussed at some length. Planning a program, considering how to make the most of the living arrangements, and acting sensibly during the first critical weeks of college are important to the success of every college student.

As high school students and their families take their first tentative steps toward identifying suitable colleges, they move into a world shrouded in vagueness and mystery. They see before them a number of perplexing myths that this book intends to dispel.

One myth suggests that the more rigorous the admissions standards of an institution, the better the education its students receive. This book argues that the enormous gap between the admissions standards of highly selective colleges and those of other collegiate institutions often bears little relationship to the quality of the undergraduate education.

Another myth that has gained recent ascendancy is that of the "hot college." The more applications an institution receives, the more popular it is, and supposedly the better the quality of the education it offers its students. So runs the hot-college argument. Nonetheless, students and their families will soon discover that there can be a discrepancy between the quality of education at an institution and the number of applications it receives for each available space.

Yet another myth often believed by applicants is that the interview is all-important. Students sometimes think that their interpersonal skills will help offset a mediocre record and that, if only they have a chance to present themselves adequately at the interview, a favorable admission decision will result. This book goes into some detail to explain that by and large admissions decisions are holistic judgments in which a number of factors are considered simultaneously: school record, teacher recommendations, school recommendations, standardized test scores, the student's application, and, in some cases, the impressions of an interviewer.

One of the most misleading myths abroad today concerns the importance of standardized tests. Able and insightful journalists have exposed some of the flaws in the testing process in recent years, but even though the tests have now been shown to be fallible, students still spend too much energy and money taking test preparation courses in hopes of improving their scores and gaining admission to their first-choice college. In doing so, they are running the risk of weakening their non-academic credentials, as well as undercutting their academic performance, by devoting far too much time to test preparation.

Another widely circulated myth holds that the selective-college admissions process does in fact find the best candidates. This is not always the case. Admissions officers are not clairvoyant. The admissions process is a very human one, subject to the weaknesses of our species, to all the errors of omission and commission we see in everyday life. Nonetheless, admissions officers are an ethical and dedicated group, and candidates who adequately present their strengths in their applications as well as in their other credentials can be assured of a fair hearing. Everyone needs to bear in mind that admissions officers do not admit or reject *people,* they admit or reject *applications.*

Finally, there is the myth that the admissions process is totally confusing and cannot be approached through rational analysis. This myth enables candidates and all others who may subscribe to it to rationalize away the real educational opportunity that applying to college can provide. Indulgence in this belief often encourages frivolous or devious behavior; at the least it gives rise to a fruitless cynicism. It is in reaction to this particular myth that this book is written. Students and their families who resolve to move beyond the myth of irrationality have an immense amount to gain from the college application process.

Students who are guided by this book may come to a new appreciation of their talents and their potential, not just for college work itself, but for establishing themselves as worthwhile citizens in the community. In coping with the issues of independence from family and home and departing from the relative security of adolescence, college students can move to a higher appreciation of themselves, their parents, and the enlightening role that education can play in a happy and productive life.

Parents too can benefit from the college admissions process. By treating their children as equals in decision making and planning, by crediting behavior and ideas that are new and different, and by sharing the values and experiences they have accumulated in the course of a lifetime, they can form the basis of an adult relationship with their children.

Both parents and young people dealing with the insights offered by this book have an opportunity to discuss important values, both educational and moral. As students progress through the admissions process, the challenges to their identity, as well as to the traditions of their particular family, become clear. Both students and their families have to consider seriously just how much they wish to transform themselves in order to meet the demands of the college admissions process. They will need to look for and respond to the positive cues in the process and allow spontaneity as well as ambitious planning to play their respective parts in the scheme of things. All in all, it should be an extremely interesting process for those who wish to give themselves over to it, learning as they move along.

Notwithstanding the broad educational experience of college admissions condensed within these pages, this is a personal book. I have attempted to distill my own experience and that of my students into a coherent and readable form. I have tried to write the text from the candidate's point of view in order to reach those who want to make the most of the student's abilities and help that student identify and gain admission to the college or university where those abilities will be challenged and brought to their full potential. This book contains much practical information for students motivated by the traditional American ideals of self-help, hard work, and service to society.

The advice in this book derives from a decade of observation of a particularly talented group of students coming to grips with the vagaries and eccentricities of the college admissions process. It also stems from close personal observation of how particular selective colleges operate. It draws on candid conversations with countless college admissions officers and interesting visits to over 100 of the nation's most prestigious colleges. For the friendship and candor of these officers around the country, I am immensely indebted. To a smaller group of counselors in the nation's high schools, I also express my appreciation. The quiet dedication and special sensitivity of Betty M. Kukesh, who has served three college placement directors at Exeter and who typed this manuscript, deserve special mention. She is one of a kind.

In writing this book, I have sought to be fair to all the institutions mentioned and to my readers. For any of the errors or misinterpretations that mortals inevitably make, I am responsible. I hope they are few. I hope too that readers will find in this book a store of useful advice and that, in the course of following it, they will realize, during their college years and beyond, the best that is within them.

Exeter, New Hampshire
Spring 1989

1

Thinking

About College

Travelers to the ancient city of Delphi who sought to find out what the future had in store for them were often puzzled by the vagueness of what the priests of the temple had to say. Many of those travelers would have been less confused had they read the motto inscribed over the temple's entrance: "Know thyself." The motto could not be improved upon as preliminary advice to the young person pondering the galaxy of questions that surround the decision to go to college. You must "know yourself."

All too often students in the process of thinking about college dwell on the importance of gaining admission to a particular school, rather than on the important questions that should precede the choice of a school. First, students need to think objectively about themselves, their interests, and their needs. Only then can they focus on the institution that will best suit their particular educational and social needs. Students have to engage in a self-assessment process, perhaps for the first time, before embarking on the process of choosing a specific college. This realistic self-assessment may be one of the most valuable learning experiences of the whole college-search process, for it enables students to see themselves, their goals, and the routes to those goals with a new degree of clarity and understanding.

Several years ago a professor at Haverford College studied the background of successful graduates of his institution. He found that one of the key elements of success in later life was the presence at a young age of a strong and realistic sense of self-awareness and understanding.

Self-Assessment
Beginning with the assumption that every person has a unique combination of skills, personal traits, goals, values, aptitudes, habits, and beliefs, let us explore some of the ways you can discover your unique combina-

tion and relate it to the proper college choice for you. First, look at some of your current skills. You might not be aware of how many you already have. To begin this process, make a log of your activities during the past 24 hours. Divide your log into two columns, one for the activity itself and a second for the skills it involved. After you have looked at the day just past, continue down the left-hand column of your log with the activities you have found enjoyable and productive over the past year. Then skip a few lines and make a short list of some of the things you would like to do in the future.

When you have completed your list of activities present, past, and future, let it cool for a while. Return to it later and indicate beside each activity the skills it involves. For example, your list might look like this:

ACTIVITIES	SKILLS INVOLVED
Yesterday & Today	
French homework	Memorization, writing, and speaking another language
Chem lab report	Understanding complex molecules and physical forces of bonding
Took out trash	No skill I can think of
Cheerleader practice	Physical coordination, sense of balance and motion, and cooperation with others
Trumpet lesson	Digital facility, knowledge of scale and melody, awareness of harmony and some theory, integration of instrument within orchestra
Last Summer	
Camped in Maine woods	Reading maps; building fires; cooking simple meals; learning how to pack and walk with a heavy load and how to observe nature; persuading parents to let me go
Repaired family stereo	Digital facility, knowledge of electrical circuitry and theory of sound reproduction
Learned to sail	Elementary navigation, some knowledge of the physics of wind and water, observation of weather and water patterns

The Future

Dismantle a jet engine	Knowledge of engineering physics, digital facility, sense of planning and organization in sorting the parts, and understanding of how those parts function together
Run a marathon	Physical conditioning, setting the proper diet, understanding the physics of the foot as it encounters running surfaces, planning for extensive training

A brief glance at your activities shows that you already have mastered a number of skills and are in the process of perfecting others. A look at the list also reveals that you have reason to feel good about yourself and your potential. As you think about college, add to the last section of the list some activities and their attendant skills that you would like to perfect over the course of the next four years.

Next, consider your personal values and the role they inevitably play in your daily life. You may not be aware of how strongly you believe in some values and how uncertain you are about others. To find out, try this fanciful experiment, called a "value auction." First, write down the following values and add to the list any others that may occur to you:

Health	Religion	Security
Family	Power	Marriage
Justice	Personal recognition	Honesty
Love	Personal autonomy	Friendship
Emotional well-being	Good appearance	Knowledge and wisdom
Pleasure	Charity	Achievement

Second, assume a budget of $1000 to spend on "purchasing" some or all of these values. Now spend the $1000 on the values on your list, and see where your money goes. What values emerged as most important to you? Which ones were less so? Which did you omit, and why? Rank your values in order of their importance to you and keep your list firmly in mind as you explore various colleges, talk to undergraduates and admissions personnel, and ponder the college literature you receive. At some point further down the road, you will want to align your personal values with those of the institution where you will be spending the next four years.

To begin this assessment of how an institution might affect your values positively or negatively, fantasize for a few moments. (Incidentally, researchers have found that fantasies have a high degree of correlation with our personal needs and ultimately our career decisions.) Imagine what you would like to have said about you in your obituary at age 80. What achievements would you choose to be remembered by? What weaknesses would you like concealed or dealt with gently? Jot your thoughts down on paper and keep them private. At the same time, consider what type of educational and career plans you might have to make to achieve the noteworthy results you outlined in your obituary. What values would you have to adhere to? Think about the type of college that might best help you to meet your objectives and refine the values you care about.

A third area of self-assessment lies in the domain of personality. What type of person are you? What kind of working and learning environment suits you best? Socially? Intellectually? Richard N. Bolles, in his clever and helpful book, *What Color Is Your Parachute?* (Berkeley: Ten Speed Press, 1987), offers a model for us to consider. He asks us to imagine a party at which people with the same or similar interests gather in six different areas of a room. As the newcomer, you are asked to identify the group with which you feel a natural affinity, the one you would enjoy being with. As you stand at the door of the party and consider which group you would like to join, you see six interesting groups:

Group A: People with athletic or mechanical ability, who prefer to work with objects, machines, tools, plants, or animals or to be outdoors

Group B: People who have clerical or quantitative ability, who like to work with data and like to carry things out in detail or follow through on others' instructions

Group C: People who like to work with others, influencing, persuading, leading, or managing them as they seek organizational goals, particularly financial ones

Group D: People who like to work with others to inform, enlighten, train, develop, or cure them, or who are skilled with words

Group E: People who have artistic, innovative, or intuitional abilities and like to work in unstructured situations using their imagination and creativity

Group F: People who like to observe, learn, investigate, analyze, evaluate, or solve problems

Make a note of the group you would most like to join. Then imagine that the group breaks up for some reason and its members go home. Which group would you join next? Which would be your third choice? Having made these decisions, write them down. Note the skills that were associated with your first choice of group. Also note how your personal values were underscored by this choice. Then proceed to your second and third choices, noting the skills, values, and degree of personal fulfillment those choices would reinforce were this a real-life situation.

Now you should consider making it just that, a real-life situation. Whom do you know and admire who fits into the groups you have just chosen? Make a list of their personality traits and values. Describe their work and the social and physical features of their working environments, insofar as you know those details. Consider calling one of them to get as much detail as you can about his or her life and work.

You should be aware that there is room for people from more than one of the listed groups in any given field. For example, in the field of medicine, members of Group D obviously would make good family doctors, but those in Group A might specialize in surgery or some aspect of medicine involving engineering. Students who are inclined toward medicine and are most comfortable in Group F might find fulfillment as research doctors in a large hospital or university.

The World of Work

After attending the hypothetical party and considering the ways in which individual skills, values, and personality need to combine comfortably and productively with the group setting, you must carry your process of self-evaluation into its next phase—consideration of the world of work.

Your exploration of the world of work need not be extensive at this point. Having identified your skills, interests, and preferred environments, you want to gather information about possible careers or fields of work in which you might function well in the future. The ideal way to begin would be to ask your guidance counselor to let you take the Jackson Interest Inventory Test or the Holland Self-Directed Search Test and then to go over the results with you. The armed services offer a test called the Armed Services Vocational Aptitude Battery (ASVAB), and it too can be interpreted by your guidance counselor. These tests will help you identify the fields of work for which you may have an affinity, but they are by no means conclusive predictors of future performance. Properly understood and utilized, they can help you identify your skills and aptitudes and focus on possible career goals.

To explore ways of reaching these goals, go to the library and look for two useful works: the *Dictionary of Occupational Titles* and the *Occupational Outlook Handbook*. Pick two careers that might be of interest to you and read about their requirements in the *Dictionary of Occupational Titles*. Then turn to the *Occupational Outlook Handbook* and consider the projected need for new workers in those fields. If the prospects look promising, make a list of all the requirements for those career choices, leaving space for other related careers.

From this list you should develop a set of questions about the careers you have chosen to investigate. Perhaps the experience you have already had in job situations will help you formulate your questions. The following lines of inquiry will be of assistance, too:

Working Conditions: What are the hours of work? Is the environment clean/dirty, noisy/quiet, dangerous/safe?

Duties:	What are four typical duties you might be expected to carry out?
People:	To what extent does your job involve working with other people? Is it satisfying to you in this respect?
Education:	What special training or certification did you have to get? To what extent did your education and previous jobs help you to find and obtain this one?
Benefits:	What are the salary and benefits associated with your work, including travel, use of a company car, research facilities, health insurance, and the like?
Disadvantages:	What do you dislike about your work, and is there anything you can do to change it?
Personal Qualities:	What are the most important personal qualities people should have to succeed in this line of work?
General:	Do you have any particular advice for me if I become interested in entering this career—contacts I should make, experience I should seek?

Having drafted a list of questions such as those above, you should seek to interview someone in each of the fields of interest you have designated. It may sound difficult, but the benefits of personal contact with adults working in the field are considerable, not to mention the experience gained in arranging a meeting and conducting an interview. Interviews often can be conducted informally with family members or friends who are involved in careers that interest you. Accompanying your doctor uncle on his rounds and then interviewing him in the car on the way to and from the hospital is not only feasible but valuable.

In the best of all possible worlds your final step in exploring the world of work is to actually do a little work related to the field that interests you. Often this can be accomplished through a summer job. Would-be engineers can seek work in the local computer or stereo store. Prospective doctors can offer their services as volunteers in the local hospital or nursing home. Aspiring businesspeople can sample the market by taking jobs as waitresses or waiters, sales clerks, shippers, or even factory workers. In each instance, looking for a job that suits you will be made easier by the insights you already have gained about your skills and interests and the kind of work environments best suited to developing them.

Thinking About Majors

Somewhere in the course of this odyssey dedicated to identifying your strong qualities and directing them toward a career, you will begin to develop some ideas about a possible college major. You do not need to make a firm choice of college major in high school, and you may want to sample a broad range of subjects in your freshman year. However, at this stage it is useful to consider possible fields of study and how they might relate to the careers you are considering.

Your uncle, the doctor, may encourage you to pursue a liberal arts program as the best preparation for dealing with the variety of individuals that a doctor encounters and must understand. A would-be pilot may be advised to major in electrical engineering and get on with the acquisition of the technical knowledge required further down the line. A prospective journalist may be told to continue the concentration on mathematics but keep on writing. This could lead to the science editorship of a major newspaper one day.

When students have identified particular subjects or majors they might want to pursue, they can turn to a number of standard sources that will direct them toward specific colleges. There are *The Index of Majors* of the College Board and *Peterson's Guide to Four-Year Colleges*. In addition, both organizations produce computer programs that enable students to locate colleges offering a particular major.

Before choosing a college, however, students have to frame a set of questions that will help them discover whether a proposed major is suited to their skills, values, and learning style. In addition, they will need to know whether their choice of major will allow them the flexibility to explore other areas while pursuing their career goals. At the college interview, the student should ask the following questions:

1) What skills are needed to pursue this major successfully? What high school courses will help me prepare myself?
2) What fields of work do students in this major enter?
3) Is there room for students to branch out into related areas while pursuing this major? Examples?
4) What college courses are commonly taken in conjunction with this major? If I major in history, will I be encouraged to take political science and economics?
5) Are there any special programs within this major, such as foreign study or internships, that could help me refine my interests and perfect my abilities?
6) To what extent is graduate school necessary to acquire real competence in this major?
7) What satisfactions and dissatisfactions might I experience as a student with this major at this college?

8) What kind of people typically enter this major and do well in it? (Think back to the groups at the "party" on page 8.)

As you receive answers to these questions from a college interviewer, alumni representative, or knowledgeable student in your field of interest, relate what you hear to your own self-assessment. Your skills, values, personality, and learning style should roughly coincide with those of your fellow students in that major at a particular college. If they do not, then you should look elsewhere.

Let us look at the example of George Matthews, who is 17 and wants to be a lawyer. George has a keen interest in history. He does some research on Donaldson College and is pleased to hear that 60 percent of the history department's graduates took the Law School Aptitude Test last spring. He is equally impressed by several courses that focus on the role of law in society. He makes a list of the skills he would need to be successful in history and, ultimately, law. He recognizes that his strong writing abilities would help him, as would his ability to organize data and make hypotheses about them. However, he would have to concentrate on his research and note-taking skills because there are lots of lecture courses and research papers in the history department at Donaldson.

George has already taken two history courses in high school and would welcome the opportunity to study the allied field of political science in college. He also wants to understand rudimentary economics and perhaps take some courses in fiscal management. He discovers that these options are available at the college. In assessing Donaldson's strengths and drawbacks, he finds he could live with the crowding at the library reserve desk and the fact that history professors are often away on sabbatical in Washington. He knows he would find satisfaction studying a subject in which he has always been interested, and one that is obviously favored by the college. (The best-teacher award has gone to a member of the history department in three of the past five years.) The Donaldson history department would provide him with stimulating professors whose national reputation might enhance his application to law school or graduate school. Finally, as George considers the type of social and intellectual situation he likes most—working with and managing people as they seek organizational goals—he becomes convinced that history is the major for him, and Donaldson is the college where he should study.

Activities and Interests

Now is the time to consider such factors as your extracurricular and creative interests. Pursuing activities and interests is an important part of college life. The history student who is also a good football player and likes to play the violin will want to locate a school where all those talents can be nurtured—one with a good history curriculum, a strong football team, and an expansive music program that welcomes amateurs as well as experienced musicians. Similarly, the student who loves to cook, someday hopes to own a catering business, and plans to study economics will have to look carefully at a college's culinary arts facilities, as well as its academic ones.

Both of these students need to consider their extracurricular activities in some kind of social context, too. The accomplished cook who used to perform cooking miracles at home will have to rely on the college's equipment now and share it with members of the Gourmet Society. This sharing may necessitate relating to other people more than in the past. An interest in cooking can thus lead to friendships outside the dormitory and the classroom.

For the football player who was lionized in high school, getting to know his new teammates off the field—in the classroom and in the dormitory—will be important. As a person who likes music and plays it on occasion, he may want to act as liaison between the football team and the band in the fall, then join the band as an instrumentalist during the winter and spring. Whatever their choices, both cook and athlete need to find a school where academics are of primary importance but their special talents are appreciated as well.

Academic Abilities

A frank assessment of your personal skills, preferred learning environment, career interests, potential major, and extracurricular talents does not quite complete the self-evaluation needed for a sound college choice. You also have to conduct a frank appraisal of your academic abilities and, if any particular weaknesses are discovered, set about remedying them during your remaining time in high school. The academic skills you will need over the next four years are already familiar to you: note-taking, the organization of information for papers, participation in oral discussion, writing, typing, and knowledge of the computer.

First, you will need to master the skill of note-taking. Not only should you be able to take notes on a lecture, but you also should be able to capture the main ideas in a reading assignment. This includes summarizing the message of the text, defining the author's key terms, and restating the author's point of view and biases in your own words.

Second, you need to know how to organize a long paper, develop a bibliography, take notes on note cards, evolve a thesis, and organize an outline. You should plan to take at least one course in high school that teaches these skills.

Third, you should develop some oral discussion skills before entering college. Although many freshman courses meet in large lectures, classes tend to become smaller as students progress and specialize. Ideally the first-year college student will have at least one seminar class in which the skills of oral discussion can be employed. These skills can be practiced in high school classes or in ordinary conversation with friends. A crucial oral skill is the ability to keep your attention on the main point of the conversation and not be distracted by digressions. When having a serious discussion with a group of people, try to keep them on track by asking them to define any new terms they employ or, when they go off the track, try to return them to the main point.

Oral discussion also calls for the ability to present ideas that may contradict without alienating others. Learning to do this naturally and smoothly comes from practice; it is an art too elaborate for description here, but one that is well worth having. Referring positively to something that a speaker has said and then relating it to your own comment and to the topic in general often will avoid offense.

At the end of a group discussion, you should practice synthesizing the various opinions that have been expressed and then pose some new questions that might not have been considered. Not all of these techniques come easily, but prospective college students should not undervalue the role of the spoken word in their educational growth. Whether in all-night bull sessions or in an introductory course on Western political tradition, your oral skills will serve to help you clarify your own ideas and assimilate new ones.

Fourth, you should enter college with some mastery of basic writing skills. Clarity, coherence, and style in writing elude all but a few of today's high school students. Their teachers assign too few written exercises, and high school curricula have also shifted emphasis away from writing courses. Television has fostered the preeminence of the spoken over the written word. Eleventh graders planning to apply to a four-year college should make it a priority to concentrate on developing effective writing skills before their freshman year of college. A conference with your English teacher is the first step. Your teacher can help you identify any weaknesses and suggest ways to remedy them. Perhaps the suggestion will involve something as simple as learning the rule for the correct use of who and whom, or how to avoid split infinitives. Or it may involve more complicated efforts: vocabulary building, outlining your thoughts before writing, studying the various ways of subordinating ideas in a sentence.

For an indication of your level of writing ability, look at a pamphlet called *About the Achievement Tests* (published by the College Board and available from your high school guidance office). Under the section on the English Composition Test, you will find a sample essay question from the exam. One recent version asks students to formulate a written response to the proposition: People seldom stand up for what they truly believe in; instead they merely go along with the popular view. Following the statement are four responses, which represent a good, an average, a below-average, and a poor response for a high school senior. You may want to write your own response to the sample question before looking at the examples. Then, when you have made your own comparisons, ask your English teacher to rate your efforts and suggest possible improvements.

Two other skills are highly desirable for a productive four years in college: typing and knowledge of the computer. Typing sounds like such a simple matter, and it is—unless you don't know how! Most college courses require typed papers, and, moreover, students who can type their own papers gain time in which they can put their papers through additional revisions before they are due.

Fortunately, typing skill is also relevant to computer operation. Many computers can be used as word processors, and college students who can type and who understand how to operate a computer quickly become adept at editing their papers on a word processor.

In addition to its editorial function, the computer has touched all aspects of learning in the past decade. Historians use computers to study the demography of communities, formulating theories about social and political change. With them, political scientists study voting patterns and predict elections. Economists use computers to analyze the stock market, and even language teachers use them to test their students' knowledge of grammatical forms.

If students understand the elementary principles of computing, how to use the computer to collect data, how to operate a word processing program, and how to connect a school or personal computer with other networks, they will find these skills useful when they are in college. To know what kinds of questions the computer can answer and how to make it supply those answers will be enormously beneficial.

The Role of the Family

No self-evaluation, however honest and far-reaching, should ignore the importance of family in shaping the college decision. Thinking about college involves thinking about the family—its expectations, its view of itself, its view of the student, and its finances. All college-bound seniors should plan several long discussions with the family members who have shaped their lives thus far, especially those—usually parents—who may be helping to pay college costs.

Often students find that their families have very high expectations and need to know more about the realities of the college admissions process. Students may have to arrange a meeting with their guidance counselor for this purpose, thus introducing an objective third party to help the family conduct a reasonable conversation and bring them much-needed information.

On the other hand, some families may have expectations that are not high enough and use financial limitations to mask that feeling. In both cases—high expectations and low—students should gather as many facts as they can so they can inform their families of the importance of choosing the right college. Being able to address the concerns of a cost-conscious parent who has a jaundiced view of the need for a liberal arts education followed by graduate school can help. For example, saying, "Dad, when I interviewed Dr. Soldowski, he told me that a four-year liberal arts education with a few science courses sprinkled in is the best preparation for medical school that he could possibly think of," can help carry the argument for a small liberal arts college as opposed to a less expensive—and huge—state university. Being able to rebut the argument that you must go to a particular Ivy League school because your parents' friends' children go there with the statement that "the aeronautical physics department at the University of Texas is better" will help defuse the high-expectations argument advanced by some parents.

Once parents know specific facts about the colleges their children are considering and understand how reasonably they are approaching the subject in general, they tend to delegate considerable control over the college selection process to them. Parents will undoubtedly ask to be kept informed, they will offer their opinions from time to time, and they will play a supportive yet subordinate role.

Philosophical Considerations

Finally, some philosophical considerations. A four-year college education begins a lifelong process of learning and changing. College is not a finite experience. It stays with you throughout your life. What you are looking for is something beyond good grades, rewarding extracurricular activities, a particular expertise, a degree, and a "ticket to the big life." You want to find a place that will enhance your capacity to think independently, appreciate the variety and complexity of the world around you, and move comfortably within it. As a college student, you should seek not only to acquire knowledge but to develop a creative and disciplined mind that allows you to be adventurous in thought and action, while at the same time feeling secure and committed.

Reflect momentarily on the enormous differences between high school and college and try to imagine the immense freedom that college brings. There is no freer period in a person's life than the four years of college. Away from home and family, able to set your own schedule of work and play, free to take a wide variety of courses and to engage in any number of social and extracurricular activities, and—with luck—free from major financial worries, you have an unlimited opportunity to construct and furnish an intellectual, spiritual, and social home of your own. It is important, therefore, that you realize why you want to be at college in the first place, so that, from its innumerable options, you make wise choices.

You should approach the college experience seriously, setting your own reasonable standards independent of the variety of attitudes and behavior you may find on campus. The lack of concern of some college students for one another and their community, the drugs and liquor prevalent on many campuses, the sexual freedom, the frenzy over grades, and the undue emphasis on career preparation at the expense of a broader education all can distort the collegiate experience for the unwary.

In the end what really matters is that you actively choose a college and course of study for the right reasons. As long as your decision is an active one and takes into consideration your own skills, interests, and personality based on a realistic self-assessment, then yours will be the right decision. Too often we look at only one side of Robert Frost's poem about the roads diverging in the yellow wood:

> I shall be telling this with a sigh
> Somewhere ages and ages hence:
> Two roads diverged in a wood, and I—
> I took the one less traveled by,
> And that has made all the difference.

We are inclined to believe that the less-traveled path is the right path. In other words, it is better to be a poet than a banker. But Frost did not say exactly that, for elsewhere in the poem he writes:

> . . . both that morning equally lay
> in leaves no step has trodden black.

Frost is emphasizing the need for free choice in our life's decisions. Like the poet, you will come to many junctions and have to make choices. The freedom to make the choices involved in going to college does not come merely from the absence of restraint; it derives from a realistic self-evaluation, a sincere commitment to the educational process itself, and an awareness that a college education imposes a certain responsibility on the student. As we look ahead to the remainder of this century and the first years of the next, we can readily see that our society will require the maximum development of individual potential. Ernest Boyer, head of the Carnegie Foundation for the Advancement of Teaching, put the task well when he wrote recently:

> This nation and the world need well-informed, inquisitive, open-minded young people who are both productive and reflective, seeking answers to life's most important questions. Above all, we need educated men and women who not only pursue their own personal interests but are also prepared to fulfill their social and civic obligations. And it is during the undergraduate experience . . . that these essential qualities of mind and character are refined. (Ernest L. Boyer, *College: The Undergraduate Experience in America.* New York: Harper and Row, 1987, p. 7)

The decision to go to college, then, entails a special commitment to the larger society as well as to yourself. Like all real decisions, it represents both a freedom and a responsibility.

2
Choosing
Colleges

Choosing a college involves blending the factors you have developed through your self-evaluation with other important criteria. It combines a look inside yourself with a look outside yourself. In reflecting on your skills, values, and learning style you have already discovered your possible field of work and the college major that should probably precede it. Now you need to talk to professionals, your guidance counselors, and trusted friends and come up with a list of twenty or so schools. Next you want to explore these schools in greater depth before writing for catalogs or making personal visits.

For this, you can turn to the reference literature, keeping in mind your selection criteria. You will first want to find out more about the *academic program* at a particular school. This is, after all, your main criterion. If you also want to be near home, then *location* becomes your second major consideration. You may have some preconceived notions about how large or small a college you want to attend, so *size* is a third criterion. Then comes the very significant category of *extracurricular activity:* sports, drama, cooking facilities, nationally ranked chess club, or whatever is important to you. Every college candidate should be sure that there are interesting activities outside the classroom. Next come the vital and complicated matters of *cost* and its companion, *financial aid,* with which you will have to concern yourself as you seek admission to college (see Chapter 7). Finally the criterion of *difficulty* of admission needs to be considered in the college search process.

With these criteria in mind, you will be faced with two types of general reference works to ponder. The first might be called the objective guides, which consist mainly of neutral facts about each college, often in a chart form in compact paragraphs. The second group of reference books, the subjective guides, are more judgmental. They usually rank the colleges and describe the schools in qualitative terms that leave an unmistakable impression on the reader. The intelligent college candidate will want to gather as much data as possible from an objective guide before turning for assistance to a subjective one.

A cautionary note about the subjective guides: faced with the apparent complexity and often whimsical nature of the college admissions process, many students and families are relying on these books for too much of their information and strategy. Recently the Eastern Group of Admissions Directors, representing some of the best-known colleges in the eastern part of the country, passed two resolutions that serve as useful advice to families and students contemplating the purchase of one of the now-famous subjective guides to colleges.

The directors urged, "College-bound students should rely for guidance upon secondary school counselors, professional independent counselors, admissions officers . . . *and current reference books*" in making their decisions about a college. They also encouraged applicants to make a "first-hand investigation" of the schools they were considering. Even so, the brisk sale of the subjective guides goes on. Enough said.

Selection Criteria

Catalogs and the Academic Program

Your first step is to procure a copy of the catalog of each school in which you are interested and apply your selection criteria to it. Often colleges will not send catalogs with their first mailing since they are expensive to publish and to mail. Instead they will send what is called in the trade a brochure or viewbook. If this happens, study the viewbook thoroughly. It may be quite factual and informative. If it is not, see if you can find a catalog somewhere. Your guidance office, the school library, or perhaps even a friend may have a copy of the catalog you require.

In examining the catalog, look first at the academic programs in which you are interested. Are there a fairly large number of courses you could take? Within a given academic area, are there special programs that would be accessible to you? If you are interested in majoring in the history of art and possibly going on to a career as a museum curator, does the school offer programs that involve students with nearby museums? Does it offer a study-abroad program that would enable someone like yourself to examine the art treasures of Florence and Rome at first hand? Can a major in the history of art be joined with a minor in business management?

If you are interested in combining engineering and business, look at the requirements for engineering. Are they too numerous to allow a student to take a half-dozen courses in economics, marketing, and organizational behavior? Or is there a specific program for people who wish to combine engineering with a related field? (Some schools offer a combined degree in liberal arts and engineering.)

If the academic programs at a college look reasonably good, you must then assess the opportunities for contact with teachers. Does the catalog give the average class size for the introductory courses taken by freshmen? Does it merely divide the total number of students by the number of full-time faculty members in computing the faculty-student ratio? Are there special seminars for freshmen and sophomores, or would you have to progress through a series of large classes in order to qualify for seminars in your junior and senior years? Students who intend to major in a science will want to pay special heed to the size and frequency of laboratory periods. How many instructors supervise the laboratory sessions? Students faced with the prospect of large classes will want to ascertain the availability of professors outside of class. Are they required to hold office hours? Are they encouraged by the administration to entertain students informally in their homes? If the catalog does not answer these and similar questions for you, write them down to raise later in an interview or letter.

Students who have special qualifications and may already be advanced in their particular field of interest will want to know whether a college grants credit for advanced placement courses taken in high school. Such students may also want to know if a school with a graduate program allows qualified undergraduates to take courses in it.

On the other hand, the budding physicist who has recently discovered the glories of literature will want to be assured that the physics department will allow him to take a number of courses outside the department. Some colleges have what is usually called a general studies program for this type of person.

Candidates will also want to consider the flexibility of a particular academic program within the context of their other criteria. Those in need of financial aid will want to explore the opportunities for employment during the term, as well as during the summer. Talented athletes will have to look carefully at programs with long laboratory requirements that may interfere with team practice.

Having established that the college has both sufficient flexibility and challenge in the department of interest, you need to assess the quality of the education being offered. You have already looked at your own academic interests and developed a set of questions that attempts to match your requirements and personality with the qualities of the college to which you might apply. Now you should focus on your area of major interest, for instance, history. Scrutinize the catalog description of the college's history courses. How many of them look exciting? Are there any courses you would like to see but don't?

Next, look at the number of professors in the department compared to the number of students. Remember that the popularity of a department may have drawbacks in terms of class size and amount of contact with professors. Often departments that are slightly underenrolled are more stimulating than the more popular departments because they are trying to attract students with special programs and course offerings.

You should ask the admissions office for literature describing individual departments.

Other Resources

In assessing the quality of an academic department, you can also turn to sources other than the official literature. At many institutions, undergraduates publish a confidential guide to courses. This publication, frequently photocopied and sold in the college's bookstore, assesses course difficulty and quality, evaluates the books used, summarizes assignments, and appraises the quality of the teaching of the professor and his or her assistants. If a college does not have such a publication, you could ask some undergraduates studying in the same field for their informal advice.

Another line of inquiry lies in professional journals. Pick a topic within your field of interest, such as cellular biology, and then look at professional journals in the field to see if any members of the biology department at the college you are considering have published articles or are mentioned in footnotes. A student interested in pursuing medicine could look in the *New England Journal of Medicine;* one interested in the history of industrial relations could consult the journal *Labor History.* If you pursue this line of investigation, make sure your overview of the literature is fairly broad and thorough; conclusions drawn from a sketchy search can be misleading.

Finally, students interested in evaluating the quality of teaching in a particular field can contact someone practicing in the field, seeking an informed opinion about the academic departments of the schools they are considering. (These could be the same people who have already helped you in the course of exploring the world of work.) If you have decided on business, you should ask your aunt who majored in economics in college and is now a personnel manager for a large corporation what she thinks of the economics departments of the schools you are looking at. If you wish to pursue the study of ecology, ask the president of the local environmental engineering firm for an opinion about the graduates of the small engineering schools in the central Atlantic region. This will provide a quick way of helping you form your judgment of those schools. (Caveat: Any one person's opinion may be biased or dated or simply based on incomplete information. Talk to as many people as you can to get the most complete view possible.)

Academic Facilities

Catalogs also describe an institution's academic facilities. You should pay careful attention to all the information about a school's library, not just to the number of volumes. It is accessibility of the library's collections that counts. Are students able to get at the books? What parts of the collection circulate to students? What are the provisions for taking books out, and how long can they be kept? Does the library have an ample reserve collection so that sought-after volumes are available to students? What are its hours? This question is very important, for there may be times when the dormitory becomes too noisy for study. Is a certain section of the library open all night, for instance? You should determine the number of seats in the library in relation to the number of students. If there is room for no more than 10 percent of the total student population, then the library will undoubtedly be overcrowded around exam time. Are there ancillary libraries on campus that are open to students? Do dormitories have small libraries, or do individual departments allow students to use their books? In that connection, does the library have a good collection of primary sources? History buffs will want to know if the library has the *New York Times* on microfilm and perhaps some other major paper as well, the *Chicago Tribune,* for instance. Musicians will want to know the number of classical music recordings and whether tapes are available for loan to students.

All college students will be using the computer in one form or another and will want to determine the number and location of terminals that can be used by students. Those with an interest in science should pay special attention to what the catalog has to say about laboratory space. If there are 50 stations in the chemistry lab and over 500 students enrolled in the department, crowding will invariably result. Limited laboratory facilities for behavioral experiments will be a drawback for the candidate who plans to major in psychology. On the other hand, prospective mechanical engineers should be impressed by an engineering department that possesses a giant stress machine. This device will be an asset when they test the models they build in the laboratory.

Once you have completed your survey of a college's facilities, you should record your impressions. You will want to refer to them when comparing this college's facilities with those of other colleges.

Extracurricular Activities

Extracurricular activities must be evaluated, too. Students with particular talents should ask questions about extracurricular activities similar to those they asked about academic programs. How much contact with coaches or directors is there? What is the institutional commitment— philosophical and financial—to the given activity? To be specific, athletes will want to make sure that there are on-campus facilities for their sport. Divers need to know if there is a separate diving pool or if the divers and swimmers share the same one. Ham radio operators will be concerned with the wattage of the shortwave radio station's transformer. Clarinetists will want to be sure that the orchestra is large enough to accommodate a few new players every year. Budding actresses and actors will want to read about theater facilities. Is there a practice theater or an experimental theater? And what about courses for the theater, opportunities for involvement in community theater, chances to attend the theater in a nearby city? Are there extra charges for participation in any of these activities? And so on.

As candidates consider possible extracurricular activities in college, they should think about which facilities and programs are open to those without sufficient skill to participate at the higher levels of their chosen activity. If you would not qualify for the varsity tennis team, are there jayvee and intramural teams that would allow you to continue to enjoy your sport and be challenged by other players? Students interested in acting might look into what happens if they do not make a major production. Are there student-directed plays offered in a smaller theater? Are there such things as dormitory or house plays in which they could participate? In other words, be sure that there are different levels of a given activity so that students of differing abilities can participate. This is especially important if you are expecting to undertake a new activity at college. Make sure that there is a beginner's level.

Social Life

College is not all books and activities, though. Students should give some thought to the social life they will encounter on campus. Finding out what kind of students attend each college is essential. These are the people you may be living with for four years, so it is crucial to discover whether you would be comfortable and happy in their company.

In order to focus on these people, their interests, and their personalities, consider the following suggestions. First, you should read closely what the catalog has to say about dormitories. Are there a variety of living arrangements, both coeducational and single-sex? In particular, is there enough space? How many students are assigned to a room? Do a fair number of students move off campus for some reason, and why? Is it crowding, or expense, or both? Is there a mechanism for dealing with dormitory living arrangements that turn out badly? What about fraternities and sororities? Are they encouraged or discouraged? What percentage of the students are members? (If more than 50 percent of students join fraternities or sororities, you can assume that these groups are a major force in campus life.) Does the college have a variety of meal plans, and can students experiment with cooperative arrangements?

Moving beyond the living conditions on campus, you should try to discern what the social ambience of the campus is. How do students treat one another? What is the relationship of faculty members to students? Do they see a lot of one another or not? Under what conditions, formal or informal? Is there any hostility between the college students and the local community?

Try to find out what students do in their free time. Do many of them own cars? If so, do they vacate the campus on weekends? Are there big campus events, such as a rites of spring celebration or winter carnival? Do most students participate? If not, who is left out and why? What is the role of athletics on campus? Does football dominate the fall and therefore define the social life of that season? Develop some sense of the cultural life on campus. Is there a current list of visiting lecturers, concerts, and plays? Are students involved in planning these affairs, or are they the responsibility of a faculty committee?

Photographs in the catalog and viewbook will tell you something about the social ambience of a college. Study them closely. Do the pictures appear staged or not? Do they portray a variety of social activities? Do they show informal student interactions as well as more formal ones, such as dances or excursions?

One suburban school in the East recently devoted ten full pages of its catalog to pictures of life on campus. But on close inspection one found that the shots had actually been taken in a nearby city—where another prominent school happens to be located. This selection of photos suggests that the college feels dominated by both the city around it and the other prominent college. Without meaning to, the catalog gives the impression that the college's students choose to spend much of their time away from the campus.

This sort of lack of candor is quite common, as schools attempt to show their best faces in videos and slick brochures with well-chosen pictures. So read catalogs and judge videos and photographs critically. Generalize from both what you see and what you don't see. A catalog from a small college in upstate New York that has only two pictures out of thirty showing snow is not being honest about the weather, since the average snowfall for that region is about 40 inches a year. Students interested in an unfamiliar location should ask questions about its annual rainfall and average temperature, the percentage of sunny days per season, and the presence of any local peculiarities, such as smog.

Costs and Aid

All students and their families will be interested in the cost of a favored school and how its fees are constructed. In looking over the costs, be sure to figure in transportation to and from the college. Note whether there are separate fees for student activities or use of the gymnasium and laboratories. If there are, compare them with those of the other colleges you are considering. You might want to ask if there are penalty fees for early graduation or for living off campus.

In this era of escalating college costs, you also should be interested in the financial health of the colleges you are considering. Some schools are not on the firmest footing, and, where this is the case, tuition could go up and scholarship aid down in the future. It is, therefore, perfectly legitimate to ask a question about the college's projections for tuition and scholarship assistance in an interview with an admissions officer.

Prospective candidates for financial aid should develop a list of questions after discussing the family's financial situation with their parents. They will want to know how much grant aid is actually available from the college, what the average grant per student is, and what the ratio of college grant aid to loans and government aid is in the average financial aid award. Beyond that, families who qualify for a merit-based award will want to know whether such awards run for four years or one, and whether the total financial aid package is adjusted when a student receives merit-based aid. Some parents will want to know about parent loan programs and the availability of long-term financing. Others will have questions about prepaying their child's tuition. Most colleges have very specific literature on all these topics.

School Size

The choice of size of school rests almost entirely with the individual applicant. It is important, however, not to fall prey to any of the several myths that surround the criterion of size. For example, many people equate size with diversity and assume that small schools cannot be as diverse as large ones. Some candidates also assume that small schools have the advantage when it comes to forming close and numerous social relationships. Not necessarily. Some large schools nurture the same degree of familiarity and sense of community as small ones do. Some small schools are cold and aloof.

A similar assumption applies to contact with professors. Candidates often believe that large schools encourage students to work on their own and leave professors to their own research, while at small schools professors are obliged to have an open-door policy. Not always true. Finally, you should not assume that at large schools your access to extracurricular activities would be more difficult than at a small college. Intramural sports, for instance, may be supported more vigorously at a large school than at a small one. The converse could also be true.

By setting aside preconceptions about the effects of school size, students can make a more realistic determination of the real and varying impact of size in relation to their own needs. They should read catalogs closely with an eye to the qualities that meet their own expectations, be it at a large, mid-sized, or small school.

Admission Difficulty

The final criterion to consider is difficulty of admission, or the D-factor. Most college reference books have a paragraph and some statistics about the D-factor. Begin with those, comparing them to what the college catalog says. Regrettably, the catalog often will say little, but it should say *something* about the admissions process itself: how folders are read and evaluated, the role of the interview, and the number of students admitted compared to the total number of applications. Most of the reference books will tell you something about Scholastic Aptitude Test (SAT) or American College Testing Program (ACT) scores for the entering class, e.g., "Of those admitted, 60 percent had an SAT verbal score above 560." Since numbers do not play an overwhelming role in your college selection process, you may not want to go much further than this. Admissions "profiles," which most colleges produce for high school counselors and for their own alumni, elaborate on the SAT and ACT score statistics. They give mean Achievement Test results for the entering class; they also show the relationship of class rank to admission. In addition, geographical distribution, minority enrollment, and yield statistics (percentage of students who accept the college's offer of admission) are reported.

The difficulty factor is harder to quantify at the most selective colleges. This is because the selective colleges, with large and perceptive admissions staffs, are able to apply a variety of nonnumerical criteria to each candidate. They are very interested, for instance, in such personal qualities as character and leadership potential. They frequently move beyond test results and grades to look for individual creativity in the arts, or even in human relations. Because such colleges are deluged with applications from outstanding candidates, the summary figures for SAT and ACT scores, class rank, and the like will be impressive, but they cannot suggest the sophistication of the selection process and should be treated with a fair amount of caution.

In reading catalogs and examining other pieces of printed and visual information about colleges, candidates should keep in mind that such documents have two purposes. They are designed to convey information, and they are shaped to give a favorable impression of the institution. Candidates should not hold the colleges culpable for their image making; however, they and their families should be aware of it and be sure to obtain satisfactory answers to all their questions before making final application.

Selective Applications

After reading the catalogs, visiting the colleges that look interesting (discussed in the next chapter), and talking to a member of the admissions staff, students at the college, parents, guidance counselors, and friends, the candidate comes face to face with the task of selecting the group of schools he or she wishes to apply to. How many will there be? Which ones will they be?

Before students answer these questions, they should ponder the strategy of selective applications. On the assumption that applicants may not gain admission to all the colleges to which they apply, we then erect a simple theory: A range of colleges should be selected that will guarantee a choice of acceptances. The greater the number of choices desired, the more conservative the list should be in terms of the difficulty of the schools applied to. However, in no case should students apply to one "safe" school and a parcel of very difficult ones. This may leave them with only one choice, the safe school. Students who have at least two letters of acceptance in April of the senior year have a genuine choice to make, and they will feel much better about attending the college they eventually select than will those who have been forced into a corner and must "select" the backup school.

Establishing an order of preference for your college applications is a bit like playing the game of diplomacy. The diplomat makes a list stating what his government most wants to extract from negotiations with a foreign power; then he makes three or four more lists stating what he would accept if his first proposals were to meet with resistance. These additional demands are arranged in order of preference, from most preferred to least preferred. By arranging the colleges you have selected from your first through fifth choices, you, like the diplomat, will then be able to arrange all your options before you.

From the college directories and catalogs, focus on the admissions criteria for each of your colleges. Develop a rating scale of one to five. One will represent the most difficult to gain admission to, five the easiest. The ratings will incorporate your credentials as they compare with the admissions standards of the colleges you seek to enter. In determining this rating, you will want to consider the SAT and ACT scores of candidates accepted in the previous year, your rank in class, the difficulty of the program you have pursued in high school, and finally the types of students from your school who have been selected by the college in the past.

At this point it might be helpful to write a brief admissions profile of yourself:

Profile

Academic: SAT—math 590, verbal 640; Achievement Tests—English Composition 620, Math II 700, American History 640; B+ average (3.6); top 15% of high school class in a highly rated suburban school. National Merit Semifinalist, National Honor Society. Wish to major in history in college and become a lawyer.

Extracurricular: Goalie for boys' varsity soccer team, Life Scout, camp counselor for three summers, construction worker for one, play the trumpet well in school band and won a regional talent show last year. Do some acting and like it, want to continue in college. Also write music and drama reviews for school's newspaper.

Personal: Liked and admired by friends; enjoy being with people and managing them; also value family, personal honesty, and hard work. While not always a leader, I am conscientious and well organized in everything that I do.

Now write the colleges in which you are interested along the left-hand margin of a piece of paper, arranging them in descending order of difficulty of admission. List your criteria across the top: Academic Program, Location, Size, Extracurricular Activities, Cost, and Level of Difficulty. In the first column rate the quality of the academic program of each college on a scale from one to five, with one standing for the strongest and five for the weakest. Do the same for the attractiveness of the location and the size of the school. If a school is attractive in all respects except that its size is too large for you, then it must receive a size rating of four or five.

The extracurricular category refers to the availability of activities that you will want to become involved in at college. If you are a moderately good field hockey player, and the college's team had a fair season last year and will probably be looking for players, then the college gets the highest rating of one. Cost comes next. The cheapest school gets a one, the most expensive a five. Last is the level of difficulty of admission, the D-factor. Now total each college's ratings.

School	Academic Program	Location	Size	Extracurricular Activities	Cost	Level of Difficulty	Total
Hanover	1	2	3	2	4	1	13
Gold Coast	2	1	4	2	5	1	15
Capitol U.	1	1	2	1	3	2	10
Sunbelt U.	3	2	4	4	2	2	17
Midwestern U.	2	2	2	3	3	3	15
Gateway	2	4	1	2	3	4	16
Atheneum	2	3	1	3	3	4	16
State U.	2	4	4	3	1	5	19
Small College	3	5	4	2	2	5	21

You are now ready to make distinctions among the colleges and reduce your list to five choices. Already you know that Hanover is going to be your toughest school to get into. Last year the students who were accepted from your school had scores in the high 600s and were in the top 10 percent of their class, except for the varsity basketball center, who was accepted from the waiting list. Even so, you may be able to impress Hanover with your talent as a musician, with your solid record in tough courses, and with your wide involvement in school life.

Although Gold Coast's profile is much like Hanover's, its curriculum is somewhat weaker in the social sciences, according to an alumnus who has just come to work in your father's office. Gold Coast was the most beautiful school you saw last summer, but it is also a little on the small side, and you are looking mostly at larger colleges. Moreover, Gold Coast is rated five on cost. It does not offer very much financial aid, and your family will probably qualify for aid when your sister enters college in two years. Besides, Gold Coast has a higher overall score than Hanover, and a low score wins. Hanover is your number one choice.

From the schools you have ranked at the second degree of difficulty you should choose Capitol University. It has a total score of ten, whereas Sunbelt University, the other school in this category, has a high score of seventeen. Capitol, you will have noted, has the lowest score overall, but it is not your first choice. It should be first according to the rating system, but you have dreamed of applying to Hanover since you were quite young. No rating system can adequately express your fervor for Hanover, so it will remain your number one choice. If you don't make Hanover, and the chances are pretty good that you won't, the rating system has told you that Capitol University is just as good as Hanover except for that intangible emotional factor. In addition, your high school has a particularly good relationship with Capitol, since your predecessors have done well there. There is no doubt that Capitol should be your second choice. Its curriculum allows you to construct an area studies major, which is what you want to do; if you pursue international law, you would be able to focus on one particular area of the world, such as Africa or Asia.

Initially you liked Sunbelt University, even though it is somewhat small and does not have any special programs for history majors. It is, however, easier to get into than Hanover, your top choice. But now your enthusiasm for Sunbelt pales in the light of the ratings you have given Capitol. You have also learned that Sunbelt's admissions standards are rising due to an intensive public relations campaign that resulted in a high volume of applications this year. So Sunbelt should be scratched as a number two choice.

Midwestern's case speaks for itself. Although not in the best location, it is an ideal size—around 4,000—and its history department is good, surely better than Sunbelt's. Furthermore your scores, grades, and the other elements of your profile definitely put you in the group that Midwestern will accept. "If you keep your work up to your past standards, you ought to make it," your counselor says. You decide to apply.

Although Atheneum has as many points as Gateway, your father graduated from Gateway in 1960. This fact will greatly enhance your admission chances at Gateway, as will your high school record and SAT scores. Even if your grades decline slightly as you shoulder the increased responsibilities of senior year, you still ought to make Gateway. You have no alumni ties to Atheneum, and you might have a little trouble getting in there. So Gateway clearly becomes your number four choice.

As your backup, or safety choice, you select your state university rather than pick Small College, which is located in a picturesque Midwestern town and which may be in need of students next April. State University is very near home, but your parents have said they would pay for your room and board on campus. Moreover, close scrutiny of State's catalog reveals that its history department has quite a variety of courses, as well as internships in government offices. You also decide to apply to State because you feel you would receive more of a challenge in a school of its size (5,000) than in a smaller liberal arts college in a rural setting. Finally, State University is cheaper by far than your other choices! It therefore meets the standard test of a safety choice: "If all else fails, it is a place where I would be willing to go and do my best."

Filing your applications selectively gives you peace of mind, for in selecting five schools within the range of your abilities, you are almost assured of at least three admissions. Consequently you will have a genuine choice to make at decision time in April. With the confidence this gives you, you will be able to focus most of your attention on gaining admission to your first and second choices. Finally, you are in a position to say to your first- and second-choice schools: "Look, you are one of my two top choices. I am not shopping around; I really want to come." Students often underestimate how much their desire to attend a school can persuade a college to favor them with an offer of admission, especially if their credentials look like those of a lot of other candidates. After all, if you look at it from the college's point of view, they are interested in students who will turn up in September and register as freshmen. They do not want to send out thousands of admissions letters only to be turned down by many of the students who receive them. The more competitive the college's approach to admissions, the more a student's desire to come figures positively in the admissions process. Even though the college-bound population is expected to decline in the early 1990s, competition at selective colleges is expected to increase steadily, giving this generalization even greater validity than it has had in the past.

Early Decision, Early Action, Rolling Admissions
Students can make their desire to attend certain colleges known to these colleges by applying under several early admission plans. The simplest and most well known is the Early Decision plan operated by most private colleges and some public universities. Under this plan students submit their credentials early, usually by November 1 of the senior year, and sign a statement that they will accept the college's offer of admission if tendered. Students then receive word of their status by December 15. If they are denied early admission, then in most cases the colleges will defer final action on their application until March.

In recent years, the high quality of Early Decision applicants has led a number of colleges to accept more students. However, students with marginal records need to beware. As Karl Furstenberg, dean of admissions at Wesleyan University, warns, "There is a slightly better chance of being accepted early, but the pool is also stronger" ("Education Life," *New York Times,* 8 Jan. 1989, Education Section).

Some universities have adopted a one-sided version of Early Decision, which they call Early Action (originally offered only by Brown, Georgetown, Harvard, Massachusetts Institute of Technology, Princeton, and Yale). Under this plan a student need not accept the college's offer of admission but may file other applications. Students considering Early Action must bear in mind several important features of this plan. First, Early Action candidates can be rejected. Under most Early Decision plans candidates who are not admissible in December are deferred for consideration in March. Second, no financial aid awards are made to Early Action candidates until April. Third, Early Action is a very discriminating admissions process, so if your record is not superior in every way, you should wait until the regular deadline in January to apply to any of the schools that have this plan. Fourth, candidates who really want to attend a particular school should not regard Early Action as the most effective expression of keen interest. A first-choice letter similar to the one below could send the message more effectively.

Rolling Admissions bears some resemblance to Early Action, only its calendar is different. This program, offered by many state universities and other schools, allows candidates to submit credentials at their convenience up to a certain date, often January 1. They receive a letter of acceptance or rejection within four weeks of filing their application. Many ambitious candidates use Rolling Admissions to gain early acceptance at a school they regard as a backup choice and then concentrate on their top one or two choices. Whatever the motive, students should pay careful attention to published deadlines. Rolling Admissions at the University of Michigan, for instance, begins after September 1 and concludes on February 15 of the following year. Some colleges that accept students on a rolling basis fill up their freshman class before the final application deadline, so students should find out what each college's Rolling Admissions timetable really is.

Candidates who cannot decide which colleges they really want to apply to should not feel pressured to apply early to any of them. Those whose clear decision on a first-choice college comes later can write a letter to the dean of admissions in February and indicate their preference. A brief, simple letter will suffice:

> 34 Webster Street
> Westchester, New York 10783

Mr. Charles A. Smith
Director of Admissions
Coburn College
Harwick, New York 13321

Dear Mr. Smith:

Ever since I first heard about Coburn two years ago while working with an undergraduate who was a fellow camp counselor, I have wanted to come to the school. Recently I completed a thorough investigation of a number of colleges, and I still favor Coburn over the others. The special program for engineering students, the nationally recognized swimming team, and the opportunities for continuing my interests in drama and music all appeal to me particularly. I just wanted you to know at this point, when you are considering my application, that I really do want to be accepted. If I am, I will definitely come. I know I have much to learn, but I think I have something to contribute too.

> Yours sincerely,
> Martha A. Prentice

Ensuring Success

Students frequently respond to the inconsistencies of the college admissions process by filing a large number of applications in hopes of receiving multiple admissions through sheer luck. This is called the shotgun approach. What these students do not realize is that in applying to a number of schools with difficult and very similar admissions standards, they may be maximizing their chances of rejection rather than increasing their odds of acceptance. Admissions committees are staffed by professional admissions officers and discerning faculty members, and schools that are equally difficult to get into will react similarly to candidates whose credentials do not come up to the mark: they will reject them.

Candidates who file a plethora of applications cannot take the time to develop an approach tailored to the requirements and the style of each college. Such candidates often do not have enough time to research their colleges sufficiently and to see where they might fit in to a particular academic or extracurricular program. Thus they do not *match* themselves very well with the colleges to which they are applying. Also they do not have sufficient time to consider just what their special merits are as candidates, and so are unable to develop an *edge* over other candidates in their category. (The concepts *match* and *edge* are discussed in Chapter 5.)

In the multiple-application, or shotgun, approach, any tactical error, such as a weak personal essay, will be repeated on all applications, because candidates essentially are submitting the same application everywhere. So the risk of rejection increases rather than decreases. Filing numerous applications also puts candidates in the position of not being able to signal their first choice. Because they devote equal and insufficient energy to all, they are not able to focus on the one school they really want to attend. They may not even have a first choice! The message: Select five or six colleges across a range of difficulty, and stay with them.

By the time you come to the end of the selection process, having figured out which colleges you intend to apply to, you also may have come to the realization that the distinctions among the colleges are not that significant. That is a reasonable and proper outcome. You have in fact made a number of slight distinctions based on academic program, cost, size, location, and the like. You have judged the colleges, physically and philosophically. You have ascertained what life at the school is really like. You have developed a list of schools, all of which are similar and appropriate for you. You *know* your colleges, and also *know* yourself.

When you receive your acceptances and decide which of the schools you will attend, you will do so with the knowledge that this college is the place where *you* are going to exercise the prime responsibility for educating yourself. The college will provide the environment in which learning can happen, and you will take the responsibility for making it happen. Jean-Jacques Rousseau once remarked, "It is not the difference in the quality [that matters], but the quality of the difference." You are going to be making that difference during the next four years. Whatever catalogs promise, whatever rating methods the guidebooks employ, whatever judgments guidance counselors pronounce, you have the final say about whether your experience will be a productive and successful one. If you have approached your selection of colleges methodically and confidently, the odds that your college experience will be the best four years of your life are very high indeed.

3

Visiting

a College

It was a little after 3 p.m. one day in late August, and Laura Richards was afraid she would be late. Laura and her mother had just turned off the thruway and had 18 miles to go before reaching the campus of Coburn College. If they did not lose their way, they might be on time for their interview at 4 p.m.

As Laura mused about Coburn, she tried to remember some of the facts about it that she had read in one of the college guidebooks, but the statistics for Coburn and the other small liberal arts colleges she was considering all blurred together as she tried to read road signs and carry on a conversation with her mother. Laura wished she had remembered to ask for a catalog when she called up to arrange her campus visit a week ago. She also lamented the fact that she had not found the time to talk to some Coburn undergraduates who lived near her home in Westchester. Somewhere, too, in the deep recesses of her memory was her guidance counselor's suggestion that she take along a copy of her high school transcript to show to her interviewer. Laura regretted that she had forgotten it, especially since she had had a successful eleventh-grade year, and her principal had told her that she was in the top 20 percent of her class.

Now Laura and her mother were on a secondary country road, and they both had to keep a sharp eye out for the signs to Coburn. They pulled into the admissions office parking lot shortly before 4 p.m. Laura headed directly for the receptionist to announce herself. Her mother followed somewhat awkwardly. When the admissions officer came out to greet Laura, he encountered her mother first. Laura was in the ladies' room touching up her makeup. When she emerged, she noticed that the interviewer was dressed casually, and she wished she had thought to wear comfortable clothes rather than her voluminous print dress and high heels. After the preliminary introductions and some discussion of what Laura's mother would do while the interview was in progress, Laura and her interviewer went off to his office for a brief chat about her interest in Coburn.

Planning a Visit

Laura's hurried and poorly planned visit to Coburn suggests several ways to arrange for a successful visit to a college campus. When students make their initial contact with a college, whether by letter or telephone, they should make sure that they request a catalog and schedule a tour of the campus before going in for an interview. They should also ask for any special materials that may be pertinent to their own interests—a list of off-campus internships, a copy of the campus newspaper. The paper at least will acquaint them with important issues on campus. Candidates may want to consider asking the admissions office for the names of current undergraduates who live near their home, in order to discuss with them the kinds of academic and social challenges they might encounter at the college.

Students who already know their particular field of interest might ask the admissions office for the names of faculty members in their field. They then can write to these instructors or meet with them during the campus visit itself. Sometimes admissions offices will set up appointments with faculty members. Ask.

Martha Prentice goes to the same high school as Laura Richards. She planned her visit in a much more sensible fashion than Laura. She began by writing the following letter to the director of admissions at Coburn:

34 Webster Street
Westchester, New York 10783

Mr. Charles A. Smith
Director of Admissions
Coburn College
Harwick, New York 13321

Dear Mr. Smith:

I am very much interested in visiting the Coburn campus and having an interview later this summer. I will be finishing my job as a waitress on Martha's Vineyard about the twentieth of August. It would be very convenient for me if I could come to Coburn between the twenty-fifth and the twenty-ninth of August.

I would like to arrive in time to take your last morning tour, then have lunch with any students who might be on campus.

Since I am reasonably sure that I want to enter the engineering field, I would appreciate an opportunity to talk to one of the engineering faculty members after lunch. Then if you could schedule me for an interview at two o'clock, I would appreciate it.

I realize that you have many requests for interviews and materials at this time of the year, but I would still appreciate it if you could send me the following information: (1) a catalog for Coburn, (2) a copy of the campus newspaper, (3) any special literature you have about the engineering programs at the college, and (4) a list of the Coburn undergraduates who live near me in Westchester.

Even though I will be on the Vineyard, you may reply to this letter at my home address above. Thanks very much for your assistance.

Yours sincerely,
Martha A. Prentice

If Laura Richards had written such a letter she might have spent a very productive August day on the Coburn campus. Instead of arriving at the interview harried and short on information about Coburn, Laura would have had ample time to make a preliminary survey of the college. She would have read the catalog from cover to cover. She would have gleaned from the campus newspaper what the main issues on campus were. She would have learned from current Coburn students what they thought about the quality of undergraduate life there. And from her conversation with an engineering professor she would have been able to make some assessment of her interest in the field and her ability to handle the engineering program at Coburn.

Martha Prentice's Visit

But it was Martha Prentice who got Mr. Smith's reply, in which he told her that a Coburn sophomore named Sarah Chapman lived near her home in Westchester. When she got home, Martha telephoned Sarah and arranged to meet her for a snack downtown. Martha and Sarah liked each other immediately. They found that they had several friends in common and that they were both interested in the sciences. Sarah was majoring in Coburn's special program in animal behavior and liked the science department. She had played field hockey at her high school and was a member of Coburn's field hockey team. Martha also played field hockey, as well as basketball, and she wanted to find out about women's sports at Coburn. Since Coburn had been coeducational for only ten years, Martha did not believe all the claims the college made in its special pamphlet on women's sports at Coburn.

In the course of their hour-long conversation, Martha was able to get interesting answers to some of her pressing questions, among them:

1) What attracted you especially to Coburn? Has it lived up to your expectations? What has surprised you about the school? What has disappointed you?

2) Do you know any girls who are majoring in engineering? What do they say about the program?

3) Have you gotten good academic and career advice at Coburn? How frequently do you see your faculty adviser? Can you change advisers easily if you need to? Have your teachers and adviser suggested courses and research topics that have helped you proceed toward your graduate work in veterinary school?

4) Tell me about life in the dormitories. I know there are all sorts of living arrangements—single-sex, coeducational, the communal kitchen idea—as well as a few off-campus apartments, but what I really want to know is how you like where you live.

5) In the same vein, do students seem to care genuinely about one another? Is the social life relaxed yet interesting, or do you feel pressured into going to the football games on Saturday afternoons? What about your other female friends—how do they feel? And the boys? Have you met some nice ones?

6) Can we talk about sports for a minute? Frankly, I don't believe all that I read in the Coburn catalog about "individualized instruction," "spacious and well-equipped facilities," and the "enthusiasm of fellow participants." What has been your experience with the field hockey team at Coburn? Has it been relegated to second place because of Coburn's prominence in football? Does it play a rigorous schedule? Does it compete in any regional tournaments? Could you tell me about the actual facilities for women—the locker rooms, uniforms, and equipment? Are there female coaches for most of the women's sports? Finally, since I know I will only be able to play one varsity sport at Coburn and I am interested in both basketball and field hockey, what is your opinion of these two teams and their coaches? Do people enjoy playing these sports on the intramural level as well?

Before Martha knew it, an hour had flown by, and Sarah had to go back to her job as a lab technician for a local veterinarian, which her zoology instructor had helped her find. This impressed Martha, as did Sarah's positive responses to her questions. Martha looked forward to visiting Coburn and asking some of the same questions of her student guide and the other Coburn students with whom she would have lunch.

As Martha rode her bicycle home, she formulated some of the questions that she would ask the engineering professor. She was impressed with the engineering offerings at Coburn. There were only 3,000 students on the campus, yet the engineering department offered four degree options: a Bachelor of Science in Chemical, Civil, Electrical, or Mechanical Engineering; a Bachelor of Science in Engineering—a much more general degree program that allowed interdisciplinary work; a five-year program that awarded a Bachelor of Arts or Bachelor of Science in the liberal arts and engineering; and an integrated bachelor's and master's program that led to two degrees at the end of five years. Martha's mental list of questions came together as follows:

1) **The Future.** What advice would you offer someone entering the engineering field today? What specific areas of engineering appear to be crowded? What areas appear to need students? From my own reading I would judge that aerospace is overcrowded and environmental engineering is underpopulated. What would you say?

2) **Flexibility of Program.** I know that I will enjoy the basic engineering courses in civil and mechanical engineering and the like, but I also want broad liberal arts training. I know I want to study some economics and accounting so that I would be qualified to enter the management field if my engineering specialty ever became outmoded. Given these interests, which one of the four degree programs would you suggest I follow?

3) **Faculty Presence.** The Coburn catalog says that the ratio of students to teachers is ten to one; that figure only means something to me when translated into class size. In the engineering department, roughly what percentage of the classes have ten students or less? What percentage have a hundred or more? How many instructors does the student have access to in a given lab period? Are there opportunities for individualized tutorial instruction for undergraduates? Does the faculty have to hold office hours?

4) **Faculty Quality.** Could you tell me a little about the engineering faculty? What are some of the honors recently won by members of the department? I assume that many of them do private research. Is student research ever integrated into a professor's own area of specialization?

5) **Facilities.** Do you feel that the engineering facilities at Coburn are adequate for training undergraduate engineers? If the facilities are deficient in one particular area, what special arrangements, if any, have been made for students who are interested in that sector of the engineering field?

6) **Undergraduate Life.** What is your feeling about the undergraduates here at Coburn? Do the faculty and students mix on an informal social basis? Do you enjoy this interaction with students yourself? Do the students appear pleased with the education they are receiving?

When Martha arrived home, she jotted these questions down (leaving room to note their answers after her visit) and placed them in the manila folder she had designated for Coburn.

When Martha was at last ready to make her visit, she and her mother left early in the morning, with an hour's margin built into their schedule just to be on the safe side. Martha dressed neatly yet casually in clothes that made her feel comfortable rather than formal. When they arrived on the campus at 10:15 a.m., they found they had time to go to the cafeteria for a cup of coffee before Martha went off on the campus tour at 10:45.

Martha's mother had arranged to have lunch with a friend who lived nearby. She would rejoin Martha at the admissions office when the interview was over. She would also take the afternoon tour and spend some time in the school's art studio, since she was a commercial artist by training. That left Martha free to operate on her own. In a long and friendly conversation with her parents at the beginning of the summer, Martha had told them that she wanted to handle her college exploration herself. Martha's parents had agreed, realizing that colleges take their direct relationship with applicants seriously and are inclined to look with disfavor on parents who appear to interfere in the admissions process.

Martha and her parents had agreed that one parent might well show up at the end of an interview to demonstrate the family's genuine interest in helping her make the right decision about college. At that point, the parent could ask questions of the admissions officer. For that matter, the admissions officer might have a question for the parent. The meeting between admissions officer and parent would allow an opportunity for a brief exchange.

Martha had already drafted her questions for the student guide, and she raised those questions during the hour-and-a-half tour and the luncheon that followed. After lunch, the interview Mr. Smith had arranged for her with an engineering professor also went well, because of her thorough preparation for it.

But Martha still had to gather a substantial amount of crucial information from her visit. Most of it was qualitative: student impressions of the social life, sports, work load, teachers, and other students. Martha was also interested in the library: the breadth of its holdings, special journals in her field, accessibility of the various collections, its hours, and the terms for borrowing books.

Martha also inspected the gym carefully. Having learned from Sarah Chapman of improvements in the women's locker rooms, Martha wanted to see them herself. She asked about the gym's hours. Would she and her friends be able to play an informal game of basketball some evening in the winter? She examined the new $4-million field house, which had eight handball and racquetball courts, four squash courts, a 200-meter running track, wrestling and weight rooms, a dance studio, trainers' suites, and men's and women's locker rooms.

Martha visited a dormitory briefly to see a student room and to check how crowded the living conditions were. If she should decide to live in a coeducational dorm, would she be happy with the existing bathroom and shower facilities for men and women? Would there be sufficient privacy? Were there rooms or spaces in dormitories where students wishing to study could separate themselves from those who did not? She wanted to know—so she asked.

She also asked about interdormitory athletic competitions and social affairs, about the faculty and graduate student resident adviser program in the dormitories, and about the relationship between Coburn and the residents of the nearby town of Harwick. (What specific activities bring students and townspeople together? Are there areas of tension? What is being done to alleviate them?)

Finally, Martha looked carefully at Coburn's theater. Having long suppressed a desire to act, she wanted to try her hand at acting in college. As the tour group moved through the theater, Martha was impressed by both the main hall for major productions and the so-called "black box" for advanced and experimental student and faculty productions. However, Martha was most interested in the small theater downstairs where informal plays and musicals were put on under student or faculty direction. This was one of the facilities that would eventually induce her to apply to Coburn.

Interview Guidelines

Now it was time for Martha to have her interview, and as she approached the admissions office at the end of her tour, she tried to keep the following guidelines in mind:

1) *Assert yourself* during the interview. Make sure that your interviewer knows not only who you are, but what you have done in your high school, the courses you have taken, the sports you have played, the extracurricular activities and hobbies that have intrigued you. Be enthusiastic about the activities—including studies—that interest you and in which you have done well. Try to convey your enthusiasm in a way that reveals *why* you like a certain thing.

2) Use the interview process to *probe the nature of the educational and social experience* at the college. Make your interviewer work. For example, Coburn has 3,200 students and so is considered a medium-sized school. Ask your interviewer what he thinks the advantages of a school this size are as compared with those of a small school with 1,500 undergraduates or a large campus, such as Berkeley, with 35,000 students. Which are the better academic departments at Coburn? Coburn has only been coeducational for ten years. How would the interviewer characterize the status of coeducation at Coburn today? Is it a fact of life and no longer an issue, or do further changes have to be made? What is it like to be a student at Coburn? Would someone with your interests, abilities, and background really be happy there?

3) *Ask analytical questions,* not factual ones. For example: "Coburn is sometimes called a rather homogeneous school, with many students from the upper-middle class and from New York State. Is that true?" Ask the interviewer to describe faculty-student relationships at Coburn. The figures may be impressive, a ten-to-one ratio of students to faculty, but, beyond that, how much do students see faculty members on a one-to-one basis both academically and socially? How do Coburn students feel about the place? Is there much use of alcohol

and drugs on campus? What about antisocial behavior? On the other hand, is there a fair amount of rational behavior and conformity among the students? Are students really involved in the decision-making process at the college? Do they sit on major committees? Undergraduates do not appear to have any role in the admissions process. Is that true? Is there any prospect for change in the near future? If you want to pursue engineering at Coburn but also want to take courses in the humanities and social sciences, particularly economics, would it be possible for you to take one engineering course, one humanities course, one economics course, and a fourth course of some sort each semester? Or should you consider instead fulfilling your humanities and social science interests in the January term, or in an off-campus program?

4) *Find out about your interviewer.* Try to establish some sort of personal relationship with your interviewer without straining the bounds of good manners or the normal flow of the interview itself. Who is your interviewer? Is he or she a graduate of the school? What did the interviewer like most about the experience there? What was least impressive about the education at Coburn? Whatever questions you decide to ask, remember that ideally the interviewer should come to see a little of himself or herself in you. In that way you will be remembered.

5) *Make the match* between yourself and the college. In a way, this guideline incorporates all the others. During the interview you should try to show not only your interest in attending the college but also your ability to contribute to it. Martha Prentice is an example of someone with much to offer. She is an able student who knows in which field she wishes to study. She is a good athlete, and her interest in dramatics may ultimately translate into a skill that will enliven the Coburn community. However, it is up to Martha to make these qualities known.

She can introduce evidence of her academic ability into the interview quite naturally by taking a copy of her high school transcript. This will show the success she has had in the courses she has taken. Many transcripts also include scores on the SAT or ACT Assessment, Achievement Tests, and Advanced Placement tests. A transcript gives the interviewer something to react to, and many interviewers will gladly give a frank assessment of your chances for admission once they have examined your transcript.

To *make the match* for her extracurricular contribution, Martha can ask, "How difficult would it be for me to make a varsity team?" She can then direct the discussion toward her abilities as a field hockey and basketball player. She can also prepare an athletic data sheet (discussed in Chapter 5) to show to the coaches at Coburn. In prefacing her remarks about her interest in the theater with a brief statement about her extracurricular activities at Westchester High School, Martha can indicate to her interviewer her interest in and willingness to contribute to another area of community life at Coburn.

Finally, by asking incisive questions about the role of the undergraduates in student governance and college policymaking, Martha can show mild dissatisfaction with the status quo and express her desire to change Coburn for the better. Very often colleges are impressed with candidates who are willing and able to carry out constructive changes on the campus.

Nervousness

The following tips will help to reduce the apprehension that is normally felt before a college interview. First, remember that the interview is not designed to stress you unduly but rather to focus on your credentials both as a person and as a student. Most interviewers will proceed from what you have to say, asking questions about the points you bring up. This means that you can have a substantial role in setting the agenda of the interview and controlling its content. So prepare for your interview. Know yourself. Know your subject—the college itself. Remember, you know a lot already. This is an opportunity to show what you know and to learn more.

Second, listen to what is being said. If the interviewer asks an ambiguous question, don't be afraid to ask for clarification. Or you can break the question down into its several parts and then proceed to answer each of them separately. Treat every question as important, but don't prevent humor from coming in either. Try to see all the implications in a given question—social, academic, psychological, cultural. Then pick the particular elements you want to respond to.

Third, be honest. Often, admitting a weakness can be disarming and subtly helps to bond you to the interviewer, who after all is not perfect either. Honesty is often the beginning of a learning experience, so it is a value that colleges appreciate. Nevertheless, honesty should not take the form of an apology; you should not be overly self-critical. In relating facts or incidents that may be slightly embarrassing, remember that college interviewers will be interested not so much in what you did as in what you learned.

Fourth, pauses can be refreshing. All too often first-time interviewees rush ahead with their conversation, in fear that a pause may create the impression that they are ignorant or insecure. Wrong. Consider the following historical example. On December 12, 1941, General George C. Marshall, the Chief of Staff, called in Colonel Dwight D. Eisenhower, who had served in the Philippines, and asked him for his "on the spot" opinion of the best strategy to follow in responding to the disastrous attack on Pearl Harbor five days before. Instead of answering at once, Eisenhower paused and then asked for three hours to consider the matter, promising to return in the afternoon with his answer. Marshall was a bit taken aback, but agreed. As he thought about it he became very impressed that Eisenhower took his question so seriously and wanted to give the most careful answer he could. From then on Marshall took a keen interest in the career of this intelligent young officer who "thought before speaking."

Perhaps Eisenhower carried the pause a bit further than a student in a college interview can, but the point is the same. A pause can also be used to ask for clarification. In addition, a pause can be used to regroup your thoughts before pushing on with your line of argument. Very often when you are having a conversational disagreement and are slowly trying to build your own case, a pause can help each of your points to stand out more strongly than if they were rushed together in a lengthy speech.

Fifth, look for the telltale signs that it is time to shift your tactics—the interviewer's body language and eye movements. Fidgeting, clenching or unclenching of hands, crossing and uncrossing of legs, and a faraway look in the eyes are signs that you had better change your tactics quickly. Bring your response to a close. Ask the interviewer a question. Allow a natural pause to take place. Somehow break the stream of conversation so it can go in a more fruitful direction.

Remember that if eye contact is not maintained all the time, it does not necessarily mean that either of you is bored. Very often when people are explaining something or venturing their own opinions, they are not quite sure of what they are saying. Thus they tend to look away from the person to whom they are talking. If, on the other hand, the listener in a conversation tends to look away, then the message being sent is often one of boredom or disagreement. By contrast, when speakers look directly at you, they are frequently confident of what they are saying and are therefore seeking confirmation from you. They are often signaling that they are willing to be interrupted and are eager to hear your thoughts. The rule for the novice interviewee? Act naturally and maintain a healthy degree of eye contact with the interviewer. Be yourself above all else.

Martha Prentice's Interview

Now let us consider an interview between Martha Prentice and David Walenski, an assistant director of admissions at Coburn, in which both parties learn much about the kind of experience Martha would be likely to have as an undergraduate at Coburn.

Walenski:	Well, how did your tour and lunch with the students go? Did any questions come up that I could answer?
Martha:	Yes, I enjoyed the tour and my talk with the students. Both experiences answered many of the questions I had, but I did want to find out from you what you feel to be the advantages of a relatively small school like Coburn for an undergraduate education.
Walenski:	I'd say there are two or three distinct advantages to this

institution. First, the size of Coburn is ideal. With 3,200 students, we can put together a class that has variety and quality in a way that a small college with half as many students cannot. So what you have here is a heterogeneous student body that is neither too big nor too small. You are going to get to know all sorts of different people here, and you will learn a lot from them, inside the classrooom as well as outside.

Second, I think the facilities at Coburn are exceptional. The unlimited access to the library's collection, the spacious playing area provided by the brand-new field house, and the three different types of theaters, not to mention the facilities over at the engineering school, really do impress me even though I'm very used to them by now.

Third, I think that your contact with teachers here will be of genuine and lasting value to you. The teachers here are just that—teachers. They like students. They want to spend time with them. If their primary objective were to publish, then they would be at a big university. Basically they come here to teach, and you will see a lot of them if you so desire. They are invariably available outside their office hours, and they really want to help the individual student do well enough to get into a good graduate school or land an interesting, responsible job.

Martha: You mention that you are used to the facilities here. How long have you been here, and what has been your experience?

Walenski: I came to Coburn seven years ago as an undergraduate. I had been picked up on a football scholarship. I had never heard of Coburn until one of the leading businessmen in my community of Altoona, Pennsylvania, suggested that I apply. I had done pretty well in high school, and the football coach here took an interest in my case after I sent him some newspaper clippings. At any rate, I came, majored in government, worked for a year and a half in Washington as a result of a job I had had during the Washington semester here, and have come back to work in the admissions department.

I may go off to graduate school in a year or so, but I'm going to have to wait for my wife to finish her nurse's training at the hospital in Buffalo. But you asked what my experience here had been. I love this place. I came from a small-town background. Neither of my parents went to college. I was very grateful for the scholarship I received.

I worked quite hard here and I feel I got something out of it. I met a lot of different people. One of my room-mates was a champion swimmer from Winnetka, Illinois. Another one was a science wizard from Baltimore. I had visited both their homes before I graduated. I also had the opportunity to take a variety of courses, some in fields I never knew existed. I even took that special Japanese history course for nonspecialists. I also learned the French language—you know you have to meet a language requirement here—and that was a great experience for me. I think that in a big university I would have been lost. I would not have gotten to know so many people. Here I also had the chance to shine in a couple of areas, and I met some people who will be my friends for the rest of my life.

Martha: That's a pretty persuasive argument. Many of the things you said are of interest to me. I want to get to know new people. I want to take a variety of courses, but I also want to finish here with a special skill in at least one area. Can you tell me which the strong departments are here and which the weak ones are? Is engineering really that strong?

Walenski: To be honest, I don't think that music is terribly strong here. The department has failed to obtain a couple of grants that would have helped it a good deal, and several of the younger promising teachers have left. However, I think you are in good shape if you pursue engineering with a minor in economics. Several of the engineering professors have had nationally acclaimed articles in the *Journal of Professional Engineers.* Because our engineering facilities are not as extensive as those at, say, a place like the University of Michigan, we do not get all that fancy government money to build a mock-up of a lunar capsule. However, our engineering professors are nationally recognized—at least, several of them are—and I would add that the college's Glickenspiel Award for distinguished teaching has gone to a member of the engineering department in three of the past five years. That's really something.

Martha: I am certainly impressed with that statistic. However, could I shift the subject for a moment? I would like to find out a little something about the social life here. I know it may be hard for you to answer, but what is your impression of the role of women here? Have they been

fully integrated? How about the fraternities and sororities? Do they dominate the social life here?

Walenski: I will take the latter question first. Fraternities and sororities exist on a take-it-or-leave-it basis here. About half the
students belong to a fraternity or sorority, but since
freshmen all have to live together in three dormitories,
and since there is not sufficient room for all fraternity
and sorority members in their houses, students do not
tend to break off into house cliques. If you do not want to
join a sorority, fine. If you don't, you'll probably get
invited to many of their parties anyway. I wouldn't worry
about fraternity or sorority domination one bit. Now on
the question about the role of women, that is pretty hard
for me to answer. We have been coeducational for about
ten years. Not quite 50 percent of the undergraduates
here are women. Certainly I did not sense any discrimination against them when I was an undergraduate here.
Since the competition for admission to Coburn is
sharper among women than among men, the women
tend to be a little bit brighter, and sometimes even more
dynamic, than the men. So they can more than hold
their own, even though technically they are in the minority. I would say quite frankly, though, that the main problem for Coburn in regard to women has been to attract
and then to retain competent women faculty members.
We still need to make progress in that area. For instance,
no woman has won the undergraduate teaching award
yet. There just aren't enough of them!

Martha: What is the ratio of male to female faculty members?

Walenski: Actually now it is about 20 percent female, and as you can
see this is under half the percentage of women students.
So what this all boils down to is that there aren't as many
role models, as the sociologists like to say, for the young
women here as there are for the young men. But other
than that, I would say that women here have a fulfilling
experience. There are undergraduate women resident
advisers in the dormitories; there are women on the
boards of most of the campus organizations—last year
the editor of the newspaper was female; and women artists and politicians are featured in the special events that
often occur on the campus. Jeane Kirkpatrick, former
ambassador to the United Nations, received an honorary
degree here last June, for instance.

Martha: From what you say, I gather that the role of women at

Coburn is not a particular issue. What, then, are the social and academic issues that have come up on the campus during the past year?

Walenski: I would say that the role of women is an issue, and one that the school is sensitive about. That there has not been a public outcry about women's rights should not obscure the fact that the administration cares very deeply about according women an equal place on this campus. You can see that from the special pamphlet on women's athletics that was sent to you along with the catalog.

If you looked at the campus newspaper, you probably know that the big issue last year was the investment of Coburn funds in companies doing business in South Africa. Both blacks and whites raised the alarm on that issue.

Martha: I saw that, but what did the school do about it?

Walenski: After a series of articles in the newspaper and interviews with trustees, the treasurer came out with an itemized statement of all of the school's investments. That was in late February. In early March the concerned students and staff, of whom I was one, held a huge rally in front of the administration building. We had megaphones, a sound truck, placards, the whole lot. Faced with our opposition, the trustees agreed to withdraw school funds from companies having a poor track record on integrating their work force in South Africa. It was a great victory.

Martha: It must have been exciting. I have given a lot of thought to this issue, since I may well end up somewhere in the business sector after graduation. But I feel that educational institutions ought to go pretty slowly on this whole question of investment in countries that abridge the civil rights of their citizens.

Walenski: You do?

Martha: Yes, I do. I feel that the maintenance or withdrawal of investments in countries like South Africa is closely related to American foreign policy and not entirely the concern of educational institutions. I think if the President believes that it would be in the American interest to withdraw investments from a country like South Africa, or indeed any of the black African countries, then he and Congress ought to take steps to implement that idea. For individual institutions to be constantly juggling their investments based on their own definition of what is politically desirable may well distract them from their essential purpose of educating undergraduates and result in mixed messages to the country in question. In terms of our foreign policy, it may well be of greater advantage to the United States to maintain all its investments and then threaten to withdraw them unless certain civil liberties are observed, rather than have individual institutions withdrawing funds in hopes of bringing greater rights to the oppressed inhabitants of those countries. I think we need a more coordinated approach and more leadership from our government, frankly.

Walenski: You do have a point there, and I don't know that I had thought about it in that way before.

Martha: Well, when I get in I'll have to see what I can do about changing Coburn's position. I have another question that relates to one of my interests. If I were to be admitted to Coburn, just how difficult would it be for me to win a place on the freshman field hockey team? We play pretty good field hockey at Westchester. Last year our team made the state semifinals, but I have heard that Coburn's field hockey team is pretty good too.

Walenski: Yes, it is. Last year the Coburn team went up to the semifinals in the state playoffs and managed to get to the semifinals in the East Coast tournament at Mount Holyoke as well. If you are as good as you say you are and your particular position is not overcrowded with candidates, I think that you could make the freshman team and plan to play about a third of the time. If you hung in there, you would probably make the varsity team the following year when some of the kids drop out because of academic or other interests. I will ask Sharon Cushman, the varsity coach, to drop you a line and give you the team's recent statistics. Sharon is a dynamic lady.

Martha: Thanks. If I am a potential field hockey player, will that enhance my chances of admission?

Walenski: Yes, it will. Every year we try to take a handful of people for each varsity sport. There is no formal rating system or coaches' quota system such as you might have at a state university, but athletics is a concern. We make no secret about that. If Sharon backs you, it will help.

Martha: In that connection, I hope you do not think it too bold of me to ask, but how do I look as a candidate for Coburn? I really am interested in the school, and I have brought along my high school transcript for you to look at if you wish.

Walenski: Well, I can say frankly from our conversation here today that you are a reasonably strong candidate. Let me see what courses you have had in high school . . . This transcript looks pretty strong to me. You have paid attention to the solid courses that we look for: English, a foreign language, mathematics, and the sciences. Do you plan to take a second semester of either physics or chemistry?

Martha: Chemistry is not my best subject, and the physics course is very hard, so I was considering separating them and taking one in each semester of my senior year. I do plan to take physics, which I like very much. Also in the fall I plan to continue with English, to take a course in current events, to begin calculus, and to take the French Advanced Placement course.

Walenski: Except for the current events course, those decisions all make sense to me. I would suggest that in view of your interest in engineering, you take physics in the fall. Then you would be far enough along to take the Achievement Test in January and submit that as a part of your application. Thus you would have the English Composition, French, Mathematics Level II, and Physics Achievement tests. If you got all 600 scores or better, you would look pretty good to us.

Martha: I will consider that suggestion seriously. Is there anything besides grades, scores, and ability to contribute to athletics and extracurricular activities that you and the committee are looking for in an applicant to Coburn?

Walenski: I'd say that we are definitely looking for an intangible quality of dynamism in a candidate. That can come out in a field hockey game, in an aggressive hook shot from the center of the field toward the goalie when there is little time left on the clock. It can come out as a statement, such as "I really don't understand what you are trying to show me, Professor So-and-So; could you go over that again?" Or it could be a statement made at a student-faculty forum, something similar to what you said to me a moment ago about South African investment policy; for example, "I wonder if it is the responsibility of a small college in central New York State to withdraw its investments from South Africa unilaterally when it perceives that civil rights in that country are being abridged. I wonder if we ought not to heed the advice of the State

Department and consult with our fellow institutions before attempting to deal with a social injustice 15,000 miles away."

In short, we are looking for people with vitality, imagination, and a sense of responsibility to themselves and to the community around them. I always remember a line from Alfred North Whitehead. He said, "The task of a university or college is to weld together imagination and experience." The professors here, the libraries, the facilities, they all add up to experience. What we are looking for is a group of students with imagination and a constructive interest in challenging their teachers and this institution as they move through it. If we can compose a class of varied individuals who are bright and spirited, yet aware that institutions and society often change slowly, then we will have done our job.

Martha: Thanks. In my application I'll give some thought to the points you raise.

Walenski: Well, thank you too for coming up today. I think we have to wind up this interview because we have gone overtime. I am very glad to have had the chance to talk with you. I shall look forward to reading your application. In the meantime, if there are any questions that come up, here is my card. Please do not hesitate to get in touch with me.

Martha: Thanks again.

Naturally interviews will vary enormously in their style and content. One can only hope that they proceed as smoothly as the one between Martha Prentice and David Walenski. Even if they do not, they will probably have a positive impact on the candidate's chances of admission. A recent study by a national testing organization found that the impact of the interview on the admissions decision "was even greater than most colleges realized themselves" (Herbert F. Dalton Jr. and Thomas C. Hayden, *Preparing for a Successful College Interview.* Princeton, N.J.: Peterson's Guides, 1984, p. 10). Therefore it seems safe to argue that a reasonably good college interview can make a difference, especially at a selective college, and particularly when the candidate is at the margin of the acceptable group.

Applicants should keep in mind, however, that a wonderful interview does not guarantee an admission. A good interview cannot overcome a poor academic record or minimal involvement in extracurricular activities or weak personal recommendations by your teachers or your school. Colleges will admit mainly those students who have made the most of their educational opportunities, rather than those who show charm and an ability to converse at the interview.

Nonetheless, students contemplating their first college interview should look on it as an excellent opportunity to present their unique personal traits, academic abilities, and special talents to the college. In many instances the journey to a college campus far from home in order to have an interview is a statement of interest and enthusiasm that is not lost on the admissions office. So, with the proper attitude, students can make the interview serve their end—enhancing their application to a particular school.

Bear in mind that the interview also serves important ends for the college. It gives them an opportunity to describe strong programs, courses, instructors, and athletic and artistic facilities to the public. Obviously, it offers admissions officers an opportunity to "convert" good candidates to their school's "cause." Even at selective colleges at which the chances for admission are slim for many, the interview has real significance. One compassionate admissions officer at a very selective college put it well when he said, "I look on the interview as the first and last opportunity a lot of kids will have to make contact with my college. I want the opportunity to be as pleasant and as productive as it can be."

Given the opportunity of a college interview, students should show a natural enthusiasm about themselves and their credentials; they should plan to control as much of the content of the interview as seems reasonable; they should listen to their interviewer so that they can give thoughtful responses to questions and come to know something about the interviewer as a person; they should be honest about their failings as well as their opinions and not tailor their remarks to suit what they think the interviewer wants to hear; they should not fear pauses but use them to their advantage; and finally they should watch for telltale signs in eye movement and body language so that they can shift the conversation if necessary and keep it on a productive course.

They might remember, too, that in every good interview there is at least one instance of the unexpected. In Martha's conversation with David Walenski, the digression about Coburn's investments in South Africa brought both the interviewer and the interviewee to a new level of understanding. Walenski discovered that the neatly attired upper-middle-class girl from a wealthy suburb of New York City had a mind of her own and wasn't afraid to speak it. In fact, as he said, David Walenski had not thought about the problem of overseas investments in quite that way before.

Martha herself came to understand that the "climate of free discussion" described in the catalog really did exist at Coburn. She found Walenski's reaction to her statement a reasonable one, and that impressed her.

After Martha left the room, David Walenski jotted down a few notes on Martha's interview report form: "Sensitive, intelligent, mature young woman who knows what she wants but is open to the ideas of others. Reasonable scores, very good grades, probably a contributor to field hockey and may also turn up in student theater productions. I was impressed with this fine young woman. I hope she applies and that we can find a place for her."

Martha's interview was a success.

4

Timing

and Testing

Some of the older readers of this book will view it as sacrilege to suggest that the freshman year in high school is not too early to begin thinking about college. Admittedly college lies well ahead of the ninth grade, and overconcentration on college planning at this early point in a student's education could distort the emotional and intellectual growth that adolescence should bring. Nonetheless, a little college thinking during this important year will go a long way toward making that growth as smooth as possible.

Freshman Year—Becoming Aware

Once the challenge of high school seems manageable and life has settled down to a routine, ninth-grade students should think about what subjects they particularly like, what outside activities give them pleasure, and what areas of study and vocational skill they might like to explore during the next four years. Often guidance counselors can help students clarify their thoughts or direct them to courses and programs they might want to pursue, but students can also explore on their own. A young woman who loves helping with her mother's catering business on the weekends and who is a whiz at math takes an optional cooking course in the spring term of her ninth-grade year. She also decides to go to the school's computer center to look at software that would enable her to help her mother do some simple bookkeeping on the family computer. Who knows what might happen next? What is important is that the young woman took some initiative with respect to her future and may someday bring together in a college program her talent for math and her experience in food preparation.

Ninth-grade students may also want to talk to older friends who are in college and find out what it is like, asking, for example, what advice they would give to someone beginning high school or what they would have done differently. If there is a college near home, they might visit it on an informal basis, perhaps to attend a sporting event or look at the library. They might try to picture themselves at that college.

Finally, as a ninth-grade student, you should have at least one talk with your parents so that they know that you are interested in going on to college, if indeed you are. Your parents know your strengths very well and may have some ideas about what skills still lie dormant in you. They may have some specific colleges in mind where they think you would be happy. If there happens to be a difference of opinion, perhaps the family could visit certain colleges during a vacation the following summer. Then you would have specific examples to discuss.

Having done these things, you should turn back to the enjoyment of being a freshman and to the myriad activities, both social and academic, that will make high school a productive and happy experience.

Sophomore Year—Self-Analysis

In the beginning of this book there was a lengthy section advising students to focus on their talents, inclinations, and personality. The tenth grade is an ideal time to begin to look at these areas—to explore yourself—and then to begin to focus on a possible career. Start the tenth-grade year with an interview with your guidance counselor. Find out if your school administers tests to assess preferences, to inventory interests, or to identify personality traits. It may be necessary to go to another school to take these tests or to seek the assistance of an educational counselor in order to find out what you are good at, what kinds of social situations bring out the best in you, and how you approach challenges.

Discussions with your friends and parents already may have helped you come to a preliminary judgment about the kind of person you are and what your apparent talents are. To add to this the formal results of a preference test, a skills assessment, and some kind of personality profile would help enormously as you begin to think about your possibilities for the future. After you get the results of these tests, you should have a general idea of what fields of work you might want to explore. Ask your counselor to show you the career reference section of the guidance office, so that you can look at the qualifications necessary for some of the careers that interest you. There are also a number of computer programs that assist students in exploring careers. If your school does not have one, the guidance counselor may be able to access a career program on a state or national database.

At this point sophomores might want to consider taking the P-ACT+ test, which is offered by the American College Testing Program. This instrument is not a formal practice test for the ACT Assessment, but rather a device that helps students "initiate and sustain the process of making postsecondary plans, identify and acquire the academic . . . skills they will need to make a successful transition to postsecondary education or work, . . . [and] effectively demonstrate their academic skills on national college admissions tests . . ." (P-ACT+ pamphlet. Iowa City, Iowa: American College Testing Program, 1988, p. 1). There are four skill areas in the test format: writing skills, mathematics, reading, and science reasoning; scores are reported for each on a scale of 1 to 36 (which is similar to the ACT Assessment). Moreover, a quartile rating is given for each subscore, so that students will know where they fall compared to others who took the test, and they can identify areas that need strengthening. The P-ACT+ is new, and it will ultimately help students to look at the relationship between their high school grades and their skills, as well as to look ahead to their possible ACT results.

The Preliminary Scholastic Aptitude Test (PSAT) can also be taken for practice in the sophomore year. Guidance officers can help with registration for the test, which normally is given in late October. They will also distribute copies of the answer sheets once the tests have been scored. Literature accompanying the test results helps students interpret their responses and scores. When the test results come back, students should schedule an appointment with the counselor to review them.

During the sophomore year students should have a more extensive conversation with their parents than they had the year before, informing them of the results of the various tests and relaying the insights of their guidance counselor. They should also raise the subject of the financing of their college education, so that both student and family can begin to plan for this, if they have not already.

In addition, students should begin to build up a small library about colleges, concentrating on reference works rather than specific catalogs. *Peterson's Guide to Four-Year Colleges* and *The College Handbook* of the College Board are both relatively inexpensive, and either will serve students well.

As students begin to make the connections between their aptitudes, skills, and personality and possible careers, they should be sure to take any high school courses that will highlight those skills and illuminate those career possibilities. Guidance counselors can usually help students pick the courses that suit them best, while ensuring that the proper complement of college-preparatory courses is pursued. If in doubt, students should take the most demanding program they can handle.

Junior Year—Setting Strategy

Everyone knows that the plot thickens in the junior year, when the time comes to get serious about college planning. If some of the objectives for the sophomore year were impossible to meet, then get them done in the fall of the junior year. Also begin your testing program, keeping in mind two salient points. First, the timing of the tests should be keyed to the courses you are taking. Take your Achievement Tests when you have come to the proper point in your courses, and take the SAT or ACT on the other available test days. Research has shown that the Achievement Tests are a valid predictor of college success, so concentrate on doing your best on them.

Second, do not take the tests too many times in hopes of improving your scores. Your scores will not improve significantly, and the colleges will not necessarily be impressed by five SATs (all with nearly the same score) and four sets of Achievement Tests. Obviously, if you are sick on a certain test date and feel you could do better with another opportunity, then take the test again. Or if you have taken one of the SAT preparation courses or extensively reviewed the subject matter covered by an Achievement Test since you were first tested, then you should attempt the tests again. Otherwise follow this rule of thumb—SAT or ACT twice, Achievement Tests twice, and leave it at that. There are other things to do on Saturday mornings besides taking tests.

A college-planning calendar for your junior and senior years should include the following:

October   Take the PSAT, making sure you have read the materials describing the test's content prior to the test date. When you get your results, discuss them with your counselor, who can help you interpret your scores.

January   Take the SAT or the Achievement Tests in subjects you have completed in the first semester of your junior year. For specific information on the Achievement Tests, consult the pamphlet *About the Achievement Tests,* available in your guidance office.

February   Take the ACT Assessment if you believe it reveals your strengths better than the SAT or any of your college choices require it. If you take the ACT, get ahold of a pamphlet called *Preparing for the Enhanced ACT Assessment* from your guidance counselor, and review the suggestions for the subject-area tests.

     Make sure that you know the layout of the guidance library—where the catalogs, career guidance materials, and any helpful audiovisual and computer programs are located. If you have not done so already, conduct a search for colleges that offer the majors and the extra-curricular activities that you are interested in pursuing. Use the section on majors in *Peterson's Guide to Four-Year Colleges* or the College Board's *Index of Majors.* If you like to use computers, then you may want to try Peterson's College Selection Service or the College Board's Explorer program.

March   Possible SAT test date if you took Achievement Tests in January.

April   Make an appointment to talk with your guidance counselor about applying to colleges. Research the colleges the counselor suggests in the catalogs in your school's library. Write for additional materials from the colleges that intrigue you. During your spring vacation, if you have one, visit a college near your home and take the guided tour. Talk to students if possible.

If you have chosen to take the ACT and did not take it in February, take it now.

May   Take the Advanced Placement tests if you are enrolled in advanced courses and your teachers approve.

June   Take Achievement Tests in subjects you will not be continuing in your senior year. Also take Achievement Tests in Latin, Hebrew, German, and European History and World Cultures if you are taking one of those subjects and doing well. These Achievement Tests are administered only in June and December. Consult your instructors for advice on taking all these exams. Proper timing of tests is important. You may want to take the SAT again, but do so only if you feel you can better your first score significantly! June is also another time to take the ACT, if you wish to and have not already done so.

Summer Vacation   Plan to visit and have interviews at colleges in which you are genuinely interested and which are too far from your home to be visited easily in the fall. (See Chapter 3.)

Senior Year—Active Engagement

September/ October   Many colleges will undoubtedly send representatives to your high school or to your area. Most will conduct group meetings rather than personal interviews. Attend these meetings to make yourself known to the college representatives. On weekends, plan to visit nearby colleges in which you are interested. Schedule yourself for a campus tour, followed by an interview. Procure application forms from all the colleges to which you might apply. Keep your college counselor informed of your plans and any new developments, such as honors and awards that have come your way or specific words of encouragement from college coaches or admissions officers. Remember to complete and file applications to state schools with early or rolling admissions deadlines. The increased popularity of "the state school option" has caused many state universities to fill before their final filing dates.

October also presents the first opportunity for taking the ACT as a senior.

November   Take the SAT for the last time—your second or possibly third try. Submit Early Decision or Early Action applications by November 1 or November 15. Visit a college campus during your Thanksgiving vacation. Begin to fill out your regular college applications. Do the easiest first. Allow three to four days for each one. Send off applications to schools with early deadlines.

December   Most seniors will take their final set of Achievement Tests this month. Note that the English Composition with Essay Test is given only on this date, and some colleges like you to take it. The Latin, European History and World Cultures, German, and Hebrew Achievement Tests can also be taken in December. Distribute teacher recommendation forms to those teachers who have agreed to help you.

The ACT is also offered this month. Those who did not take it in October should do so now.

January   Send off your college applications by January 1 or January 15, the final dates for most applications. Submit portfolios, musical tapes, or other supplements to your application at this time. Take the SAT or Achievement Tests late in the month if you did not complete your testing in December.

February   Submit any special letters of recommendation from coaches or prominent alumni by the first of February. If you have a first-choice college, write to the admissions committee and inform them of your preference. Colleges are making tentative evaluations of students at this time and may notify your guidance counselor informally of your chances of admission. Listen to what your counselor has to say. Read between the lines. File additional applications if the horizon darkens.

March   Nothing to do but wait, but try to avoid agonizing. Keep your academic work up to your previous level; improve it if you can. If you are placed on a waiting list later on, your midwinter record will take on great importance.

April   Colleges notify applicants of their decisions. If you have tough choices to make, plan to revisit the schools in which you are interested. Be sure to talk to students this time. If financial aid figures in your decision, ask the colleges that accepted you to explain their offers thoroughly.

May   Reply to the colleges that accepted you and choose the one you think will be best for you, not one your parents or friends think you ought to go to. If by chance you have been placed on a waiting list, follow the suggestions outlined in Chapter 9.

The Tests Themselves

Achievement Tests

In planning for your standardized testing, remember our two rules: time the tests to coincide with your courses, and try to limit the number of times you repeat the tests. Because timing is so important, build your test schedule around the Achievement Tests. Take the SAT or ACT at a sensible interval once you have decided where your Achievement Tests will fall.

If you want to take the Mathematics Level II exam, for instance, do so at the point at which you have concluded your study of algebra, solid and coordinate geometry, and trigonometry and functions, not after you have begun your study of calculus. Likewise, you should take the French Achievement Test at the point at which you have covered all of French grammar, most standard French vocabulary, and the various styles and levels of written French. In other words, you should be able to read French quickly and understand the author's point of view, the feelings of the characters, and the mood or tone of the work. Clearly it would be a mistake to attempt the French Achievement Test before you had completed at least two years of intensive study of the subject. Three years would be better. However, it would also be wrong to defer the French Achievement Test until you had reached the Advanced-Placement-level course in your high school. By that time you would have gone beyond the critical point for the Achievement Test. Your memory of the proper grammatical forms might have become clouded by the fact that you had been doing more reading than writing or speaking. You would probably achieve a decent score on the test, but it could be lower than if you had taken the test a year or two earlier.

For an introduction to the tests, study the pamphlet called *About the Achievement Tests,* which is published by the Admissions Testing Program. Your school's guidance office should have a copy. This pamphlet describes the material covered by each test and gives sample questions.

The final decision to take a given Achievement Test should lie with your teachers. They should know what the content of the Achievement Test in their particular subject is and how well the course you are currently taking covers the test material. Many excellent high school courses do not teach specifically for the Achievement Test, nor should they. At one eastern boarding school, for example, the American history course does not cover the factual material required by the American History and Social Studies Achievement Test. Instead the course concentrates on primary source reading, writing, and analytical skills. If you find yourself in such a course, it may be necessary for you to do some special preparation for the Achievement Test. For example, in American history, students might profit from a review of the College Outline Series pamphlet on the subject or by intensive study of a short textbook on American history before taking the fact-oriented exam.

Often teachers who want their students to do well on the Achievement Tests will offer minireview courses or give advice about specific areas of the subject matter that require further study for success on the Achievement Test.

If an Achievement Test has been taken at the proper point in the student's course of study and good results obtained, it may not have to be taken again. If the student is not continuing the study of a particular discipline, then taking the test once will probably have to suffice. Often, though, students are going ahead in, say, French, math, or biology and may want to take the Achievement Test again in one or more of these areas. Several guidelines should be kept in mind for repeating tests:

1) Take the test again if you are in the process of completing another course in the subject. For example, if you took the French Achievement Test after three years' study of the language—and scored 600, say—and are now taking a course requiring you to read certain French playwrights in the original, then you should probably take the Achievement Test a second time. On the other hand, if you have taken the Biology Achievement Test once and are currently studying histology, you should probably not take the Biology Achievement Test again. According to *About the Achievement Tests,* the Biology Achievement Test covers cellular structure and function, organismal reproduction, development, growth, nutrition, genetics, evolution, systematics, ecology, and behavior. The test also calls for an understanding of "basic scientific methods and laboratory techniques." Histology is not included on the test; it is too specialized. Unless you have an opportunity for extensive review of the biology topics just mentioned during winter or spring vacation, for example, you should probably stand on your original biology score and not jeopardize it by taking the test a second time.

2) If you believe that you can improve your score significantly by taking the test again, and if you do plan to select your college major from the same general area as the material covered by the test, then try to take it again. An applicant to Princeton, for instance, who obtained a 600 on the Biology Achievement Test and who is intent on pursuing the study of microbiology in college should plan on taking the Achievement Test again. A quick look at the profile of Princeton's admitted students last year reveals that the average score on the Biology Achievement Test was 630. So this applicant should consider taking the next level of biology in the next term at high school and reviewing carefully for the test.

3) If you have achieved a score of 700 on an Achievement Test, rejoice and be satisfied with that; do not risk getting a lower score on a second attempt at the test. On the other hand, if you scored below 500 the first time you took an Achievement Test, you ought to try to take that test again, even if you are no longer studying that particular discipline. Demanding colleges look askance at scores below 500 and are generally impressed with scores over 700.

If you are really worried about what to do, you can always call the admissions office of the college to which you are seeking admission and ask for advice. Or you can ask the guidance counselor at your high school and then make your decision. In the meantime, study the schedule for the Achievement Tests in order to make your choice with time considerations in mind. (See page 64.)

Scholastic Aptitude Test

Allowing the Achievement Tests to set the test schedule, students have ample opportunity to take the SAT on two occasions if they so desire. The normal pattern is for students to take the SAT for the first time in the spring of their junior year and a second time in November of their senior year.

The subject of taking the SAT again brings up the question of using coaching or preparatory courses to improve scores. Readers of the national press will be aware of the battle that arrays a small but vocal group of critics against the College Board and its testing affiliate, Educational Testing Service. The critics argue that the SAT has a "code" and that it can be broken. Some of these people run so-called cram courses that promise inordinate improvement in scores. Students considering such courses should bear a few points in mind before plunging wildly ahead.

First, colleges are becoming increasingly chary of the validity of the SAT. This is not to say that they have lost faith in it; they have not. But many college admissions officers now feel that it is not as accurate a predictor of student success in college as they once thought.

Second, any college that is worthy of its name as a selective school will consider the SAT in the broader context of other tests, such as the Achievement Tests or the ACT; grade point average; school support; teacher recommendations; and the student's application itself. The SAT is not the sole factor influencing admission to a selective college.

Third, students' scores will normally fluctuate 20 to 30 points per test from one administration to another. Even though the test makers try to standardize all the tests, they are not always able to achieve absolute equivalency. So the tests vary slightly, and the scores will reflect that. One of the more famous of the preparatory courses promises a score improvement of from 110 to 150 points. Even if this proves true, the shrewd buyer of these services should remember that 50 to 60 of those points represent a normal variation from one test administration to the next.

A Guide to the Achievement Tests

Subject	Achievement Test	Recommended Course of Study	Recommended Test Dates	Comments
English	English Composition	3 years of high school English	May or June of grade 11; December of grade 12	Early date applies to good students only.
	English Composition with Essay	3 1/2 years of high school English	December of grade 12	Given only in December.
	English Literature	3 1/2 years of high school English	December or January of grade 12	Good students only; must have skills and the terminology of literary analysis.
History	American History and Social Studies	1 year of high school survey course, preferably in grade 11	June of grade 11; December of grade 12	Review a good American history text; all factual questions.
	European History and World Cultures	1 year of European history, 1600 to present; other courses in the history of the Middle East, Latin America, and Asia helpful	June of grade 11; December of grade 12*	Questions on political, diplomatic, intellectual, cultural, social, and economic history; graph and cartoon or two.
Classics	Latin	2 to 4 years of high school Latin	June of grade 11; December of grade 12*	3 to 4 years of study; grammar and forms, prose, poetry, and reading.
Modern Languages	French	2 years of high school French; 3 to 4 years preferable	June of grade 11; December of grade 12	Only superior students should take test after 2 years' study.
	German	2 years of high school German; 3 to 4 years preferable	June of grade 11; December of grade 12*	3 to 4 years' preparation; grammar and vocabulary are stressed.

Modern Languages (continued)	Hebrew	2 years of intensive study; 3 to 4 years preferable	June of grade 11; December of grade 12*	Consult instructors before taking test; half the test takers have studied for 10 years.
	Spanish	2 years of high school Spanish; 3 to 4 years preferable	June of grade 11; December of grade 12	Only superior students should take test after 2 years' study.
Mathematics	Math Level I	2 years covering algebra, geometry, trigonometry, functions, number theory	January or June of grade 11; December of grade 12	Recommended for average or weak students.
	Math Level II	3 years of math, advanced algebra, plane and solid geometry, vectors, sequences, functions, limits, logic, probability	June of grade 11; December or January of grade 12	Narrower and deeper than Level I test; recommended for good students with 3 years of high school math.
Science	Biology	1 year of high school biology covering cells, reproduction, nutrition, genetics, evolution, ecology, behavior, basic lab skills	June of grade 10; June of grade 11	Take test after good general survey course (college prep), not after specialized course.
	Chemistry	1 year of college-preparatory course (not introductory) covering molecular theory, matter, formulae and equations, bonding, various types of chemical changes	June of grade 11; December or January of grade 12	Consult instructor and *About the Achievement Tests* before attempting test; laboratory experience helpful.
	Physics	1 year of college-preparatory course (not introductory) covering mechanics, electricity, magnetism, optics, waves, heat, kinetic theory	June of grade 11; December or January of grade 12	Consult instructor and *About the Achievement Tests* before attempting test; no calculators or slide rules.

*Test only given in June and December.

Fourth, there is much that students can do to maximize their own scores, without outside help. When signing up for the SAT, students should ask their counselor for a pamphlet called *Taking the SAT*. It contains a sample test and answers for the student to consider. Students can even time themselves and arrive at a tentative score on their own. Then they can move on to the books *SAT Success* (Joan Davenport Carris with William R. McQuade and Michael R. Crystal. Princeton, N.J.: Peterson's Guides, 1987) and *10 SATs*, published by the College Board, and study several tests on their own. (Students also should be aware that they can request a copy of their completed SAT from the Admissions Testing Program in Princeton, New Jersey. A small fee is involved, but a large educational benefit can result from a close inspection of just where you went wrong.)

There are also a growing number of computer programs on the market, such as Peterson's SAT Success for Micros, that can be bought for a reasonable price and perhaps shared by families with college-bound children. In selecting a computer program, keep in mind three questions: (1) Does the program have a mechanism that tells students where and how they went wrong? (2) Does the program have graphics or sound capabilities, and if so are they helpful or distracting? (3) Are there accompanying materials, such as workbooks, practice tests, and perhaps a manual that complement and expand upon the program itself?

Fifth, if you do decide to take an SAT prep course, focus on one that will teach you skills and information, rather than a technique to "beat the system." As Dona Schwab, assistant principal of Bronx High School of Science, says:

> Taking a course with other college-bound students can be a stimulant. [It] encourages students to perform better. . . . But the best preparation for the SATs is long-range skill building. Read, read, read! Long-term skill building pays off. Beating the system may pay off for the moment, but it is not the way to go. If you have already developed the skills needed to succeed in college, your SAT scores should reflect this. (Sandra F. MacGowan and Sarah M. McGinty, *Fifty College Admission Directors Speak to Parents*. New York: Harcourt Brace Jovanovich, 1988, p. 110)

Sixth, aside from formal preparation, students should realize that the SAT is not unrelated to what they may be studying in mathematics and English. Continuing to do well in their courses (particularly by studying English vocabulary, if that is a weak area) can often help students improve their performance on a subsequent SAT exam. Also, the simple process of growing socially and intellectually can often have a positive impact on SAT results.

Remember that there is much to be gained from a sensible scheduling of the SAT and Achievement Tests. By planning ahead for their testing, students can eliminate some of the anxiety from the outset. By leaving intervals between the tests, there will be time to correct any deficiencies that may arise. Furthermore, planning for the tests and taking some of them in the junior year will give guidance counselors some preliminary data on which to base their advice. Even though they may not want to hear that advice, at least wise test scheduling allows students some time to act on it before applications must be filed.

Moreover, students who begin the testing process in the junior year are able to report their scores informally to colleges during summer interviews with admissions officers. Results of standardized testing enable students to make reasonable college choices so they avoid applying over their heads or beneath their abilities. Test scores help students distribute their choices over a range of colleges, thus ensuring a number of affirmative responses at decision time in the spring. This is the real objective of the college admissions process, maximizing the number of colleges that say "yes" in April. Intelligent planning for tests forms an important part of the process that leads to those affirmative results in April.

ACT Assessment

The new ACT Assessment Program goes into effect in the fall of 1989, and students who are considering taking the test will be able to prepare for it by procuring a copy of the pamphlet *Preparing for the Enhanced ACT Assessment* from their guidance counselors. In this pamphlet, they will find a detailed description of the new test. Sample items will be accompanied by a detailed discussion of the correct and incorrect answers, and students will also be instructed in strategies and activities useful in preparing for the test. The test itself, which will be given five times a year in October, December, February, April, and June, is divided into four sections: English, Reading, Mathematics, and Science Reasoning. It will also continue the successful career-interest section of its predecessor.

The English portion of the test will contain 75 items, with subscores in usage/mechanics and rhetorical skills. The first score yields an insight into how well the student understands the mechanics of punctuation, grammar, and sentence structure, while the latter reveals the student's knowledge of organization, style, and appropriateness of expression.

The Reading Test replaces the old Social Studies Test and, in the course of its 40 questions, examines how students apply their skills of reasoning and referring to a broad range of texts in such areas as prose fiction, humanities, social sciences, and the natural sciences.

The Mathematics Test is a 60-item, 60-minute test that assesses the student's level of understanding in elementary algebra, intermediate algebra, and plane geometry/trigonometry. The mathematics section measures quantitative reasoning rather than memorization of formulas, special techniques, or computational skill. Each item in the test poses a problem, suggests several alternative solutions, and offers the choice "none of the above."

The Science Reasoning Test is just that, a 40-item, 35-minute test that measures the student's ability to interpret, analyze, evaluate, reason with, and solve problems posed by scientific facts. As it touches on concepts in biology, physical sciences, chemistry, and physics, the science portion of the test seeks to assess students' ability to understand data presented in graphs, tables, and charts; to focus on the interpretation of experimental results in "research summaries"; and to deal with conflicting viewpoints that arise from different hypotheses.

Registration for Tests

Registering for the ACT, SAT, or Achievement Tests does not have to be complicated, although some students make it so. Most high school guidance offices have registration forms for the tests, envelopes addressed to the Admissions Testing Program in Princeton, New Jersey, and copies of a pamphlet called *The Student Bulletin.* Very often *The Student Bulletin* also contains the registration form and envelope. The ACT Assessment application comes in a self-addressed envelope. If your guidance office does not have one, call 319-337-1270 and request an application.

Two months before the date on which you plan to take a given test, obtain a copy of *Preparing for the Enhanced ACT Assessment* or *The Student Bulletin* and the registration form and envelope from your guidance office. Fill out the form in the privacy of your study room or the school library so that you can be certain to complete it properly. Remember the following simple points:

1) Always spell your name the same way, using the same first name and initial.

2) Remember to put down your school code for the ACT, SAT, or Achievement Tests. This is the same six-digit number normally listed on a poster in the guidance office.

3) Be sure to distinguish the school code number from the test center number. This is essential. Even if you take the tests in your high school gym, the test center number will be different from the school code number. The test center numbers for the SAT and Achievement Tests have five digits, and those for the ACT have four digits. The appropriate numbers are listed in the back of *The Student Bulletin* or the ACT Student Registration Packet. If your school does not offer the SAT, ACT, or Achievement Tests on a testing date when you wish to take the exam, then you will have to locate another test center near your home where you can take the test. Enter the number for that test center on your registration form so that you will have no difficulty being admitted there. When you receive your ticket of admission, which should be about two weeks before the test, check your name for proper spelling, your school code number, and your test center number. If any of these items is incorrect, indicate the error on the correction form that comes with your admission ticket. Mail the correction form back to the Admissions Testing Program or the ACT so that

errors can be rectified. For any other changes you desire, phone the Admissions Testing Program in Princeton or the ACT Assessment Program in Iowa City, Iowa.

4) Select three schools from the medium-to-safe end of your list and enter their names in the portion of the registration form that asks where you wish to have your scores sent. The final test report form, which is eventually sent to the colleges you specify, has all your scores on it anyway, so why be bashful? You never know; you may do exceptionally well, and the colleges that receive your scores may respond by asking about your interest or by sending you a catalog and application.

5) Fill out the Student Descriptive Questionnaire/Student Profile part of the registration form. About 91 percent of test takers do so. This questionnaire asks for basic information about your family background, academic record, extracurricular interests, and plans for college study. Students who complete this questionnaire are likely to receive mail from colleges seeking to identify students they may wish to recruit. If, for instance, you are a minority student interested in the study of business or economics, you should be aware that institutions with good business programs and scholarship funds for able minority students may purchase a list of suitable candidates from the Admissions Testing Program or the ACT Assessment Program in order to send them literature describing the opportunities available at their schools. Similarly, special scholarship programs, sometimes unknown to both students and guidance counselors, may use information from the questionnaire to identify and make contact with candidates who may be worthy of support.

Finally, check to see that you have completed all the items on the registration form. Then enclose your check or money order in the stamped envelope, and you are ready to mail your registration form.

Test Anxieties

With these details out of the way, turn your attention to the matter of taking the SAT, ACT, or Achievement Test. A month or so before the test, ask yourself the following three questions:

1) How do I really feel about taking tests?

2) How might I rehearse for the test I plan to take?

3) What special skills will I need to employ in the test situation itself?

In response to the first question you may well answer: "Well, I feel fine about tests until I encounter the first question I can't answer. Then I just tighten up, and I can't go on. I'm stuck, and it's all over! I'll never get anywhere in life."

Or you may say: "I am the kind of person who gets hypnotized by the clock. I watch the minutes tick away and become more and more tense until I can't work anymore. I consequently never finish tests on time and always leave them with a sense of deep frustration. I have worked hard and concentrated, but I have disappointed myself and others. I just wish people would stop asking me my scores and start to appreciate me for the person I really am."

Or you may be like the student who complained: "In test situations I just can't focus on the test! I keep thinking how much fun I am going to have next Saturday afternoon as center on the girls' basketball team at the state championships in Springfield. I never study enough before-hand."

These comments may all seem pretty similar to you, but they are not. Some of them relate to the sources of test anxiety; others are merely an expression of it. It is important to deal with the *sources* first. Divine and Kylen have identified four main sources of test anxiety: (1) concerns about self-image, illustrated by the person hypnotized by the clock; (2) concerns over how others will treat you if you do poorly, illustrated by the same example; (3) concerns about future security, as in the first example; and (4) concerns about not being prepared for the test, as in the last instance (James H. Divine and David W. Kylen, *How to Beat Test Anxiety.* Woodbury, N.Y.: Barron's Press, 1979, p. 12).

If you have concerns about test anxiety, try taking them up with your guidance counselor. If that proves awkward or impossible, sit down by yourself and try to list, in order of their importance, the sources of your test anxiety. Then make a list of appropriate responses to each source of anxiety. For instance, if you are concerned about your future security, list the example of your grandmother, who, although she never did well on tests, somehow rose through the ranks of the local bank before retiring with a nice pension. Think of as many responses as you can to counter each concern and write them all down. This exercise will help you become more rational about your anxiety and make you feel much better about yourself and your prospects. Perhaps you will only have responses to two of the four concerns—fine!

Next, we come to your actual feelings and behavior in the test situation: "clutching," letting your mind wander, staying too long on one particular question or section. Again list these behavior patterns on a piece of paper, as in the following example: "(1) Difficult questions make me panic, (2) The length of tests scares me, and (3) I can't make the fine distinctions when given four or five possible answers to a question."

Now think of some sensible ways of dealing with these problems, again writing each one down. For example, a response to the panic you feel when confronted with a difficult question might be: "I will not be able to answer all questions correctly anyway. Wrong answers cost only a quarter of a point on the SAT and do not count on the ACT. Still, the best policy is to jump over difficult questions and go on. Perhaps I will return if I have time, perhaps not."

If the length of the test intimidates you, your strategy should be to figure out a time schedule for each test you take, even determining approximately how many minutes to spend on each question. Then stick to your schedule no matter what, even skipping responses if you have to. *Preparing for the Enhanced ACT Assessment* suggests practicing with a kitchen timer to keep yourself within the time allotted for the tests.

If you have trouble making up your mind about multiple-choice questions, determine to go through each section of the test with all deliberate speed, then returning to the questions that puzzle you. After crossing out responses that are obviously wrong, translate into your own words the answers you cannot choose between, then select the one that best responds to the question. Try not to read too much into the various choices; don't make them more complicated than they really are.

A Group Approach

Sometimes schools will offer group counseling, where problems of this type can be dealt with efficiently and painlessly. Students are asked to share their experiences (and counselors may share theirs), and these experiences are listed on the blackboard. The group then suggests remedial techniques for each student's problems, which are recorded in a second column. The counselor should make sure that the techniques recommended in each case are directly related to the individual student's problem and that they actually can be carried out by that student. Foisting inappropriate solutions on people will only increase their anxiety.

The next thing the group does is to conduct a rehearsal of test taking. What students want to find out is how they behave while taking a test, so that they can eliminate inefficient and counterproductive behavior. They must use a sample test, such as the ones found in *About the Achievement Tests, 10 SATs,* and *Preparing for the Enhanced ACT Assessment.*

The group appoints an observer and proceeds with the sample test. At the end of the examination period, the observer describes each person's behavior during the test period; for example, "Dave appeared stone faced and stared into the middle distance a lot"; "Joan bit her nails and pencil unmercifully"; "Tom kept crossing and uncrossing his legs, then scrunched up in the chair and perspired a lot, especially after consulting the clock."

At this point, the behavior observed for each student is entered in a third column on the blackboard. The group gives specific suggestions for modified behavior for each person, noting those suggestions in a fourth column. What results in this last column is an individual recommendation for each student and an overall model for correct examination behavior. (Students should transfer what applies to them in each column to four separate index cards.) For the behavior noted in the preceding paragraph, the fourth column might read: "Dave should keep head and neck flexible, focus on the test paper, look up only occasionally"; "Joan should keep her hands as still as possible and perhaps chew gum, if permitted, to avoid mutilating her pencils and distracting herself"; "Tom should sit in a more relaxed, upright position and look at the clock only when he has come to the end of a section."

Columns two and four yield the combination of mental strategy and physical behavior that students need as they cope with their anxiety about taking tests. Supplementing these skills with a few simple muscle-relaxing techniques will only enhance their ability to cope successfully with the tests that lie before them. John Emery of the Human Resources Institute in California has suggested the following muscle-relaxing exercises for people approaching anxious moments in their lives (John R. Emery, "Systematic Desensitization: Reducing Test Anxiety," in John D. Krumholtz and Carl E. Thoresen, eds., *Behavioral Counseling: Cases and Techniques.* New York: Holt, Rinehart and Winston, 1969, pp. 270–272):

1) Settle back in your chair and relax. Take a few deep breaths and begin to let yourself go.

2) Now extend both arms straight out and clench your fists more and more tightly as you count slowly to five. Then relax and let your arms drop. Concentrate on the differences you perceive between the tension phase and the relaxation phase.

3) Focus on your forearms. Extend your arms as above, and push out on a slow five-count as before. Relax again. Do the same for your biceps, flexing your arms toward your body and then relaxing after five seconds.

4) Concentrate on your forehead. Wrinkle your brow, hard, on a five-count. Relax.

5) Close your eyes tightly as you count to five. Then relax slowly.

6) Do the same for your neck and shoulders, sitting up rigidly, then relaxing. For each exercise, conclude by contemplating the difference between the tense feeling and the relaxed feeling that follows it.

7) Do the same for your stomach muscles. Then let them relax, and try to spread this relaxation throughout your entire body.

8) Now move to your thighs. Straighten out your legs and turn your toes up toward your face on a five-count and relax.

9) Unlimber your calf muscles in a similar way, turning your toes away and down as hard as you can as you count to five. Then relax again. Repeat, turning your toes up.

10) Finally, in a relaxed position, close your eyes and review your exercises, trying to "spread that relaxed feeling" outward from each particular muscle group throughout your whole body.

On an intellectual level, you can approach the anxiety of taking tests by inventing a simple game. Reward yourself for good behavior, that is, behavior that is conducive to handling tests in a calm and rational manner. Dave, who blanks out and stares into the middle distance during tests, might promise himself a solid ten-minute break after taking a mock test if, and only if, he does not look up and blank out for ten minutes while taking the practice test. Joan might reward herself by having something decent to eat if, and only if, she is able to abstain from chewing her pencil while taking a practice test. Tom could decide to limit his clock-watching to two time checks per test section and reinforce this by promising himself the dazzling shirt he recently admired in a shop if, and only if, he succeeds in controlling his test behavior.

Alternatively, you might punish yourself for continuing bad patterns of test behavior by denying yourself free time, a certain kind of food, or a shirt that you like. This negative approach may be too discouraging for most, but it may work better than a reward stimulus for some. The important idea to bear in mind is that you must discover and then employ your own techniques for combating anxiety. The more individual and reasonable the reward or punishment system is for you, the more effective it will be.

First Time Out

With your anxiety reduced through awareness of what your test problems are and how they can be overcome, you are ready to make your appearance at the designated test center on a given Saturday morning and run the gauntlet for the first time. Here's what you need to remember:

1) Take your ticket of admission with you to the test center. Make sure that you have entered any corrections on the second sheet of the test ticket *before* going to the examination room.

2) Take two or three sharpened No. 2 pencils with you. Make sure they all have adequate erasers.

3) Take at least one photo identification card with you, such as a driver's license or a student identification card issued by your school. If you don't have either of these documents, ask your guidance counselor for advice. He or she may be proctoring the examination and thus will be able to supply visual identification.

4) Plan to arrive at least 15 minutes before the scheduled time—a half hour if you are unfamiliar with the test center. It may be that only one door to the test center is open that Saturday morning, and you may have to walk around one or more large buildings in order to find your way in. Allow time for such contingencies. If you are really apprehensive about finding the test center, call the school or college where the test center is located and ask directions. While you are at it, ask the name of the person to whom you should report. If you are planning on "walking in" to the test without prior registration, it is especially

important to notify the director of the test center that you are coming.

Standby registration for the SAT or Achievement Tests is a last resort, to be used when students forget to register in advance. (The ACT does not allow walk-in/standby registration.) Students in this predicament should follow these steps:

1) Obtain a copy of *The Student Bulletin* from your school's counseling office. Fill out the test registration form before going to the test center.

2) Write a check for the test fees, adding $30 to the basic fee listed on the back cover of *The Student Bulletin*. The check should be made out to the Admissions Testing Program. Cash will not be accepted.

3) Contact the test center in advance. Although test monitors will not know how many spaces are likely to open up, there may be special directions for standby candidates.

4) Take positive identification (photo ID) with you to the test center.

5) Arrive at least 45 minutes early. Standby registration is not guaranteed, and often walk-ins are accepted on a first-come, first-served basis.

Once you arrive at the test center and pass through the registration line, you will be assigned to a particular test room where you will confront the test itself. If you are taking the SAT and have read the pamphlet *Taking the SAT,* you already know that the test is divided into six sections: two 30-minute verbal sections with a total of 80-odd questions, two mathematical sections with a total of approximately 60 questions, a test of standard written English with nearly 50 questions, and one experimental section (which will not count toward your score) from any of the three categories above. If you are taking the ACT, you know that there are four sections, two of 35 minutes each, one of 45 minutes, and one of 60 minutes, for a total of 2 3/4 hours. As with the SAT and the Achievement Tests, each ACT section is preceded by at least a half hour of instructions.

As the test instructions are being read, or earlier if you have time, review your muscle-relaxing exercises. Then go over in your mind the specific negative behaviors that you have discovered in yourself through group discussions or your own private reflection. Accentuate the positive as you bring these thoughts to mind. Think of what you will reward yourself with if you successfully manage your behavior: that delicious sundae, that smashing shirt, or the party invitation you told yourself you would accept if, and only if, you could find the courage to skip over the hard questions and finish each test section.

With the test in front of you and the answer sheet to your right (if you are right-handed), begin the exam. Read carefully, working slowly and methodically. Every ten questions, check to see that you are blackening an answer space that corresponds to the number of the question you are answering. Some sections will have more spaces on the answer sheet than there are questions. Do not let that disturb you.

Blacken each answer space thoroughly as you have been instructed. The No. 2 pencils that you have brought along are sufficiently soft to do that easily. If you want to change an answer, be sure to erase your first response thoroughly. Otherwise the computer will record two responses for the question, and you won't get any credit for your answer.

Use the test booklet for any scratch work you may need to do. This is both perfectly legal and desirable. By no means should you think that scratch work is appropriate only for the mathematics problems. As you read through a long passage in a reading comprehension section, you may want to underline the main idea or put a question mark in the margin of a paragraph that puzzles you. You will undoubtedly be asked about the author's point of view or the tone of the passage, so if you run across a phrase or sentence that reveals either or both of these, mark it accordingly, e.g., "tone" or "p. of v."

Remember that on the SAT you neither gain nor lose points for questions that you do not answer, so do not hesitate to withhold a response if you are unsure. Remember too, as a rule of thumb, that if you omit 20 percent of the questions and give correct answers to all of the remaining 80 percent, you will score 700 on the test. Do not guess wildly just so you can answer every question. The rule for guessing at an answer holds that it is reasonable to guess when you know that two of the suggested answers are wrong. Random guessing is unlikely to increase your score.

On the ACT, wrong answers do not count. So it makes good sense on both tests to answer the easy questions first; both difficult and easy questions carry the same credit. Skipping the difficult questions as you go through the test section the first time, then coming back to them as you review the section, is the best way to make the most of your abilities.

When the test is finally over, make sure that there are no extraneous marks on the answer sheet. Double-check to be sure that the answer sheet has the same number as your test booklet. If it does not, inform the examination proctor. Collect your pencils, and you're off, one hopes, to enjoy the reward you have earned by your calm and sensible approach to the exam.

Interpreting Your Scores

The SAT

In about five weeks you will receive the results of your exam on a sheet called "The College Planning Report."

Now you, your parents, and your college counselor need to interpret the results and reexamine your college choices. By scrutinizing the test report form, you will be able to ascertain what areas need attention before you take the SAT again.

Passing over the first section of the report, which contains your vital statistics and the name of your high school, you move quickly to the reported verbal score. Let us say it is 540. Whew! Not too bad! You will then notice that the score of 540 is broken down into percentiles for reading and vocabulary in the summary section below. Your raw score for reading comprehension is 55. Looking at the percentile breakdown below, you see you are in the 50th percentile of college-bound seniors. Fifty percent of the students who took the test scored lower than you. That is not many, when you think about it. You recall that the average verbal SAT for Coburn College is 600, with a reading comprehension raw score of around 65. You realize that you have to do some work on your reading comprehension if you are going to come up the 10 points you need in order to meet the standards of Coburn. You then see that your vocabulary score is in the 75th percentile for college-bound seniors, and you can relax a bit. Studying the list of words that you have laboriously compiled in the back of your English notebook for a year and a half has paid off.

A brief glance up to the right of the report reveals that a 540 verbal score places you in the 85th percentile overall nationally, in only the 75th percentile among the nation's college-bound students, and in the 80th percentile among your state's college-bound students. These figures tell you that admission to a competitive college will depend on doing better on the SAT next time. You resolve to study *Taking the SAT* again, to buy *SAT Success* or *10 SATs,* and to consider obtaining a computer program to help you sharpen your skills. You also decide to speak to your English teacher to see if he or she has any books to recommend for a reading program that parallels your other efforts. You resolve that while you do your reading, you will make a list of all the unfamiliar words that you encounter and look them up in the dictionary. If you really want to increase your vocabulary, you may want to make a flash card for each new word. If the word has more than one meaning in the dictionary, write them all down, since the SAT test makers often present vocabulary words in the form of analogies, which test your knowledge of the variety of a word's meanings. To improve your reading comprehension, ask your English teacher to suggest authors representing a variety of styles and points of view so you will be able to address both comprehension and vocabulary as you read.

Now the math score—it is 650. Terrific! This places you in the 91st percentile of your national high school class. In other words, only 9 percent of all students taking this test did better than you. However, you are in only the 85th percentile for college-bound high school seniors. You got 110 points less on the verbal portion of the test, yet managed to make the 75th percentile of the college-bound group. This means that you ought to brush up on your mathematics skills also before taking the SAT again. Because you are now taking trigonometry and functions and are well beyond the level of the mathematics aptitude portion of the

SAT, you should review the mathematics section of *Taking the SAT, 10 SATs,* or *SAT Success.*

You are not finished yet. Check your score on the Test of Standard Written English (TSWE), just to the right of the math score. You obtained a score of 56 (60 is perfect). That result may raise some eyebrows in college admissions offices. With the national decline in competence in reading and writing the English language, colleges have become concerned about the writing abilities of the students they admit. Many colleges, in fact, have had to design remedial courses in English grammar and composition in order to bring undergraduates up to a decent standard of literacy. These courses are expensive to run and somewhat embarrassing to a prestigious college. As a result, many college admissions officers will look askance at a TSWE score below 60.

If you know that the mean entering TSWE score is 58 at one of the colleges you have investigated, you have to get busy and sharpen your grammatical skills. Where to begin? You might look at the examples of correct and incorrect syntax in Strunk and White's *The Elements of Style* (New York: Macmillan, 1979) or William Zinsser's *Writing to Learn* (New York: Harper and Row, 1988) for a more wide-ranging approach to the writing process. Or you might take the mock TSWE in *SAT Success* and go over your errors with your English teacher. Perhaps the teacher has some exercises that you can complete on your own time.

There is no question that an able and interested student who likes to read can improve his or her TSWE score to the 90th or higher percentile with some effort and concentration.

Achievement Tests

Let's assume your score report also gives the results of your testing on two Achievement Tests, Mathematics Level I and American History and Social Studies. You can interpret these results just as you interpreted the results of the SAT. Say your score for Mathematics Level I is 610. Alas, not too good. In the columns to the right of the score you see that among the college-bound you are in the 75th percentile. Suppose that the mean score for students entering three of the five colleges you are interested in is 650. Something must be done. You have made honors grades in math for the past three years. Perhaps you did not review the material sufficiently and should now go over it again in order to achieve better results on your next try. Perhaps you have gone too far beyond the material of the Mathematics Level I test and should have taken Mathematics Level II instead. Although it is a harder test, the standard deviation measurement, which is used for scaling the scores, is lower for the Level II, and this tends to help good students score higher. Consult your mathematics instructor for advice on what you should do next—prepare for the Level I again or reach for the Level II. If you wish to major in economics in college, you will certainly want to improve your score, as admissions officers will want to see a much higher score on the Mathematics Achievement Test for potential economics majors.

Fortunately your American History score of 650 is another matter entirely. It places you in the 85th percentile of the college-bound group taking the test, very good by national standards and, indeed, by the standards of virtually all the colleges in which you are interested. As you do not plan to major in American history in college, this score will not help you in the admissions process all that much. But it still looks good, and it gives you a hint of where some of your abilities lie. In other words, once you are in college, it might be a good idea for you to consider taking some history courses as part of your program. Your 650 on the Achievement Test suggests that you would have success in college history courses. Think about this. The Achievement Tests often tell students where their competence lies, and if that competence can be made to coincide with their academic interests they can look forward to promising college records and professional careers.

The ACT

In interpreting your ACT results, you need to consider a number of different scores. The composite score, an average of the four subtest scores, lies on a scale from 1 to 36. Each of the four subtests is scored on a 1–36 scale as well. A score of 18 will be the mean score for the nationally representative sample of students who take the test. Similarly, on the seven subscores, which will also be displayed on the report form the student receives when the tests are evaluated, the scale runs from 1 to 18, with a mean score of 9 for the national sample. On the report form, the student will also find the percentage of students who received the same or a lower score, both in the state and in the nation at large.

Using these scores and percentages, students will be able to ascertain how well they are doing in a variety of academic skills and content areas and, in consultation with their guidance counselors and teachers, can work on techniques for improvement. High scores in certain areas may suggest a good chance of success in certain college majors and particular careers. Low scores may indicate that you need to concentrate on improving some skills before moving on to college.

As with the SAT and Achievement Tests, colleges that use the ACT Assessment will give some indication of ACT composite or even subtest score averages or ranges in their school profiles. Colleges are generally impressed with the predictive validity of the ACT. In a current example given in *Using Your ACT Results,* 78 percent of the students whose ACT scores placed them in the top 20 percent of their class did in fact have an A or B record during their first term of college. Yet, "there are many low-scoring students who beat the odds," the authors of the pamphlet go on to say. If they reflect on their scores and take steps to improve their performance, students in this category can still look forward to productive college careers.

Once you have analyzed your scores on the SAT, the Achievement

Tests, or the ACT, you are ready to go on to the next step in the testing process: reviewing your weak subject areas, planning to retake the tests at the next available opportunity, and rejoicing in the successes that resulted from your careful planning.

5

The Application
Makes a Difference

College candidates today have many opportunities for productive discussions about college. Their guidance counselors have much to offer, as do peers and, especially, college students whom they know. Nonetheless, one of the most important opportunities for examination of yourself and your suitability for a particular college comes in the admissions packet. It is called the college application.

Students sometimes underestimate the importance of responding carefully to the questions on their applications and being sensible about neatness and organization. One reason for this oversight is that so much of the information requested on an application seems routine and straightforward. Another reason is that counselors and students seldom discuss applications because the counselors don't often see them. In most instances, the student writes directly to the college for the application form, fills it out, and returns it to the college. The counselor meanwhile focuses on the school's recommendation form, which normally is sent to the college separately.

Colleges rightly expect applications to be completed solely by the student. So candidates should allocate enough time to respond fully to the application essays and pay sufficient attention to the short answers. Occasionally an optional essay is requested in terms such as these: "To help us understand you better, take this opportunity to express your interests, your background, and your aspirations. If you believe your other credentials represent you fairly, feel free to leave the space below blank." In spite of the option to omit this essay, students should take the request seriously and respond to it. Most of the other candidates undoubtedly will. The application is the student's only representative before the admissions committee and therefore requires the most complete effort.

The comments below will give you some idea of the importance colleges place on students' self-presentation on the application. Comments of this sort are commonly recorded on the jacket of an applicant's folder; these particular remarks are the final judgments of the admissions officers at a fine small college in New England.

> *Nope.* Despite A's, summer courses at the Wharton School, and nifty scores, the raves aren't uniform. The "person" is missing in the essay and in the extracurricular activities (War Games and Model UN). May be brilliant and precocious, but he is also narrow and limited.

> *Wait List maybe.* Proctor (student leader in dormitory), math team, varsity water polo, and New England champion swimmer. Termed "diligent," "shy," "responsible" by school. Essays show ambition and drive but lack the depth or perspective we usually see. A caring kid who takes his job as proctor seriously. At least he is other-directed, even if the essay is flat and nonreflective.

> *Admit this kid!!* Art, hockey, lacrosse, guitar; a favorite of the counselor, who likes her warmth, integrity, and creativity. Perceptive essays show she is a strong person who would make maximum use of opportunities here. Still growing personally and academically, but impressive application all the same.

These perceptive admissions officers are not only looking for candidates who are academically talented; they are also seeking candidates who have given in their application a strong indication of themselves as people and as potential contributors to the community.

Therefore, before you even begin to fill out an application, you should review your academic and extracurricular interests, your thoughts about careers, and your personal values. Then you should think about how these three elements can be related to one another and presented as a coherent whole. If you have visited the campus of the school, had an interview, and read the literature, you may begin to see how you would fit into that institution both academically and socially. As you fill out your application, you can relate your interests and background to the academic and extracurricular opportunities at the college. Admittedly, some of the connections may be subtle or even tenuous, but the more you can relate your strengths and interests directly to those of the college, the more forceful and persuasive your application will be.

Competition and Constituencies

College candidates for the most selective colleges, both public and private, should realize at the outset that they will be competing in the admissions process against other candidates of similar interests and abilities, not against the whole applicant pool. Therefore, in their application students should attempt to identify themselves subtly as members of one of the five admissions constituencies described below. This is called *making the match*. Then they must try to set themselves above the other candidates in their particular constituency. This is called *developing the edge*. Neither of these two tasks is easy, yet the concepts of "match" and "edge" ought to be understood by students as they shape their application to college.

The categories used here were first described by Richard Moll, former director of admissions at the University of California at Santa Cruz, in *Playing the Private College Admissions Game* (New York: Times Books, 1979, pp. 126–129). Although the following scheme of constituencies inclines toward the practices of the private colleges, it is also useful for a general understanding of this aspect of the college admissions process. State universities also have their constituencies: in-state, out-of-state, minority, athlete, and scholar.

The Scholar Category

Well over half of four-year colleges have merit scholarships to attract bright students. The faculty of every college is legitimately interested in attracting the best students it can find. Professors want able, creative, and, in some cases, unorthodox minds in their classrooms. So they tell admissions directors to deliver "scholars." These are generally the candidates with SAT scores averaging 700 or ACT results of 29 or higher, three Advanced Placement tests with a score of 5 on each, and National Merit Scholarship Qualifying Test scores of 210 or better. These candidates may not be very lovable; they may be prickly people who seem to know all there is to know about computers or Indians or Shakespeare or cytology. Yet they are the kind of students who will animate college classrooms. They will ask the tough questions of professors. They will spend long hours in the library researching a minor point, and they will be elected to Phi Beta Kappa and probably win a traveling fellowship after graduation. They may even go on for a Ph.D.

However, they may not contribute much to activities outside their narrow field of expertise. They probably will not root vigorously for the football team or the field hockey team. Their major contribution will be to the intellectual energy of the institution, and that is why they will fare well in the admissions process. High school seniors who feel they fall into this category of highly able candidates should not draw back from identifying themselves as "scholar" applicants. (Some of the sample essays later on in this chapter will reveal the kinds of topics such candidates will want to address in their applications.)

The Special Talent Category

Every college and university has its need for special skills among the students who are admitted. Where would the radio station be without any freshmen who are interested in broadcasting or the maintenance of electronic equipment? Where would the football team be without depth in its line—three tight ends, eight guards, and a couple of good centers? The admissions office of every college must ensure that all the varied activities of undergraduate life will have students able to sustain them. In this respect college admissions is no different from the U.S. Army. Every year the army needs so many riflemen, so many cooks, so many clerk-typists, etc., in order to operate. Colleges are similar.

The smaller the college, the more important this special talent category is apt to be. If Coburn College cannot find three female divers to admit to each freshman class and thereby ensure that the swimming team has at least one good new diver each year, the whole women's diving program will be in jeopardy.

Candidates with special talents should ask their counselors about the needs of the colleges to which they intend to apply. Then they can attempt to match their talents with those needs. A few years ago, the director of admissions of a small selective college had little reluctance in revealing what special skills his school needed that year. He told the inquiring counselor, "We just have to find a hockey goalie, since our backup goalie is going to spend his junior year abroad. And we desperately need an oboist, too. Have you got either?"

Special talent applicants must realize that although the number of other applicants with whom they may be competing is small the competition is nevertheless intense. The college that seeks an oboist may have among its 4,500 applicants only three candidates who play the instrument, but all three may play it well. A candidate who believes she is able to play the oboe well enough to win a place in the college orchestra should shape her application to draw attention to her musical talents. She should also make a tape of her playing and send or take it to the director of the college's orchestra and ask for his or her help in gaining admission. Similarly, athletes should prepare athletic data sheets (discussed later) and establish contact with college coaches.

Special talent candidates need not worry as much as other students about deficiencies in their scholastic record. If our applicant is a sufficiently good oboist and an oboist is what a college is looking for, even the most selective will tend to de-emphasize Cs in mathematics and a 550 score on the Mathematics Level I Achievement Test. The basketball player who is involved in his sport 3 hours a day and on weekends is not expected to have quite as high an academic average as other admissible candidates. The match of the college's need and the student's talent will likely result in admission.

Candidates may not want to approach all of their college choices as a special talent applicant. The competition may be too intense at some schools. At others the student's special talent may not be a factor in the admissions process; for example, the school may have a good orchestra, but not go looking for any of its musicians. Therefore, the oboist should approach one or more of her colleges as an all-around candidate, and in those instances she should be sure that her scores and grades meet the norms for those colleges.

The Family Category

Usually the family category means that there are alumni connections. It is, after all, the alumni of the private colleges who provide essential financial support. In the public sector the alumni are also active in the political and economic life of a university, but the influence of alumni families tends to be a bit less than at the private schools. At public institutions, it is mainly public monies that provide for university operating costs.

Occasionally the family category can be interpreted to include groups other than alumni. It can mean that the school has a special interest in candidates from a particular region. Harvard, for example, has always considered the Greater Boston area as a kind of extension of its own community of Cambridge and so looks with favor on applicants from that area. The history of Stanford is tied in with the impressive growth of California, and, quite naturally, California students fare well in the admissions process there. The family category can also embrace what are called "development cases," individuals from whom there is the potential for large donations to the college or university.

Applicants who are alumni children—whose parents or grandparents attended the college to which they are applying—will have to handle their special relationship carefully. Most applications have a question about the connections of the applicant with the college. If this question is missing, or the response it calls for is too brief, then the applicant should indicate the connection in a succinct sentence or two.

Bear in mind that the more difficult the admission standards of the college, the closer the alumni tie will have to be in order to influence the admissions committee. Having a great-aunt who went to Radcliffe or the University of Michigan will not impress admissions committees at those competitive schools very much. The Ivy League schools will only be influenced by the tie to an alumni parent, sibling, or close relative, such as an uncle, aunt, or grandparent. At most of these institutions about 40 percent of the "legacies" are admitted, and that is considerably better than the overall average for acceptances. Obviously, however, a large number do not make it.

Therefore, candidates for the family category will have to meet reasonably high standards in order to gain admission. It may well be in their interest to consider shaping their application so that they fit one of the other categories of admission, if they can; then if they fail to qualify under that category, they may still have a chance as an alumni case. In some admissions offices athletes may be considered in one session of the admissions committee and alumni children in another. So the hockey goalie who is the son of a prominent alumnus may wish to emphasize his talents as a goalie in hopes of being admitted in the athletic round of decisions. Then, if that fails, he has a second chance to gain admission in the alumni round.

The All-Around-Kid Category

The all-around constituency is the toughest of all to delineate. Most applicants, like most people in the world, fall into this category. So be it. Colleges still need lots of all-around kids. These are the people who come to campus with a strong interest in challenging themselves academically and who want to make a contribution to the college community. Although they may never be scholars, they realize the relevance of education to a fulfilling life. They may also have definite career aspirations and know just what major they wish to pursue in college, thus setting an example for other students who are less definite about their career plans. Or they may not be at all certain about their career, but want to explore the college's curriculum. Whatever the case, all-around kids typically bring liveliness and stability to their colleges.

These all-around candidates also realize the importance of extracurricular activities in an academic community. They have usually played an active role in their high school community, and they want to make an extracurricular contribution of some kind to their college. They may not be sure just what form that contribution will take, but they will do something—open a grill in their dormitory or host prominent visitors to the campus—something. They should indicate this willingness in their application.

These candidates also offer promise as loyal alumni of the institution. They are good people who want to do well and who will appreciate the education they receive and the experiences they have at college. As graduates, they become enthusiastic alumni and elicit favorable reactions to their school by virtue of their integrity, competence, and enthusiasm.

All-around candidates should be encouraged by their large numbers in the candidate pool, but they should realize that the rate of admission is lower for their group than for any other. As a result, they will have to pay special attention to developing an individual edge in order to ensure admission to the college of their choice.

The Special Group Category

Since the 1960s colleges and universities have attempted to respond to the social and economic disadvantages of certain groups of Americans by admitting qualified candidates from these special groups. Often defined in racial terms—black, Asian, Hispanic—this category is sometimes defined more broadly to include women, foreign students, or other ethnic Americans from disadvantaged backgrounds.

Most colleges have appointed to their admissions staff one or more minority members whose special responsibility is the recruitment and evaluation of minority students. They also have admissions officers who travel abroad to recruit international students. As happens within other constituencies, students belonging to one of these subgroups must compete with members of their own group—blacks with blacks, Asians with

Asians, and so on. The competitive dimension of this category is sometimes less great at colleges whose location or lack of recruitment capability fails to attract special-group applicants in sufficient numbers. The admissions committees at these schools are inclined to look with favor on minority candidates or international students with modest records who show a sufficient desire to make the most of the opportunity to attend their college. However, at the very selective colleges, competition among special-group students for places can be as intense as that in any category.

In applying as a special-group candidate, students should not trumpet their special status in front of the admissions committee. Nor should they obscure it. They should think honestly about what their minority or special status means to them and what part they want it to play in their education—does it influence their potential for contributing to the college they wish to attend? One black student handled this rather well in responding to a question about an academic experience that had been a significant influence:

> The academic experience that has meant the most to me has been reading the book *Bury My Heart at Wounded Knee*. This book has affected my outlook on the oppressed Indian nation and the great injustices it has borne. The book stirred my emotions, and I related to the injustices that are quite often inherent in being a member of an oppressed group. Being black myself, I can truly relate to the plight of the American Indians and understand their reactions to their oppressors.
>
> My good fortune in being chosen to attend the special summer school set up by my state's governor allowed me to meet people from a variety of social and economic backgrounds. The experience has given me a perspective on life in America today, and it will enhance all future personal relationships that I may have.

Developing an Edge

When college candidates determine the constituency to which they belong and present their own personality, academic interests, and extracurricular interests to the college as a member of that particular group, they succeed in achieving a *match* between themselves and the school. Some readers may react to this suggestion by saying that candidates with average scores and grades will have no chance of admission if they follow this route. Others may object on the grounds that such a conforming approach robs candidates of their individuality. These reactions overlook the second dimension of the application process, namely, *developing an edge* or advantage within a certain category, so that the application reveals the candidate's uniqueness as a person and as a potential contributor.

Before going any further, candidates and their families must recognize the underlying assumption here: Honesty must be paramount in presenting yourself to the colleges. Admissions officers can tell when students have gotten too much help on their essay or are striking an insincere pose. I remember vividly a moment when, after completing a strong oral recommendation for a boy I knew and respected, I was told by a seasoned admissions officer that the student's application had sounded a hollow and false note. "His essays were contrived and self-serving," the admissions officer said. "I didn't get the feeling that he believed what he was saying or that he really liked anything." In his desire to project what he thought was wanted, this boy had succeeded in masking himself. He had probably been afraid that he would sound a little trite or uninteresting if he described himself in a plain and simple way, so instead he constructed a more elaborate, false identity in his application, and the perceptive admissions officer had seen through it. Thus, a candidate who was in all other respects an excellent student and a fine person, with a scintillating sense of humor, was not admitted to the college he desperately wanted to attend.

So as an applicant you must not only *know yourself*, to repeat the phrase from Chapter 1, but *be yourself*. This is the first rule to follow in developing an edge. Look at this forthright statement from a college candidate:

> My goal is to become as educated a person as possible. I certainly plan to become a productive addition to society through some profession, but I believe in the sovereignty of my spirit, and its enlightenment is the ultimate goal. Everything is "grist for the mill" for me: the hard-rock guitar of Guns n' Roses, the versatile artistry of Wynton Marsalis, the full-voiced choral music of Handel. I enjoy reading Shakespeare and "Doonesbury," going to the Matisse show at the Museum of Modern Art, and delivering a good cross-check during a spirited ice hockey game.

The candidate shows himself honestly and forcefully in this passage. He sets himself off from other candidates by his vivid and varied examples and by his honesty about himself. He has thereby developed his edge.

The second rule for developing an edge is: Set yourself off from the other members of the group by letting the college know of your talents. If you fall into the scholar category, tell the college what it meant to you to build your own telescope and explore the universe, or how you wrote a poem in Spanish that won a national competition. If you are sincere, your natural enthusiasm will effectively convey your intellectual interests and illuminate your accomplishment in the process. One boy wrote about a special project he was doing on the poetry of T. S. Eliot:

> Investigating Eliot's early works, the reader sees a growth and budding of Eliot's faith from the self-doubt and questioning of "The Hollow Men" to the cogent, assured speeches of Thomas à Becket in *Murder in the Cathedral.* To me, this progression of thought is not merely an impotent intellectual inquiry. It has found a parallel in my own life and that of countless others. Eliot's search for a plausible personal definition of God and the meaning of the lives we live is important to me. I have many questions: Who is God? How

does He affect our lives? What is immortality? Eliot has helped me formulate some tentative answers to those questions and shape my own odyssey.

If you are an excellent swimmer and thus fall into the athlete category, you should describe your accomplishments fully in your application. Tell how you have participated in the local YMCA program and that you have entered the AAU competition in the summer, winning your event. Submit your times in a few events to document your case. In addition, you should suggest seriousness about academic matters. One champion female swimmer wrote at the end of her application:

> Even though I love swimming immensely and spend 2 hours a day at practice, I do it primarily as a diversion from the arduous routine that my heavy course load imposes on me. From swimming, I have learned the value of self-discipline and of practice and how to win and lose with graciousness. But I have tried to transfer these insights to the pursuit of my chosen career, veterinary medicine. I think I have made good progress at Wheelock High School and that I can continue to excel as a swimmer and as a student at San Jacinto.

The third rule is: Show a desire to contribute to the college community. This element is especially important for family, all-around, and special-group applicants. One son of an alumnus described on his application how he encouraged his music teacher to begin drilling the school marching band so that they could perform at the fall football games and elicit stronger support for the team. In an essay entitled "The Spirit of '88," he wrote:

> This endeavor added new spirit and life not only to the varsity team but to the student body. They cheered the team on to five consecutive victories. At the last game, every student was present.
>
> For me this development of spirit in the student body is the best thing that can happen to a school. It makes for a close and friendly relationship among the students. It even attracted faculty to some of the games. I would hope that there would be a similar opportunity for me at college, for I really think there is nothing finer than a whole community of different individuals working together toward a common goal.

The daughter of another graduate responded to the question about her significant extracurricular activities:

> Hoping to combine social concern with personal achievement, I became actively engaged in class activities and student government. As class president, I organized various activities that, with student participation, have raised money to support worthy causes: Greenpeace, relief for victims of the earthquake in Armenia, and help for our local homeless. Candy sales, pancake festivals, fairs, dances, prize money from a statewide school spirit contest, and other such enterprises have brought into our school treasury over $3000. These funds will also be used to reduce graduation expenses for some of

the less well-off members of my class in a large urban high school.

A minority woman applying to a large university talked about what participating in religious activity had meant to her:

> Every Saturday I go to Branch. During the meeting we sing, we pray, we study God's teachings, and we have fun. Sometimes we go swimming or ice-skating or Christmas caroling and meet with other groups so that we can share our faith with non-Christians. I hope that there is a group like this at Hanover. It has meant a lot to me, and I believe that religion can help bring a community together.

The final rule is: Present yourself as slightly unconventional within one of the constituent categories. Such an approach takes delicacy and good sense, so proceed with caution.

Here is part of an essay that did not work because it presented too rough an edge to the college. The candidate was not admitted:

> People often call me eccentric, and you know what? They're right. I like to be different. I once wore the same suit jacket for a whole month, just to see if any of my teachers would notice. I once did not study at all for a Latin exam, just to see if I could pull it all together on the test. And I got a C. My friend studied until 2 a.m., he told me, and he got only a B–. I watched the Bears play the Colts until the same time and got only a slightly lower grade.
>
> I didn't do this, though, just to "beat the system." I did it, rather, to set a challenge for myself, to see if I would crumble under the pressure of not having studied for the exam.
>
> Another thing I like to do is impress adults in conversation. I know quite a bit about politics and I frequently make political predictions to see how adults react to them. Sometimes what I say is pretty outrageous, yet the adults always take me seriously and try to make sense out of what I am saying. I get a kick out of watching them try to formulate a serious response to my outlandish statements.

On the other hand, the following essay enhanced the candidate's chances for admission because it made him different but still reasonable:

> Quite frankly, I have encountered some difficulty at Wimset High School because of the restrictions of the school's curriculum and the demands of the coaches that I play football and lacrosse. Sports have cut into my genuine desire to be by myself and read and paint. I find myself torn between the school's demands that I achieve success in traditional channels and my own interests, which extend beyond the walls of worthy Wimset. That makes me a little eccentric, I guess. But I have been artistic since I was young and I have not been as productive in this area as I would like to be. So I intend to continue with this interest in college if I can.
>
> Some people regard me as being a little aloof or pompous. This is because I once gave a little speech to our art class. One day we had no teacher, and everyone was throwing things around or doing nothing, and someone proposed that we go to the corner store for a

snack. I told them that they could do as they liked, but that I did not regard the art class as a "creative playtime period." I wanted to finish a particular painting. That brought a lot of catcalls, but the painting did take a second prize in the student art show, so I am not sorry for what I said. I think one can balance studies, sports, and the creative arts, and I hope I can do this successfully in college.

The maturity of outlook and the honesty of this essay gave the candidate an edge that caused him to be accepted at all the colleges to which he applied. He honestly believed himself to be different, but he was able to see his own uniqueness as an individual in the context of a society that made legitimate demands on him. His ability to strike a balance among his various talents, while developing his mastery of them, gave him an edge that made him an ideal prospect. A discerning admissions officer could see that not only would this boy make a contribution to his college community, but he would not be afraid to question its prevailing values. He could help his college to change and improve, given the right situation. He had a very special edge, indeed.

Peccadilloes Can Spell Trouble

Two simple rules can eliminate much of the harm that applicants bring on themselves when they approach a college application hastily. First, before you fill out the application, write your responses in pencil on a separate sheet of paper. This reduces the likelihood of messiness and minor errors on the form itself. You may want to photocopy your application and actually fill out each blank in pencil, then move back to the original application. Second, always move from the simple to the complex. Fill out your easiest application first, then tackle the ones that ask more detailed and sophisticated questions.

College applicants often ask, "Do you type your responses or write them in longhand?" There is no simple answer to that question. If you can type, then by all means type your application. If you have neat handwriting and do not type, then answer the long essay question in your own hand. If you tend to write more than is required, you will probably be able to squeeze in more words in your handwriting, but if the squeezing makes the application hard to read, avoid it at all costs. If you, like me, have terrible handwriting, your best defense is a good offense. Use the typewriter. Brown University believes that handwriting is a vital part of a candidate's presentation. It requires that the essay portion of the application be filled out in the applicant's own handwriting. A quick look at applications from Yale, Berkeley, and the University of Michigan reveals instructions to write neatly in black pen or to type the essay. This is a good practice for any school.

If you do fill out your applications by hand, use a felt-tip pen or a fountain pen and black or blue-black ink. This makes for maximum legibility—helpful at 12 midnight, when the tired admissions officer may come to your application. Any decision about the mechanical part of the application should pass the "midnight" test. Be smart. Put yourself in the admissions officer's position. Avoid doing anything that would make his or her job harder or longer. Remember, always put your name on any extra sheets your essay may require.

Details

When completing the first section of the application, strive for uniformity. Always give your name in the same way, which should conform, incidentally, to the way you gave your name on the SAT or ACT. If you do not customarily use your middle name in full, give it only where it is expressly called for, and use your initial otherwise. Likewise, give your parents' names as they do in their formal correspondence.

Normally your home will be your mailing address, unless you are at a boarding school. Be precise: give the number and street, apartment number, and whatever other details may be necessary to ensure that your communications from colleges do not go astray. Be precise about your parents' employment as well.

In the section that calls for information about your school, enter the six-digit school code number of the Admissions Testing Program/ American College Testing Program. Give the name of your guidance counselor. If the application asks for your principal's name and makes no mention of your guidance counselor, also give the guidance counselor's name. Indicate your rank in class. Some schools rank according to the decile or quintile system. Find out your most recent rank and put it on your application. Other high schools do not rank their students. If this is true of your school, then say so; e.g., "Atlantic High does not have class rank."

In the section asking you to specify a major, you may be intimidated by the number and specificity of the choices, especially if you do not know what your major will be. On applications that permit you to do so, rank your interests rather than checking the response boxes for "general liberal arts program" or "undecided." If, on the other hand, you wish to combine economics and French in preparation for graduate work in international business, then you should append a footnote stating that information. You can also address the topic of your college major in the personal essay portion of the application. In designating a major, you should try to *match* yourself with the specific programs offered by the college, and the format of the application should not stand in the way of this process.

Extracurricular Activities: Extent, Quality, and Value

In representing their extracurricular activities, many students are confused and annoyed by the amount of space given on the application. It may be either too much or too little and is seldom just right. Before you begin this portion of the application, list on a sheet of scrap paper those organizations that have meant something to you and that you have contributed to. It would be misleading to mention the chess club if all you did was occasionally play a few moves of chess during lunch hour over the past two years. If, however, chess is a prominent activity at your school, and you have gone to evening meetings and played in competitions with other schools, then you should mention it. Use this format if none is given on the application:

Chess Club	3 hr./wk.	three years	First Board, District Winner 1988
Basketball	12 hr./wk.	four years	Captain, *City Chronicle* "Player of the Week"

In presenting your extracurricular activities to the colleges, you want to show: (a) the amount of time per week you devoted to them, (b) the number of years you have been involved in them, (c) special awards or honors you have attained in pursuit of them, and (d) leadership experience you have gained while participating in them.

You also want to be sure to include your community activities, such as scouting or church work. If there is insufficient space for this on the application, or the question is not asked, prepare a separate sheet for this information and send it along with the application. (See also Chapter 6.)

On many applications work experience is closely related to extracurricular activities. Present information about your jobs in tabular format and include your earnings:

Waiter	Blue Dolphin Restaurant	July and August 1988	45 hr./wk.	$600
Salesclerk	Gift shop (mother's)	Saturdays during school years 1987–89	8 hr./wk.	no pay

Many students worry that they are not involved in enough activities at school or that they are too young to have had much work experience. Applicants should remember that a small number of activities or jobs is not necessarily a bar to admission to a selective college, particularly if they are academically gifted or if their extracurricular activities are limited because financial hardship compels them to work after school.

In general, colleges understand that students differ widely in their extracurricular activities. What can give a candidate an edge is the depth of commitment to the particular activity undertaken. The chess player who works after school so she can earn enough to travel to the national championships in Des Moines; the young man from a rural background who stays home weekends to care for his Rhode Island Red chickens, which consistently win regional 4-H championships: these candidates are far more interesting than students with a large number of traditional activities, none of which has challenged them very much.

A few years ago I met a young woman whose great love, after her pet pigeon, was Russian cooking. She was gifted academically; she avoided athletics. She spent the bulk of her time amassing Russian recipes and cooking them for her friends. After a year or so, her Russian instructor suggested that she publish a cookbook of her favorite recipes in Russian and English. The young woman managed to accomplish this during her junior and senior years in high school. She described it thoroughly on her college applications and submitted a copy of her book with each one. She was admitted to most of her top choices. Her edge was this single accomplishment—the only extracurricular activity listed on her application!

Leadership

In addition to depth of commitment, leadership matters a good deal to college admissions officers. After all, they are trying to identify and attract the leaders of the next generation to their colleges. "We seek candidates who demonstrate a willingness to take an interest in others," says Harvard's catalog, "who place themselves in situations that call for personal initiative and leadership." Students filling out college applications should review their activities at school, in the community, and during the summer, focusing on those in which they used their leadership skills. It may sound trite to say that you were an assistant cabin leader in a summer camp or that you led your volleyball team to the state finals, but it is in situations such as these that your appreciation of ethical issues is often developed. An appreciation of ethical issues will be very important when you graduate from college and venture forth into society. Without an educated and ethical cadre of people to lead it, society will not be able to cope with the substantial challenges it faces in the future.

So whatever the extracurricular activity, it is quality not quantity that matters. As a great authority on college admissions has warned, "The biggest single mistake that applicants to selective colleges make is thinking that being very active will impress college admissions officers, when actually a long list of activities may suggest some weakness, indecision or lack of commitment." Indicate what you like to do, describe your activities thoroughly, and leave it at that. Remember that leadership in one activity is more important than following in several—that the depth of your commitments is invariably more important than their breadth.

Essays: Is Longer Better?

Now that you have dealt with all the questions requiring brief responses, you are ready to go on to those that call for longer answers—the essay questions. These questions are of two types: those that require a specific response and those that are open-ended, allowing you some latitude in your response. Notice the variation in the examples below.

Sample Essay Questions

"Provide a brief essay about your activities, interests, achievements, and talents. The goal of the essay is to help us to get to know you as an individual. Point out your strengths, and explain any inconsistencies in your record. You might comment on your experiences at school, in the community, or at work."

University of Michigan

"Describe a humorous experience."

Johns Hopkins University

"On the following page . . . please write a brief essay of 200–500 words. You may choose ANY topic about which you would like to write: your family, friends, or another person who has had an impact on you; the unusual circumstances in your life; the best or worst features of your secondary school; a recent development in your community; a scientific or other problem which you would like to solve; travel or living experiences in other countries; a question we should have asked in our application; a discussion of ethical issues which interest you or pose a challenge to you. Any subject of 'direct personal importance' is a good choice."

Harvard and Radcliffe Colleges

"[The essay] allows you to provide information about your academic achievements and unique attributes and experiences that is extremely valuable in the admission and scholarship evaluation processes. For admission purposes the University is seeking information that will distinguish you from other applicants in terms of your goals, aspirations, and achievements. You should discuss these areas in your essay, as well as what is important to you and the reasons why, your main academic interest and why you chose it, and your educational and career objectives. Please also write about your life experiences that have influenced your intellectual and personal growth."

University of California at Berkeley

"If you had to formulate the perfect admissions question, what would it be and how would you answer it?"

Dartmouth College

"Please select one of the following: (1) Briefly describe how Ripon College can help you to achieve your academic and personal goals, or (2) What experience or event has had a significant impact on your life?"

Ripon College

In evaluating the written responses to these varied topics, colleges look for evidence of your writing ability, motivation, creativity, self-discipline, character, and capacity for growth in these areas. But remember, too, to reveal yourself in your essay, because what admissions officers are really looking for is the human being behind all those grades and test scores and stellar accomplishments. No reasonable admissions officer expects an essay to describe a perfect person, brilliant scholar, and champion athlete. The reader might be suspicious of such a presentation—and should be.

Consider this response to an essay question that asked the applicant to imagine interviewing a famous historical figure:

I would want to invite Theodore Roosevelt to dinner, because of all the people in history I know of I have the most empathy for and interest in him. I was initially impressed with the fact that, even though he was born to wealth and prominence, Roosevelt had to overcome many hardships of his own. His struggle to strengthen his body is well known, but people often don't remember that T.R.'s first wife and his mother both died on the same day. His son Quentin was killed in World War I, as well. Those experiences strengthened Theodore Roosevelt in a different way. They gave him a compassion for others. I would like Roosevelt's advice on how to express human compassion in the hard and cynical world of politics today. How would he balance American interests against Palestinian and Arab nationalism in the Middle East, for instance?

I would also be fascinated to talk with Theodore Roosevelt, the intellectual. He wrote about history, he loved the natural world, and he was a keen student of politics. Where would he draw the line between the interests of big business and the need to protect the environment? As the person behind the conservation of government lands for the use of the general public, would he despoil those Wyoming hills he loved so well in order to mine the coal beneath them? Would he dam the Penobscot in northern Maine? What about the Greenhouse Effect and the destruction of the South American rainforests? What would he do to furnish America's energy needs? Impose a sizable windfall profits tax?

There are many questions of this sort that I would like to ask Mr. Roosevelt at our dinner. But I would also hope that he would do some talking on his own. I would want to hear his high-pitched voice and great laugh. He was a great raconteur, and I would want to hear his version of some of the legends that surrounded him. What was his reason for walking through the White House lily pond with the Japanese ambassador? Why did he bring a horse into the White House?

I also would want to find out Mr. Roosevelt's reactions to the famous people of his day: Admiral Mahan, Elihu Root, George Washington Carver, Jane Addams, Kaiser Wilhelm, and—dare I mention him?—Woodrow Wilson.

Whatever happened and whatever T.R. said, I hope I would come away from the dinner with some new ideas of my own about how to achieve change in the American political, social, and economic system. For Teddy Roosevelt, above all else, was a "Conservative as Liberal," that is, he sought to change America within the existing framework as he understood it. Because he was so resourceful in doing this, because he managed to do it with humor and style, he has always intrigued me. Even though he has been dead nearly seventy years, he is still relevant. It would be fascinating to spend an evening with him.

This essay, written by a young woman applying to an Ivy League college, is somewhat uneven, but it does show writing *ability*. It also reveals her capacity to think critically and her *motivation* to ask intellectual questions of her subject. She wants to know about ecology, world politics, and history. The essay does not convey much *creativity*, but that can be addressed in the free, personal essay or in other parts of the application. So can *self-discipline*. *Capacity for intellectual growth* is forcefully suggested here, however. The questions asked of Mr. Roosevelt have a strong intellectual thrust. There is a kind of open-mindedness in the writer. She does not prejudge any of the answers that Roosevelt might give. Fortunately, too, this young woman's interest in Roosevelt stems naturally from her proficiency in American history (A– average) and her current course in world politics. (Admissions officers tend to make these kinds of connections.)

The essay reveals more than a little *character*, too. The author mentions sensitivity to others. She is concerned about world peace. She cares about nature. She has a capacity to appreciate and value other people. The admissions officer who reviewed this application saw the writer as being especially well suited for a special subdivision of the college's curriculum called the College of Social Studies. So this essay provided match as well as measure, and the candidate was admitted.

Here are three essays selected from applications to three colleges. Read through them, evaluating them for evidence of ability, motivation, creativity, self-discipline, character, and capacity for growth. (Hint: One is particularly good, one is good, and one is deficient.)

A) "A Home away from Home"

The experience that has moved and taught me most was the experience of going on assignment to a shelter for runaways as a cub reporter (with an assumed name and identity) for *Philadelphia* magazine. During my four days there, I came to learn a lot about the runaways, and I found that I learned from them as well. I learned about one of the real values of life, about people taking care of each other. Despite the fact that these were disadvantaged kids, or maybe because they were disadvantaged, there was a level of camaraderie and genuine concern among them that I had never experienced before. About half the kids at the shelter were black, half white, but it seemed that racism could not exist there because the people were bound together by their struggle to survive.

These kids didn't have what so many of us take for granted—love, support, and the security of food and a warm bed every night. But there was a quality in the way they spoke and acted with each other that I admired and hoped to remember when I left them.

Though I stayed at the shelter for only four days, I came away with both a new sense of the plight of runaway kids and a new sense of hope. "They seemed at first like a strong group of oddly matched but invincible musketeers," I wrote. But, in fact, they were not invincible. They were very vulnerable.

I learned that when a person under 18 leaves home, even an intolerable home, he becomes a "status offender." He is then a ward of the state, at the mercy of the courts. The "detention" or incarceration of these kids has become a common occurrence.

Some of the kids I became friends with had been raped or knifed in the "youth study centers" the courts placed them in; many had been handcuffed and had slept in jails after running away from an insane, alcoholic, sexually abusive, or violent parent. Most had been robbed of their dignity, their self-respect, their very humanity, by the system designed to protect them.

Early on a Thursday morning I walked with Darwin, a boy from the shelter, to Family Court at Eighteenth and Vine streets, where virtually all of Philadelphia's runaways end up. We sat in Courtroom C, waiting to find out where the courts would put him, since his parents no longer wanted him. After we had waited for an hour and a half, Darwin was called in to see the judge alone. A few minutes later he was half-pulled, half-led out by a sheriff, handcuffed to another boy. Although he had done nothing more criminal than run away from an intolerable home, Darwin had become a "custody case," another number in the courtroom files, another kid for the state to put away.

In my article I tried to re-create the pain of this experience, and also its wonder and beauty. Then I tried to instill in my readers not only a sense of my rage but a rage of their own—so that perhaps they will respond, in powerful numbers, so that some small part of the system will change.

Tania Lewis

B) "Research Summers"

For this essay I would like to discuss two learning experiences that greatly influenced my interest in science. My science classes at school have all interested me, but I never realized how fascinating science could be until I worked in laboratories for two summers.

During the ninth grade I applied for and won a science scholarship. The scholarship program offers the opportunity for summer lab work to 40 high school students; admission to the program is based on a standardized science test followed by an interview. That summer I was assigned to the electron microscope lab of the university. The lab receives tissue samples from the City Hospital; preserves, mounts, and thin-sections them; and, finally, examines them with the electron microscope. During the summer I participated in every step of the process. I learned, with varying degrees of success, to thin-section and stain tissues, to use the electron microscope, to take microphotographs with it, and to develop and print the photos, all without assistance. The work was sometimes frustrating because I didn't know even the most basic lab techniques, but on the whole it was a positive experience. At the end of the summer I was asked to give a presentation to officials of the group sponsoring my study.

I spent this past summer in the biochemistry department of the University School of Medicine. The lab I was in had no routine tasks to perform; it was totally involved in research concerning cancer chemotherapy. I worked principally with a graduate student who is writing his master's thesis on this subject. After I became familiar with the techniques involved, I was allowed to conduct some experiments by myself. In addition, I attempted to synthesize B_{12A} on my own; although the experiment was a failure, I learned from my mistakes.

Last summer's experience was much more rewarding than that of two summers before. Having taken two more semesters of science and simply being two years older, I was able to take much better advantage of the situation. I not only learned how to perform the experiments but also tried to understand how and why they worked. One very useful effect of the experience was that it thoroughly taught me how to do routine basic tasks, such as making up solutions in specific concentrations, using the pH meter, and weighing chemicals. I had read about how to do all of these at school, but no amount of reading about these tasks can teach as well as actually doing them. Aside from the facts and techniques I learned, the exposure to a research lab gave me a real insight into how research is conducted. Being at the medical school gave me the chance to talk with medical students and with a member of the board of admissions. This has led me to consider medicine as a career.

The most important result of both summers came from simply being around the labs for two months. I couldn't help absorbing a feel for how science works—how research is done, how scientists communicate their findings to one another, how frustrating the work can sometimes be, and how so much often depends upon the results. Science isn't nearly as glamorous a profession as it's made out to be, but it still attracts me. I've been very fortunate to have had the chance to find that out.

George Lee

C) "The Pioneer in the World of Ideas"

Long ago I wanted to be a fireman, a policeman, or something equally dashing. I have changed since then, I suppose, and my sights aren't set so high. I would be satisfied with being a college professor or a lawyer. However, I must still have some trace of my early romanticism because I daydream every now and then of being James Bond and foiling Dr. No, or Larry Bird and scoring the winning basket as the buzzer sounds, or soaring above the earth as the astronauts do. I think, though, that if I really could choose a great adventure, I would go into the future and help explore space.

The most exciting possibility for me will be the landing on Mars. I'll be too old before they get around to the rest of the solar system, and I'll be dead before mankind is ready to take on the galaxies. For my great adventure, I think I would like to be the first person to stand on the surface of Mars. I think that would satisfy my desire for adventure for quite a while.

Failing that, I'd like to be a pioneer of some sort; I'd like to do something or discover something that has never been done or discovered before. Because most of the physical frontiers on Earth have been stormed, Mount Everest, the South Pole, a solo Atlantic flight, I am left with the world of ideas. Though in some ways a second choice, it is the best now possible for me, and I think it will satisfy my desire for adventure for some time to come, since there isn't likely to be any end to it in my lifetime.

Alton O. Rozwenc

These essays all have merit, but, in terms of providing insights into the candidate, clearly Essay A has the edge. It gave the student who wrote it an edge, too. This essay not only reveals the candidate's ability to write clearly and even movingly of her experience but also shows her motivation to deal with a social problem by using her journalistic skills. There is a degree of creativity here, too, not only in the essayist's rhetorical approach to the reader—note the irony in the sentence suggesting that we take love, support, and the security of food and a warm bed for granted—but also in her point about "the wonder and beauty" of the young children who somehow are surviving this devastating experience. The last paragraph gives a sense of her character, too.

The essay also suggests the student's capacity for growth. Elsewhere in her application she said that she wanted to major in sociology or psychology. This fact, coupled with her comment that lots of people will have to respond in their various ways in order to rectify the situation, shows that she realizes the complexity of the runaway problem and the need for the proper education of the people who deal with them. The author certainly shows a capacity for growth in her desire to see the system change and her commitment to help that change occur.

Essay B is not far behind Essay A in its forcefulness and clarity, but does not have its breadth of viewpoint. The writer has ability. He has the motivation to test and enhance his interest in chemistry in the summer laboratory program. He also has self-discipline. His words convey his joy of accomplishment but not the creativity that would mark the researcher he claims to be. Moreover, there is a narrowness about the focus of this essay. The author does not translate his experience into social or political terms. In evaluating this essay, the admissions committee of the candidate's first-choice college wondered about his social development and interest in the implications of his study for his fellow human beings. Without this sensitivity, he might grow intellectually but not personally in the course of following a liberal arts curriculum in a demanding college. This candidate would probably spend most of his time in the chemistry lab. So, even though all his other credentials were outstanding, he was not admitted to his first-choice college. He did make his second choice, however, and, after some initial adjustment problems, did well.

Obviously Essay C is the most deficient of the three, but let's not gang up on the writer. He does show motivation, even if it is generalized—he wants to be a "pioneer of some sort"—but he is not focused along academic lines. Self-discipline, at least in an intellectual sense, does not appear to be this student's strong point either. He does show some ability to communicate and has the intelligence to understand that ideas often provide vicarious possibilities for exploration. His last paragraph is opaque, however. He needs to develop his thought further. He might have talked about how he planned to use his imagination creatively to "explore the universe of books" in college. If only he had said that he wanted to explore the curriculum of this fine college, or that he liked the idea of being a pioneer in combining different types of ideas, for example, the biological and historical. Moreover, the remark "I am left with the world of ideas" creates the impression that he regards the world of academe as being in some way subordinate to the real world of action. While in one sense it may be, the world of ideas can always inform and orchestrate the world of action. Had the writer of Essay C even glimpsed this relationship and articulated it in his essay, he would have shown a greater capacity for personal and academic growth. Moreover, the writer of this essay has given no indication of his values or character. He seems like a nice person—a reasonable sort—but even so, the admissions officers wondered where he would fit. There's no match to this essay, much less edge.

Mistakes to Let Others Make

In filling out your application, and particularly in planning and executing your long essay answers, do not seek too much help from your parents, friends, or teachers. It will show, to your detriment. Asking a friend or parent to suggest a topic for an open-ended essay is quite different from having that person correct grammar and imagery. The former is permissible; the latter is not. You must stand on your own in presenting yourself to colleges.

By no means allow your mother's or father's secretary to type the application. Do it yourself on a typewriter or word processor. If you make a typing mistake, erase it neatly and go on. No one is perfect, and as long as the essay gives an indication that it was done with thought and care, the readers will not count a couple of typos against you. On the contrary, a "sanitized" essay done on the office IBM without an error—or an original thought—could weigh against you.

Pay careful attention to the instructions on the application. Some colleges want all responses written on the application itself; obey their instructions. Others are more flexible, in which case you can run over suggested word limits and include extra pages. If you have visited the college and have a general feeling for the kind of school it is, then you can judge whether to take some liberties with the instructions on the application.

Do not use the same essays for all the colleges to which you apply. To do so is to jeopardize your "match." Because each college is different, the responses you give, even to similar questions, should be slightly different. If you have a basic essay that reflects the criteria of ability, motivation, creativity, self-discipline, character, and growth, then you can tailor it to suit the programs and personalities of the various schools to which you apply.

As you work on your applications, moving, as suggested earlier, from the simple to the complex and from your least to most demanding college, you will necessarily increase the sophistication and breadth of your essays in the process. Thus, by the time you reach your last and most difficult college, which is probably the one you want most to attend, you will produce your best effort.

Often colleges will include a sheet on which you can provide additional information or comments. It would be unwise to assume that this sheet can be ignored. The sheet can be used in the event that you receive an additional honor—let us say you are named a National Merit Finalist or are elected to the National Honor Society—or to mention community activities, if not specifically called for on the application. Significant accomplishments can then be amplified by personal essays, if you wish.

If you do happen to have something special to say to the college either after you have filed your application or in the event that the college provides no form for additional information, then you should write to your interviewer or the director of admissions to tell him or her. Often students who wish to give a final thrust to an application to their first-choice school do write to the director of admissions to say that they are keenly interested in being admitted and that they would come if accepted. This letter to the first-choice school is usually sent out in mid-February, commonly after consultation with a guidance counselor. Whatever form your communication takes, be sure you keep up a dialogue with the college until the decision-making process is complete.

Other Parts of the Application

All is not quite over yet. You have finished your part of the application, but various other sections of the application have to be distributed to the appropriate parties. The secondary school report form should be given to your guidance counselor after you have filled in your name and address, your school's Admissions Testing Program/ACT school code number, and the name of the guidance counselor.

Normally your report will be sent in with those of the other students applying to a particular college. So you should not jump up and down if you receive a card from the college saying that the secondary school report has not been received. High schools often have later deadlines than students. After the deadline, just check with your guidance counselor to ensure that your school report has been sent in. Try to give the guidance office at least three weeks to process your application.

The midyear school report form should also be given to your guidance counselor, again after you have filled in the portion asking for name and address, Admissions Testing Program/ACT school code number, and name of the guidance counselor.

Teacher recommendation forms go to the teachers you have chosen. Remember to complete the top portion first. Somewhere on the teacher recommendation form the student is given the option of waiving the right to see the report, once admitted to the college. Unless it deeply bothers you to surrender this right, sign the waiver in order to give your teachers the maximum opportunity to say what they think about you. For teacher reports to have credibility, they must be complete and honest. To some teachers, knowing that students will later examine the reports puts a certain constraint on what they say, so they may fall back on cliches or unsupported conclusions that will not be particularly persuasive to the admissions officer who reads them. Don't take that chance; waive your rights. You should also give your teachers stamped and properly addressed envelopes so that they can send their recommendations to the colleges. Ask them to keep a copy of their comments, in case you call on them again to write a recommendation.

Finally, the individual colleges' financial aid forms should be completed if you are applying for aid. You should discuss your responses with your parent or guardian so that all the information you give corresponds to that on the Financial Aid Form of the College Scholarship Service or the Family Financial Statement of the American College Testing Program. (See Chapter 7 for a full description of this procedure.)

Keeping Track

Having dealt with the matter of supplementary material, you are now finished with your applications. You have generated a lot of paper, to say the least, and now you need a way to keep track of it. Begin by preparing a folder for each of the colleges to which you have applied. On the left-hand side of the folder jacket, make a chart, listing in the first vertical column each of the parts of the application, the application fee, and a space for "Other." In the second column, record the date you received each part of the application; in the third, the date you sent it to the college or gave it to a teacher or guidance counselor; in the fourth, the date the college acknowledged receiving the document; and, in the last, a space for subsequent actions.

You really should protect yourself by making a photocopy of each completed application. When you make one, attach your check for the application fee to a page that has some space on it so you will have a copy of the check as well. Otherwise, make sure that you or your parents keep a copy of the cancelled check in case confusion arises.

Keeping Track

Coburn College

Form/Item	Date Received	Date Sent (Name)	College Acknowledgment of Receipt	Photocopy Made	Subsequent Actions
Preliminary Application	15 Oct.	20 Oct.	15 Nov.	No	
Personal Part of Application	1 Dec.	20 Dec.	15 Jan.	Yes	
Secondary School Report/High School Transcript	1 Dec.	15 Jan. (Guidance Office)	15 Feb. "No"	No	High school transcript not received; another copy sent 1 March
Teacher Recommendation (I)	1 Dec.	10 Dec. (Mr. Brown)	15 Feb.	Yes	
Teacher Recommendation (II)	1 Dec.	10 Dec. (Ms. McPhee)	15 Feb. "No"	Yes	Coburn did not receive Ms. McPhee's report; she sent another 17 Feb.
Peer or Other Outside Reference	1 Dec.	10 Dec. (Coach Allright)	15 Feb.	Yes	Allright called Coburn track coach for me on 18 Feb.
Supplementary Material Athletic Data Sheet	—	28 Dec.	15 Feb.	Yes	
Financial Aid Statement	1 Dec.	10 Jan.	15 Feb.	Yes	
Application Fee	—	20 Dec.	15 Feb.	Yes	
Other Mr. Knowles (summer employer)	—	15 Jan.	—	No	Sent to Wm. Hawkins, vice president of Coburn (Knowles' ex-roommate)

State University

Form/Item	Date Received	Date Sent (Name)	University Acknowledgment of Receipt	Photocopy Made	Subsequent Actions
Application Booklet	15 Sept.	15 Oct.	15 Nov.	Yes	
ACT/SAT Scores	6 June	6 June	—	Yes	
Secondary School Report/High School Transcript	15 Sept.	1 Oct.	15 Nov.	No	
Alumnus/a Reference	—	1 Oct. (Judge Hoffman)	—	—	
Supplementary Material Athletic Data Sheet	—	1 Oct.	—	Yes	Coach Allright called State University coach for me on 10 Oct.
Application Fee	—	1 Oct.	15 Nov.	Yes	Notification of admission by 1 Feb. or earlier

The Four Cs

As you bring your application to a close and review the various documents that make up your admissions folder, ask yourself if you have met the criteria that we shall call the four Cs: clarity, candor, completeness, and contribution. Have you said everything as clearly as possible? Have you been candid about yourself, your strong points and your failings? Have you been complete in your responses to the questions on the application, even though some of them may have seemed vague or repetitious? Have you attempted to show that you can make a contribution to each particular school? Have you not only shown your match but demonstrated your edge? Simply said, do you feel good about what you have said and the way you have said it? If so, you have probably done well in this, the most difficult part of the college admissions quest.

Quite apart from whether you are admitted to the colleges to which you have applied, you have already learned a lot. You have studied the colleges and learned how to ask analytical questions about them. You have sharpened vital organizational and management skills. In the process you have learned a good deal about yourself. This knowledge will endure regardless of how the colleges eventually act on your applications. Rejoice in your new skills and self-awareness as you face the anxious days of waiting that lie ahead.

6

Course

Recommendations

and Support

There is more to gaining admission to college than merely completing a fine application. Mounting a successful college candidacy depends on several other factors, including the types of courses you take in high school; your grades; what your guidance counselor has to say about you, both orally and in writing; what your teachers say in their recommendations; and, finally, what strengths are revealed in the supplementary materials you submit on your own behalf.

Before dealing specifically with each of these areas, students, teachers, and counselors need to know that for a candidate to be successful in gaining admission to a demanding school, all parts of the application have to "fit together," to use the jargon of the admissions office. In other words, while each component of the student's application folder—grades, scores, recommendations from the school and from teachers, and the application itself—is supposed to provide different kinds of information, there must be common themes running through all these components. For example, a student with excellent test scores must have an equally impressive high school record, obtained in the school's advanced courses. Moreover, this excellence must be confirmed by what the guidance counselor and the teachers say about the student and by what the student says about himself or herself in the application. Nor should this excellence be presented in a routine way by teachers and counselors. Merely to say that a student has a fine mind is not enough. There must be proof, both through anecdote and in the strength of the language used, so that this candidate can be distinguished from other intelligent and well-qualified candidates applying to the college.

Other qualities besides sheer academic excellence should be present in an application, too. A sense of humor might be one; sensitivity to other people another; personal integrity another. When discerning college admissions officers read through an applicant's folder, they look for confirmation of such qualities in the commentary of counselors, teachers, and alumni interviewers, as well as in the student's application itself. If evidence of such qualities constantly recurs, then the folder is said to "fit together nicely," meaning that a complete and credible picture is presented.

Students pondering their strategy for gaining admission would be wise to reflect on the values they identified through the exercises described at the beginning of this book. They should try to integrate those values into their approach to their studies and to demonstrate them to the adults who will be writing their recommendations. This is a time for real honesty with yourself. If you work hard because you like your studies (rather than because it impresses others), then you should convey that fact to your counselors and to your teachers. If you have a particular passion, be it for rock music or Edwardian verse, then it is time to let other people know about it. If you feel you might have done better in a particular course had you not spent so much time doing volunteer work, then you should be sure that the teacher in that course knows what the facts are. A student who fits the foregoing description could present a convincing picture if the recommendations all spoke of "hard work" and "genuine social commitment" and the school record showed consistently high—but not always top—performance.

High School Record

At the very base of any candidacy is the high school record. In looking at a school transcript, college admissions officers want to see how well students perform with the talents they have in the learning environment available to them. College candidates should therefore try to set stiff challenges for themselves as they pursue their high school career. That means taking substantive courses across the traditional spectrum of the liberal arts: English, mathematics, history, science, arts, and languages. In the admissions lexicon, such courses are called "solids," and their opposite numbers—which may bring those easy A's—are called "gases."

Wise college candidates should try to achieve both breadth and depth in selecting their high school courses. They should try to make maximum use of the curriculum offered by their high school, bearing in mind that it is not the quality of their high school that matters most, but the quality of the work they accomplish at that school. Students should go as far as possible in their particular area of interest, be it classics or music or mathematics. If their high school does not offer sufficient instruction in their field of interest, they might want to pursue that interest at a local junior college or night school.

The Strong Transcript

The model program of Anne Marie Gregory on the next page shows a series of course decisions that have been wisely made. No college admissions officer could fail to be impressed by what Anne has done with her time at White Falls High School. She has taken English each year and has established her competence by scoring well on the English Composition Achievement Test. She hopes to repeat that fine performance on the Advanced Placement test at the end of her senior year. She has pursued math to the Advanced Placement level and will take an exam in that field in the spring of her senior year.

Anne's choice of science courses makes sense, too. Beginning with biology, she went on to chemistry and then to physics, in which she has taken an Achievement Test. Science is Anne's favorite subject, and she has managed to take all the upper-level science courses at White Falls High.

Anne has slowly built up a command of French, too. Although it is not her best subject, she has taken it every year, and her Achievement Test score is commendable.

Finally, Anne has taken solid courses in social studies during her four years of high school. A full year of American history at the Advanced Placement level and an urban political history course have made it possible for her to take the Advanced Placement test at the end of her junior year. Her score of 4 is a decent showing and will undoubtedly qualify her for placement or credit when she gets to college in the fall.

Perhaps not as obvious as the decisions that led Anne to her strong record in math, English, and science are the decisions that have led her to experiment in a variety of other areas. She has taken half-courses in elementary drawing and painting and in concert band. She has also taken summer courses in typing and data processing, skills that will undoubtedly help her in obtaining summer jobs and perhaps even jobs on campus, if she needs the money. Notice that Anne has resisted the temptation to take full courses in these areas, although doing so might have improved her grade point average.

But what if Anne had real ability in art—should she have sought to avoid courses in art just because colleges sometimes view them as less than solid? Of course not. In fact, some colleges flatly say that they want candidates to have had exposure to the arts. As long as art courses, or other courses that might be termed peripheral, are balanced by attention to the five basic liberal arts areas—English, mathematics, history, science, and languages—then all is well.

Expertise in art or music, arc welding or drama, should be documented elsewhere in a student's application, too. Just bear in mind that selective colleges are usually interested in students with expertise in specialized areas only when it is buttressed by a strong basic program of study.

The Strong Transcript

White Falls High School

Name:	Gregory, Anne Marie
Soc. Sec.:	#001-23-148 0
Sex:	Female
Parents/Legal Guardian:	William and Carole Gregory
Address:	14 Mill Crest Road White Falls, Pennsylvania 15820

High School Curriculum	Mark	Credit		
Grade 9				
English (review grammar			Class rank: 10/450	
and expository writing)	A–	1		
Math (algebra II)	B+	1	SAT:	
Science (biology)	B+	1	V590—M640 (jr. yr.)	
Language (French I)	C	1	V640—M690 (sr. yr.)	
History (modern China				
and Japan)	B	1		
Physical Education	Pass			
Grade 10				
English (themes, poetry,			Achievement Tests:	
and the novel)	B+	1	American History	690
Math (geometry)	B+	1	English Composition	700
Chemistry	A–	1	French	690
Language (French II)	B–	1	Physics	700
Economics Theory and				
Practice	B	1		
Music (trombone				
lessons)	Pass	1/2		
Physical Education	Pass			
Grade 11				
English (analysis and			Summer term:	
exposition)	A–	1	Typing	
Math (functions,			Data Processing	
precalculus)	A–	1		
Physics*	B	1		
Language (French III)	B	1	Advanced Placement Test:	
U.S. History*	B+	1	U.S. History 4	
Art (elementary drawing				
and painting)	Pass	1/2		
Grade 12**				
English (literary				
analysis)*	A–		Advanced Placement Test***	
Math (advanced calculus)	A–			
Advanced Physics*	B			
Language (French IV)	B			
Urban Political History	B+			
Music (concert band)	Pass	1/2		

*Advanced Placement or honors course.
**Marks are for first semester only.
***Advanced Placement tests in English literature and calculus will be taken in senior year.

The Weak Transcript

Name:	Ramboult, Giselle Denise
Soc. Sec.:	#001-32-5909
Sex:	Female
Parents/Legal Guardian:	David and Linda Ramboult
Address:	15C Town Hill Apartments
	White Falls, Pennsylvania 15820

High School Curriculum	Mark	Credit		
Grade 9				
English	A	1	Class rank: 4/450	
Math (prealgebra)	A	1		
Art	A	1	SAT:	
World Problems	A	1	V550—M600 (jr. yr.)	
Speech	A–	1	V600—M650 (sr. yr.)	
Wood Shop	A–	1		
Physical Education	Pass			
Grade 10				
English Composition	B+	1	Achievement Tests:	
Math (statistics)	B+	1	English Composition	550
Language Arts	A–	1	Math Level I	630
Drafting	A–	1	Math Level II	630
Typing	B	1		
Physical Education	Pass			
Music Lessons	Pass	1/2		
Grade 11				
English (style)	A–	1	Summer term:	
Business Math	A–	1	Elementary Chemistry	B
American History	A–	1		
Geography	A	1		
Drama	B	1		
Music Lessons	Pass	1/2		
Physical Education	Pass			
Grade 12*				
Communications Skills	A	1		
Cultures of the World	A–	1		
Anatomy	B+	1		
Photography	A	1		
Concert Band	A	1		
Physical Education	Pass			

*Marks are for first semester only.

The Weak Transcript

Many students do not take the time to organize a strong high school program, and some of their classic errors are demonstrated by the transcript of Giselle Ramboult. Here Giselle has chosen courses with an eye to easing her high school work load and ensuring a vibrant social life. In this program there are several mistakes that can easily be avoided by shrewd college applicants.

Giselle has selected what appear to be easy courses rather than challenging ones. By including a music or art course in her program each year, Giselle has created the impression that she is avoiding more substantive courses like history and languages. While Giselle has made use of the curriculum to a certain extent, she has really only skimmed across its top, sampling art, drafting, drama, photography, and concert band without going into any one of them in depth. Many of her courses fall into the category of gases; her grounding in the liberal arts appears to be less than solid. College admissions officers will argue that Giselle is not sufficiently prepared to undertake demanding work at the college level.

There is no question that Giselle has done well in the courses she has taken. She ranks fourth in a class of 450 (whereas Anne Gregory, pursuing a solid and more challenging program, only ranks tenth). Still, the costs in terms of college preparation are high. Giselle has taken no foreign language and has paid little attention to the sciences. The only history course she has taken is the required one in American history, and colleges like to see broader and deeper preparation in the social sciences. When it comes to Achievement Tests, many colleges require three different ones, and Giselle has taken them in only two areas, math and English. There are several institutions in the country, such as the University of California System and the University of Virginia, for which this is an inadequate range of testing. Giselle has also not presented any Advanced Placement tests, which, although not required, still have a positive impact on college admissions officers.

Moreover, Giselle has not followed any particular subject in depth. If she were genuinely interested in art, for instance, she could have focused on painting, taking courses in watercolors, oils, or other media. She could then have prepared a portfolio for examination by the admissions officers and art departments of the schools to which she applied. If her interest lay in art history, she could have taken courses that would have prepared her for the Advanced Placement test in Art History. The same would hold true for music or drama. So it is not the courses themselves that have undercut Giselle's chances; it is the lack of depth in any one field that has hurt her chances for admission to a selective college.

Academic Preparation

What these transcripts suggest is that there is a basic core of courses that high school students ought to complete as a part of their college preparation. The Harvard/Radcliffe and Princeton catalogs specify a core curriculum that many other colleges agree on:

—four years of English with a continued emphasis on writing

—four years of mathematics, preferably including an introduction to calculus

—two to three years of laboratory science

—two years of history or social science, usually including one on the United States, plus a non-U.S. course

—three or more years of a foreign language, with a preference for intensive study of one language, rather than two or more studied more briefly

—one year of course work in the fine arts

The assumption behind the nearly unanimous agreement on what constitutes strong secondary school preparation is that the best preparation for college is a rigorous high school experience. So students should pursue "rigor" wherever they can find it.

In addition to covering the academic bases outlined above, students should read widely on their own and become familiar with computers. College candidates should realize that the educated mind is continually in the process of expansion and change and does not rest when a course is completed or a paper done. Rather it is generally engaged in the process of assimilating knowledge from a variety of disciplines and experiences and applying it to the challenges of living.

Course Content

College applicants cannot rest contentedly simply because they have enrolled in the most challenging program their high school has to offer, planning to take all the courses colleges typically mention in their catalogs. Students have to be sure that the colleges know about the content of those courses. They should make it a priority to ask their guidance counselor for a copy of their high school transcript and any explanatory materials that are sent along with it to the colleges. Often high schools have a profile sheet that gives the average performance levels for their college-bound students on such measures as the SAT and Achievement Tests. It may describe the honors and grading systems as well. Students should also find out whether their high school sends along course descriptions.

When Anne Marie Gregory found out that her high school did not have a course description sheet, she decided to write her own. She went to a school pamphlet describing the courses taught at White Falls High School and from it developed the following summary:

Anne Marie Gregory:
Course Work at White Falls High School

English The ninth-grade course in English concentrates on a review of elementary grammar and focuses on instruction in basic writing skills. The course also deals with the various ways in which people interact, as revealed in dramatic scenes that students write, read, and perform.

In the tenth grade students examine various themes in novels, stories, and poetry and discuss how to develop themes in their own writing.

By the eleventh grade students are ready for critical analysis of literature. They also prepare a long biographical essay in the spring term, based on direct observation and an in-depth interview with a particular person.

The study of technique and style occupies students in their senior course in English. Here they discuss the relation of form and idea in literature, exploring it in their own writing. (My class will utilize the Advanced Placement reading list and take the Advanced Placement exam in May.)

Mathematics The normal sequence for the college-bound student begins with an introduction to algebra in the ninth grade. Polynomials and linear and fractional equations, as well as computation of algebraic expressions, are stressed. Exposure to the computer and the language of BASIC are introduced in the spring term.

In the tenth grade the student turns to a combination of algebra and geometry: linear and quadratic equations in graph form, the geometry of area and volume, and the trigonometry of right and oblique triangles.

Elementary functions, exponents, logarithms, series, limits, and probability are taken up in the spring term. Students may go on to precalculus.

In the senior year a student normally takes differential and integral calculus followed by the Advanced Placement syllabus in the spring term and prepares for the Calculus BC level examination (which I may do).

Science Biology—covering plant and animal systems, cell structure, and elementary anatomy and physiology—normally begins the science curriculum.

Students go on to take the chemistry and physics sequence in the next two years. The chemistry course covers bonding, energy relationships, chemical reactions, modern theories of molecular structure, and a description of specific chemical families and can lead to the Achievement Test for able students. The physics course begins with a study of the basic laws of conservation and the kinetic theory of gases. It goes through electromagnetism and field physics, with a detailed study of the atomic model. Like chemistry, it prepares students for the Achievement Test.

Some students go on to advanced physics, which corresponds to a first-year college course, or to advanced chemistry, which is at a similar level.

Foreign Languages The foreign language curriculum attempts to develop the basic skills of reading, writing, and speaking a language, as well as an appreciation of a foreign culture. By the end of the second year, students have mastered grammatical skills and are able to carry on a simple conversation. Then they begin reading the literature. In the final year of French, for example, the humanistic tradition in French literature is studied, and authors such as Montaigne, Molière, Voltaire, Gide, and Camus are read.

Social Studies The only requirement in social studies at White Falls is one year of U.S. history. However, students can include history in their programs every year by beginning with the history of modern China and Japan in the ninth grade. The China portion of the course begins with an examination of the ancient values of Chinese civilization, then jumps to the impact of Western imperialism on China in the eighteenth and nineteenth centuries. The first part of the course concludes with a discussion of Chinese nationalism and communism. The Japan portion of the course begins with an examination of traditional Japanese society, then moves to a discussion of the impact of industrialization and Japan's subsequent experiences with totalitarianism, democracy, and world leadership.

The economics course, which many tenth graders take, explores the classical theories of Smith, Ricardo, and Keynes, then examines three modern industrial models: the United States, the USSR, and Japan. The spring term is devoted to an analysis of world trade, inflation in the United States, and the impact of debt on economic planning.

The advanced U.S. history course is designed to prepare students for the Advanced Placement exam. The course also tries to develop effective writing skills through a series of short research papers.

The course in urban history focuses on the development of one European city—Paris—and two American cities—New York and Chicago. In particular, the course examines how people sought to arrange their political, social, and economic lives during the period between 1850 and 1960, as they wrestled with the problems of low wages, poor living conditions, and uncontrollable growth brought on by industrialization.

Art Although White Falls has no art requirement, I took the elementary art course, which focused on line drawings, watercolors, and oils. In the spring term the course introduced some color theory, spatial organization, and a few of the major historical styles of painting. Although it was only a half course, my art class was still rigorous. When considered with my music lessons and concert band class, I have had more than a year of arts.

Anne had the course description neatly typed and photocopied, so that she could send a copy to each of the colleges to which she applied.

Extracurricular Activities

Having written up her curriculum, Anne turned to a brief explanation of her outside activities. One college application had only two lines for activities, so Anne referred the reader to a separate sheet of paper on which she wrote:

Activity	Length of Involvement	Hours per Week	Offices, Honors
School newspaper (*The Clarion*)	3 years	4	staff, columnist, sports writer
Yearbook (*Pantagraph*)	2 years	2	staff writer, photo layout
Track team (winter and spring)	2 years	4	two varsity letters (high jump), cocaptain
Hospital work	3 years	2	volunteer
Underground paper (*The Bell*)	1 year	2	founder, editor
Orchestra, stage band	8 years	1	trombonist

Thereafter, if a college's application did not allow her to expand on her extracurricular activities, Anne attached this list. If there was room for her to describe her activities, she typed this information directly on the application. Since college admissions officers are keen to discover students who have the ability to influence and lead other people in worthwhile enterprises, applicants should honestly present all the activities in which they have demonstrated leadership potential. Anne did this in the fourth column of her activities sheet. Another place where students have an opportunity to expound on their leadership skills is in the essay portion of the application or in response to the frequently asked question "What activity has meant the most to you in high school and why?"

Special Talents and Abilities

Deciding whether or not to submit supplementary information about your special talents is a tricky business. If all candidates for admission to college sent in tapes, portfolios, or homemade pies, the selection process would take forever, and admissions offices would have to rent warehouses to store everything. In considering whether or not to send in supplementary materials, ask yourself if any of the following applies to you. First, is there an outstanding accomplishment or a feature of your personality that is not touched on in your application? Second, has your college counselor or a coach or teacher advised you to submit the results of your work in a particular field? Third, have you been encouraged by a representative of the college to submit supplementary information? If the answer to any of these queries is yes, then you should consider submitting the additional information. You may, for example, want to send along a tape of your tuba solo at a recent concert, or copies of your poems that won prizes in a regional competition, or an athletic data sheet showing your times in swimming or track (see sample).

Whatever you submit, it is important that you observe a few simple rules of thumb:

1) Keep it short, sweet, and to the point. Don't have twenty minutes of your tuba tape devoted to the orchestra. Edit it so that your solo is the focus of the tape.

2) Seek the advice of your coach, teacher, or guidance counselor before sending anything, and show it to one of these "experts" before you put it into the mail.

3) Send evidence, not testimony. That is to say, send examples of your own work, not rave reviews by the experts. This allows the college to evaluate your talents for itself without being influenced by what others may have said.

4) Mail your supplementary information to the director of admissions or to the admissions officer who interviewed you and ask that person to direct it to the proper person for evaluation.

Ideally, you will have discussed the procedure for sending supplementary information at the time of your interview. If it is convenient and simple to do so, send two copies of your supplementary information, one to the admissions office and one to the appropriate evaluator at the college. Ask each of them to communicate with the other about their reactions to your materials. Athletic data sheets, for instance, can easily be sent both to coaches and to the admissions office.

Whatever you do, avoid a public relations campaign. Several rave reviews of a single piece of work will merely pad your folder. Professionally printed personal brochures with pictures will only alienate the college. Use your head. Put yourself in the position of the college admissions officers who may have to read hundreds of applications between the end of January and the beginning of March. Don't give them anything to read that is not worth their time. Submit your best work in as concise a form as possible.

Robert H. Rhinehardt
Athletic Data Sheet

Home: 37 Dunbarton Drive
                    Ash Forest, Illinois 60333

Phone: 352-882-4605

Height: 6'2"

Weight: 180 lb.

School: Atlantic Academy
                    Box 566
                    Mansfield, Connecticut

Phone: 223-778-8017

Coach: Bill Storms
                    14 River Street
                    Mansfield, Connecticut 06099

Phone: 223-778-4208

I have just begun my tenth year of swimming. The first six were with the Ash Forest YMCA, an AAU team. The last three have been mainly at Atlantic Academy.

Times (all flat start)
Short Course

	50 yd.	100 yd.	200 yd.
Free	22.9	49.2	1:49.9
Back	27.5	59.7	—
Breast	28.5	1:01.8 (New England Prep record)	2:19.0
Fly	25.3	—	—
IM (intermediate medley)	—	—	2:02.0 (school record)

The breaststroke time (1:01.8) placed me fourteenth among prep school swimmers in the nation, and thus I made Prep School All-American. I also anchored a 3:17.9 free relay, which broke the school record, with a split time of 49.2. The relay time missed All-American Honorable Mention by less than two tenths of a second.

Progression of times and places in New England Prep School Championships

	1987	Place	1988	Place	1989	Place
200 IM	2:07.4	7th	2:05.2	4th	2:02.0	4th
500 Free	5:14.0	9th	—	—	—	—
100 Free (relay)	52.0	4th	—	—	49.2	2nd
50 Back (relay)	—	—	27.8	4th	—	—
100 Breast	—	—	1:04.0	4th	1:02.2*	2nd

*Set New England record in trials.

When Anne Gregory's cousin, Rob Rhinehardt, applied to college two years ago, he prepared a data sheet for his swimming skills and sent it to both the admissions office and the swimming coach of each school to which he applied. Because he was at boarding school, he listed both his home and school addresses at the top of the page and then went on to indicate his times and his awards.

Rob Rhinehardt's athletic data sheet stands out for a number of reasons. It presents specific details. It shows the development of his skills over a three-year period, and it gives the name of his coach so that the information can be verified. It is short, sweet, and to the point.

Not everyone applying to college has the noteworthy swimming skills of Rob Rhinehardt or the well-balanced extracurricular activities of his cousin, Anne, but candidates can still present their skills convincingly on a single piece of paper. Rob's and Anne's examples yield several suggestions for the skilled artist or musician who seeks to present his or her unique talents to college admissions officers:

1) Show depth, rather than scope. If you are an artist, prepare a portfolio that emphasizes your ability to look at the same object or theme in a variety of ways. Present a series of sketches of the same farmhouse from different vantage points, at different times of the day. If you are a musician, you can submit a tape of yourself playing three classical pieces on the piano. Try to show that you can do one thing well and that you have brought your artistic or musical skills to a high level of perfection in a particular area.

2) Make variety a subordinate theme. If you have worked in a variety of media, you may want to present one or two paintings or a photograph of one of your experiments with collage or sculpture in addition to your sketches of the farmhouse. As a musician, you may want to tape a short jazz piano selection in addition to your three classical pieces.

   The important point to bear in mind is that you should put your best foot forward. If colleges are going to accept you on the basis of your talent, then you have to convince them that you could fill a niche in their music or art program. Every freshman class needs its excellent pianists and its talented pen-and-ink artists. Do not give the impression of being a dabbler by spreading yourself too thin.

3) Explain yourself. Write a narrative to go along with your sketches. Introduce your musical tape with an explanation of what you are trying to achieve in your performances. Demonstrate to the viewer or listener that you are articulate about what you are doing and that you have a capacity for self-criticism and self-awareness. You don't need to brag; just state your case and let the listener or viewer decide how good you are.

   Bear in mind too that even if you are not as skilled as some other applicant, that does not necessarily mean you will be denied admission to the college. All schools need students who are genuinely interested in the arts, although they are not themselves gifted as artists. How will colleges be able to fill courses in music theory or the history of Renaissance painting if they do not have some of these people in their freshman classes?

4) Document your case. A portfolio or a musical tape should be accompanied by a recommendation from your art teacher or music instructor, who ideally has heard or seen what you are presenting to the colleges. This allows the instructor to comment directly on your work. The writer of the recommendation should also state his or her own credentials, as well as an opinion of your work and of how far you can be expected to carry your talents in college and beyond.

Whatever your special expertise, you should ask the relevant admissions offices where and to whom you should send your data sheet, portfolio, or tape. Many admissions officers like to have a look at these materials before forwarding them to the athletic, art, or music department for evaluation, in which case you would first submit your materials to the admissions office itself. If, however, your materials are to be sent directly to a named instructor in a particular department, you should request that the instructor's evaluation be sent to the admissions officer with whom you have had an interview or some previous contact by mail or phone.

Talking with Your Counselor

Many high school students fail to appreciate the important role counselors can play in the college admissions process. In part this lack of understanding stems from the fact that counselors are always so busy with the variety of tasks assigned to them by school principals and superintendents—monitoring attendance, scheduling courses, counseling families, and in some cases teaching and coaching—in addition to their traditional duties of helping students with college and career placement. In many ways the duties imposed on counselors represent society's unrealistic expectations about what schools ought to be doing for young people—not only educating them in the basic skills of mathematics, writing, scientific inquiry, historical analysis, and the like, but also providing them with emotional and social support and setting limits on their behavior.

Nevertheless, students aspiring to admission to a selective college should try to gain access to their counselors, get to know them, and then enlist their advice and aid in carrying out college plans. Remember that counselors are legitimately busy; do not waste your counselor's time. When you do go in for a scheduled visit, have your questions written down on an index card so you can refer to them during the conversation. Ask the guidance secretary such routine questions as how to request ACT information, how to get additional copies of College Board scores, or what the status of your transcripts and recommendations is. If your counselor does not schedule you for an interview automatically, ask for one directly. Try to accomplish something in between interviews, e.g., visiting several colleges, taking more tests, or improving your grade point average. Use the interview session to tell the counselor something that could not be learned elsewhere. Your counselor does not need to know that you are the news editor of the school newspaper; that is probably written down on some form he or she will examine before writing the school's recommendation to your chosen colleges. But your counselor may be interested to know that when it came to a political struggle for control of the newspaper, your editorial work was found to be too liberal, so you were not given a high post after three years of distinguished work. He or she might also be interested to learn that you were one of the two students picked by your French teacher to attend a national conference and participate in a panel discussion.

As you talk to your counselor, bear in mind that his or her major obligation to you is to write an original descriptive essay about you for the colleges. This is the school's recommendation, a document often running 500 words or more, which, if written convincingly and candidly, can go a long way in helping you gain admission to the college of your choice.

You need to be aware of what questions the colleges ask the counselor to answer in the school recommendation.

—**Academic** How would you evaluate the applicant's general academic performance? To what extent has the candidate made use of his or her intellectual potential and of the educational opportunities available?

—**Extracurricular** What is the quality of the applicant's participation and leadership in extracurricular, community, or work activities?

—**Personal** How would you and others describe the applicant in personal terms, including any special strengths or problems?

—**Other** Are there any special circumstances, background information, or other factors (positive or negative) that may be relevant? Would you care to make any additional comments, for example, elaborate on the reasons for your checks on the bottom of the secondary school report form? Do you wish to compare the applicant with other students from your school who have gone to this college?

These questions show what detailed and analytical reports on nearly all aspects of a student's candidacy the colleges expect counselors to prepare. Here is how you can help your counselor with yours:

—**Academic** Make sure that your counselor knows the exact level of the courses you are taking. When discussing your math class, refer to it by name, AP calculus, not by the number, Math 509. Make sure, too, that your counselor knows of any academic work you have done outside the school, at a local community college or art school, for example. It is not enough to send a transcript of that work to the guidance office, since it can easily get lost or overlooked. Let your counselor know what you can do academically. Offer to submit an example of your work for your file. All your counselor can say is "No thanks."

—**Extracurricular** Make sure your counselor knows about any leadership positions you have attained inside or outside of school and how much time each week you devote to your extracurricular activities. If you are an athlete and have prepared an athletic data sheet, give a copy to your counselor so that he or she can become familiar with your skills and make the school's recommendation reinforce what your coaches are saying about you.

—**Personal** All college candidates have to hold fast to their identities during a process that seems to suggest that certain traits and personalities are desirable to colleges while others are not. Although college admissions people really do strive for variety among the students they admit, it is sometimes hard to discern that when you are a candidate. Here, for example, are the personal qualities Wesleyan University looks for: "evidence of honesty, fairness, compassion, altruism, leadership . . . young men and women with a genuine sense of responsibility and consideration for others . . . [with] a capacity for commitment to society. . . ." Your counselor and your college need a rough idea of where you are on your own life agenda, how you feel about yourself and your work. So try to be both natural and honest with your counselor in describing yourself.

—**Other** Sometimes there are special circumstances in your family or in your own life that counselors need to know. You are probably the best judge of whether an incident or situation should be related to a counselor or not. If you are on the fence, discuss the matter with your parents or a valued friend. Certainly anything that might explain a slump in your high school record, a period of time away from school, or the lack of an extensive extracurricular activities list should be explained to your counselor. Then the counselor can factor such information into your recommendation so that circumstances beyond your control will not be held against you during the college admissions process.

When reflecting on how to present yourself—your accomplishments and dreams—to the counselor, you should realize that the tone of the college recommendation process is a positive one. Generally speaking, the language is supportive, and criticisms, if any, are left out of recommendations, both oral and written.

Once you are satisfied that your counselor knows you adequately, then it is time to move on to the next phase—your lobbying effort. During the fall of your senior year, you and your counselor have come to know each other. You have set the overall strategy. In December your counselor completes the school recommendation, and in January and

February colleges are considering your applications. This is when you and your counselor need to coordinate your efforts and set the tactics to implement your strategy. Ask your counselor how to approach the colleges in order to bring subtle pressure on them to accept you.

Often the counselor can best apply this subtle pressure in the form of a fact-finding phone call to the college admissions office. The purpose of the call is to find out if the folder is complete, to furnish any new information about the candidate that may have come to light, and to ascertain "how the candidate looks" in the competition for admission. If the call achieves nothing else, it will assure you that your file is complete and that all recent information has been received, and it may give you some idea of your chances of admission.

Another way to help gain admission to a college you really want to attend is to write that school a "first-choice letter." Ask your counselor whether this would be a good idea and what such a letter should say.

During the lobbying season, you may also want to discuss with your counselor any special connections you may have developed with a particular college. Parents are sometimes involved in these discussions because they have friends or other contacts at specific colleges. Students should encourage their parents to talk first with the counselor, so that all efforts can be coordinated and that "overkill"—going too far with these subtle forms of pressure—can be avoided.

Finally, if the news from a given college is not too favorable and your counselor feels that you are probably not going to be admitted, you should ask for advice on which of your second-choice colleges to approach and how. Here again, the advice and assistance of a counselor can be invaluable.

When students are admitted to colleges—usually in April—and have choices to make, they should again seek the advice of the counselor, who has been actively engaged in their quest right from the beginning. Remember that counselors are not just trying to help students gain admission to college; they also want them to succeed there. Students can gain helpful insights from consulting with their counselors before making a final decision on where to matriculate in the fall.

Enlisting Your Teachers

One of the most undervalued documents in an applicant's admissions folder is the recommendation written by a teacher. Teacher recommendations can make all the difference in an admissions decision, especially when the teacher knows the candidate well, knows his or her subject well, knows how to write well, and knows the college to which the student is applying. Although you cannot do much to affect the last three factors, you can help with the first: your teacher's knowledge of you. Consider the following method for communicating with teachers who will be writing college recommendations for you:

1) Ask teachers if they would write recommendations for you early, be-

fore they are besieged with similar requests from your classmates. If they answer yes, make an appointment to discuss your college plans with them. Before the meeting, consider what you feel is important about you as a person and a student. Make a list of your values, your strengths, and your accomplishments; then circle those that this particular teacher may be able to highlight. Think about how you can help your teacher describe you as vividly as possible.

When you have filled out the top part of the teacher recommendation forms from the various colleges, prepare an addressed envelope for each one—with a stamp! Next, make copies of your list of extracurricular activities and add to each any information that is relevant to a particular instructor's subject. For instance, if the subject is history, then you may want to note that you have traveled to a particular historical site in Europe or the United States.

2) When meeting with the teacher, begin by briefly reviewing your college plans, in particular the subjects you want to study as an undergraduate. You will probably be asking for recommendations from teachers whose subjects you intend to pursue in college. If you are not sure of what your major will be, say so. Don't worry. You have probably done well in the teacher's course; you like both the subject and the instructor. That will be basis enough for a strong recommendation.

Next, briefly describe to your teacher what the rest of your life at school and at home is like. Give the teacher a context for the recommendation. Although a teacher is only required to make judgments about students' academic competence, some colleges ask for fuller descriptions. So tell your teacher that you play two varsity sports, work one day each weekend, and are president of the debating team. At the very least, these activities demonstrate that you know how to use your limited time efficiently.

As your conversation moves along, keep in mind the specific questions that teachers are commonly asked to address in their recommendations:

—Comment on the quality and nature of the applicant's academic work. What intellectual qualities and abilities does the student have?

—What extracurricular contributions has the applicant made to the school and community? Assess the student's talent, dedication, and leadership in the areas with which you are familiar.

—Tell us about the applicant's personal qualities, particularly in regard to integrity, values, and relationships with other students.

—Do you have any additional comments that might be relevant, for example, a comparison to former students from your school who have attended our university?

—What are the first three words that come to mind in describing this applicant?

3) After the meeting is over and your teacher has written your recommendation, you should be sure to convey your thanks. In addition to the thank-you itself, a way of showing appreciation to teachers is to keep them informed of the colleges' decisions. Too often students assume that teachers know what happens to their applications. Frequently they do not, and they are interested. Involving them in your application process is a way of saying thanks and may also result in bits of friendly counsel and advice.

Coaches and Special Instructors

Students with special talents in such areas as music, art, and sports have already been advised on how to prepare tapes, portfolios, athletic data sheets, and the like. In addition to working closely with their mentors in preparing these special materials, students should enlist their support in the recommendation process. Frequently coaches or special instructors can make a telephone call to their counterparts on the college side and urge that a student be considered favorably. They can also write a short recommendation to accompany a student's work, explaining its quality and attempting to persuade the college that the candidate has a unique contribution to make. Students should facilitate this process in every way possible, asking for an honest assessment of their work from instructor or coach: "Will I be able to make a contribution to a Division I soccer team? Is it reasonable for me to hope that I can play my instrument in the orchestra or sing in the glee club at Coburn College?" If the answer is yes, then ask what role your coach or instructor can play in helping you to gain admission.

As with teachers and guidance counselors, provide instructors and coaches with some background as to your academic abilities and your other extracurricular interests and accomplishments so that these can be alluded to where appropriate in a conversation or letter. Occasionally, in the crush of applications at a college admissions office, students' tapes or athletic data sheets get overlooked. Ask your guidance counselor to check to see that your file—including these items—is complete. If it appears that your special talents are not being factored into the decision-making process, ask your coach or special instructor to call the admissions office directly to plead your case. Usually this will not be necessary, but you should prepare for it anyway.

The Concertmaster

In many ways the candidate's role in the application process is like that of the concertmaster in an orchestra. When the conductor is temporarily called away, the concertmaster, who traditionally plays an instrument in the string section, is summoned to the front to lead. When called forward to conduct, the concertmaster sets the tempo, brings all the instruments in at the right moment, and reads ahead in the score to make sure everyone does his or her part. Like the concertmaster, a student filling out college applications is first a musician playing an instrument in the orchestra. But with that primary responsibility completed, the student's role changes like that of the concertmaster become a conductor—coordinating the contributions of others to make sure that guidance counselors, teachers, coaches, and special instructors all play their respective parts. If they do so in harmony, then the performance goes ahead smoothly. If the end result pleases the audience—the colleges—then the reputation of the concertmaster is ensured, and the applause of the audience takes the form of an offer of admission.

7

Financial Aid and

Financial Planning

for College

In the past twenty years, the course of college financial aid has changed greatly. Federal, state, and private programs have expanded considerably, and as a result, access to funds has increased. By the same token, the process of applying for aid has become more complex and time-consuming. Now, in considering college choice, students and families need to consider not only the quality of the academic program but also the availability of financial aid. They also need to understand that in spite of the availability of funds from a variety of sources, the burden for financing the bulk of a student's education has shifted in the last decade from the college and the federal government back to the student and his or her family.

So any candidate for financial aid should apply to a range of colleges in order to ensure that there are financial options as well as admission options at decision time in April. A good working list might start with the school the candidate most wants to attend, regardless of cost. Next might be a college that has slightly less difficult entrance requirements and a good reputation for making reasonable financial aid offers. The third choice could be a college where the candidate's chances of admission are at least fifty-fifty and whose literature states it meets the financial need of all accepted candidates. The fourth college offers essentially the same conditions for financial aid as the third but much better chances for admission. The fifth choice will in most cases be the state university. Extremely needy candidates should select a sixth college, either one that has a cooperative education program or one to which they can conveniently commute.

Terms and Their Abbreviations

Before beginning the research necessary to make these financial decisions, candidates should familiarize themselves with the strange language of the financial aid world. The simple initials and terms in the following list describe a whole range of programs, some of which every financial aid candidate will encounter at some point.

ACT/American College Testing Program ACT's Student Need Analysis Service (Box 4005, Iowa City, IA 52243, 319-337-1200) is one of the two organizations that process financial aid forms for colleges. (The other is the College Scholarship Service, listed below.) ACT's form is the FFS (Family Financial Statement), and it is used to calculate how much a student and his or her family can afford to contribute toward a postsecondary education.

BIA/Bureau of Indian Affairs BIA grants are available to students who are at least one fourth Native American. Applications are available through each college's financial aid office.

CSS/College Scholarship Service The CSS is the processing organization of the Educational Testing Service (Box 6300, Princeton, NJ 08541, for applicants living east of the Mississippi, or Box 24670, Oakland, CA 94623, for applicants living west of the Mississippi). Financial aid applicants send their Financial Aid Form to this major clearinghouse, where a standard formula is applied to family income and assets, with adjustments for taxes, living costs, and unusual expenses. The result of the calculations is the amount of money CSS advises the colleges that a student and his or her family should be expected to contribute toward a college education. This information is sent to the applicant and to the colleges and universities he or she designates.

CWS/College Work-Study Program This federally financed program provides opportunities for students who receive financial aid to work on campus or with tax-exempt employers. The government pays for most of the student's wages; the employer pays the rest. A College Work-Study commitment is part of the financial aid package. These work programs can add both breadth and depth to a student's educational experience; can be a valuable asset when looking for a job after college; and can allow students to meet new people, have fun, and become involved with aspects of campus life other than academics.

FAF/Financial Aid Form This is a form designed by the College Scholarship Service of the Educational Testing Service. It can be obtained from any high school guidance office and is to be filled out by students and their families at the end of the calendar year. On January 1 or as soon thereafter as possible the completed form should be sent to the CSS (Box 6300, Princeton, NJ 08541).

Family contribution This is the amount that the accrediting agency (CSS or ACT Student Need Analysis Service) estimates a student's family should be able to contribute toward his or her education. The amount takes into account parent resources, as well as the student's savings and earnings.

Fee waiver A fee waiver exempts extremely needy students from the payment of fees required for processing the Financial Aid Form and for sending copies to the schools to which they apply. The CSS issues a limited number of fee waiver forms to secondary schools, and eligible applicants may obtain one from their high school guidance counselor.

FFS/Family Financial Statement Similar to the FAF, the FFS is a financial aid application form required by colleges using the American College Testing Program. Students may obtain these forms from their high school guidance counselor. When the forms have been completed, they should be sent to ACT.

Grant The grant portion of a financial aid package is the gift portion, the money that the student does not have to repay. Grant amounts may vary from college to college and thereby make one college's offer more attractive than another's.

Merit scholarship These are awarded by colleges and outside agencies on the basis of accomplishment, rather than financial need. They are becoming increasingly important to colleges as a method of attracting good students from the declining student population. A recent survey found that 85 percent of private four-year colleges and 90 percent of public four-year colleges offer merit scholarships without regard to financial need.

Pell Grant This federal program provides extremely needy families with grants ranging from $200 to $2200 a year. A student wishing consideration for this program checks the appropriate box on the Financial Aid Form or the Family Financial Statement, and the request is considered automatically by the U.S. Office of Education. The exact amount of a Pell Grant is determined by the amount of money appropriated by Congress in a given year. For 1990, Congress voted $4.7-billion, a 6 percent rise over fiscal year 1989 (*Chronicle of Higher Education,* 18 Jan. 1989, p. A22).

Perkins Loan The Perkins Loan is a low-interest loan for students with demonstrated need. Students do not apply directly for a Perkins Loan. Funds are paid directly to colleges by the federal government for allocation to students selected by the colleges. Perkins Loans are normally for no more than $4500 for the first two years up to a maximum of $9000, at 5 percent interest, with repayment limited to ten years and beginning nine months after graduation.

PLUS loan PLUS loans are available from private banks and lending institutions. They are guaranteed by the federal government and exist for the parents of dependent students. They are not need-related but are intended instead to remedy cash-flow problems that may occur when families must pay college bills out of current income. These loans are made to parents and pay up to $4000 per year. There is a $20,000 limit for each child, and payments of principal and interest begin 60 days after the loan is made. (There is a similar loan program for independent students called SLS—Supplemental Loans for Students.) "PLUS and SLS loans have variable interest rates, adjusted each year. For the 1988–89 award year, the interest rate was 10.45 percent" (U.S. Government, *The Student Guide—Financial Aid from the U.S. Department of Education: Grants, Loans, and Work-Study 1989–90.* Washington, D.C.: GPO, 1989, p. 55).

ROTC/Reserve Officers' Training Corps ROTC is a scholarship and educational program offered by the three military services of the U.S. government. In return for scholarship aid that amounts to the cost of board and room plus a stipend in some cases, students have to serve for a period of years on active or reserve duty in one of the military services.

SAR/Student Aid Report If you apply for a Pell Grant, you automatically receive a Student Aid Report in four to six weeks. The SAR will indicate your eligibility for a Pell Grant by means of a Student Aid Index. If your index number is below 1700, you are eligible. Students who qualify should be sure that the colleges to which they apply receive a copy of the SAR letter.

Stafford Loan (formerly GSL/Guaranteed Student Loan) This is a program of government-subsidized low-interest loans made to students by credit unions, commercial banks, or savings and loans. The repayment of these loans is guaranteed by the federal government. Students may borrow up to $2625 a year for the first two years of study to a total of $17,250. The interest rate is 8 percent for the first four years of repayment and 10 percent thereafter. Lenders generally allow between five and ten years to repay, starting six months after graduation, and normally deduct 5 percent as an origination fee up front. Terms for Stafford Loans change annually.

Forms

Applying for financial aid is a great deal easier than the number of abbreviations might suggest. The normal course of action begins in early December of the applicant's senior year in high school. At that point students who think they may need financial aid in college should go to the office of their guidance counselor and obtain a copy of either the FAF and the latest edition of its companion booklet *Meeting College*

Sample Loan and Payment Options

Plan	Term*	Restriction	Maximum	Interest	Fee	Repayment Period
Perkins Loan	1 yr.	need-based; limited funds available	$4500, first 2 yrs.; $9000 total	5%	none	up to 10 yrs.
Stafford Loan	1 yr.	colleges expect all financial aid applicants to apply	$2625/yr., first 2 yrs.; $17,250 total	8%/10%	5%	up to 10 yrs.
PLUS loan	1 yr.	none	$4000/yr.; $20,000 total	treasury bill plus 3.25%	up to 3%	up to 10 yrs.
Sample short-term college loan	10 mos.	none	$7500	11.75%	none	10 mos.
Sample long-term college loan	1 yr.	creditworthy $20,000/yr.	$80,000	prime rate plus 2%	up to 6%	10–15 yrs.
Sample tuition prepayment loan plan**	up to 4 yrs.	down payment minimum	4-yr. tuition charge	11.5%	varies	10 yrs.

* Renewable unless otherwise noted.
** Tuition prepayment plans can sometimes be tied to second mortgages on family homes and have distinct tax advantages.

Costs (published annually by the CSS) or the FFS and its companion
piece *Applying for Financial Aid: A Guide for Students and Parents* (distributed by the American College Testing Program). The applicant should
take the FAF or FFS home and discuss it with his or her family. The
applicant's parents are then left the sizable task of completing the form
(details follow); having done that, they send it to the CSS or to the
American College Testing Program. Copies of the resulting report are
sent to the colleges and/or programs designated by the student. In
1989–90, it cost $8.25 for the report on the FAF to be sent to the first
college or program and $6.25 for each college thereafter; fees should be
included with the FAF when it is sent to the CSS. The fees for the FFS are
similar: in 1989, $7 for the first college or program and $3 for each
subsequent college. There is no fee for the report that is sent to the
student and his or her family.

Most state scholarship programs are supported by public money and
are keyed to the FAF or FFS. In some states applicants may receive aid
automatically simply by virtue of filing the FAF or FFS. Other states
require separate applications. Normally guidance counselors will be
able to give the necessary advice about state scholarship programs.

Filling out the FAF or FFS

Students and their families should strive for accuracy when completing
their respective portions of the FAF or FFS. The student's and head of
household's Social Security numbers must be entered properly on the
form. Students who are not American citizens may still qualify for aid if
they are permanent residents or if they live in certain U.S. territories.
Students whose parents are divorced should enter the name of the
parent with whom they have lived for the past twelve months. Many
colleges will ask both parents to make a contribution to their child's
college expenses, even though there has been a divorce. The colleges
will send the noncustodial parent an FAF or FFS to complete and then
will combine the incomes of both natural parents as a basis for a financial aid award.

Parents are asked to furnish information about the number of their
dependents for the current calendar year and the number of children
they are supporting in college. Most of the financial information requested on the forms can be taken from the parents' tax return (Form
1040 or 1040A); however, other information, such as the value of real
estate, bank deposits, insurance policies, and stocks, will have to be
gathered separately. Parents will also be asked to project their earnings
for the year in which the applicant will enter college. In each case, they
should not include any money earned by their son or daughter under
any current financial aid program, nor should they project such earnings for the following year. The purpose of the form is to determine
need on an annual basis and to help college officials decide how much
aid to offer.

In cases in which Social Security benefits are involved, only those benefits that applicants and their parents receive should be included, not those received by other dependents in the family. Married students who rely on their parents' support to meet living expenses are required to include amounts received for welfare or child support, any unemployment insurance, and any living or housing allowances, whether received in cash or not. Medical expenses that are not reimbursed by any insurance plan can also be reported to offset other income, as can the amount paid for the private elementary or junior high school education of other children in the family. These amounts are then projected for the next calendar year. Then total income, taxable income, and nontaxable income are computed, and the federal income tax for the year is subtracted in order to arrive at the true income for both students and their parents.

In addition to wages (including summer earnings), the personal assets of students and their parents also figure prominently in the determination of the expected family contribution. Although not required to include any income under a previous educational assistance program or from personal and consumer loans, both parties must show the extent of their savings, the amounts kept in personal checking accounts, and their equity in any real estate, stocks, or bonds.

Students are normally expected to contribute 35 percent of their assets toward college costs, and parents about 5–7 percent of theirs each year. Although these figures may be high in instances where a family or a student owns a business or farm, students and their parents are entitled to subtract the amount of indebtedness incurred against these assets, including mortgages or loans that used the asset as collateral. In cases in which several parties are the owners of an asset or are jointly involved in repaying a debt, percentages are used to show the portion borne by applicants and by their families.

The rest of the FAF or FFS is fairly straightforward. Parents must report taxable income, wages, interest income, dividends, and various sources of nontaxable income, such as Social Security benefits. They must also provide detailed information about the expenses they bear for the education of their other children. Child support, alimony, and the income of the parent with whom the child does *not* live are requested of divorced families. Students are asked to report Social Security benefits, veterans' benefits, and other sources of income, such as summer jobs and employment during the academic year. Married students who receive support from their family or in-laws are asked to report it, as well as any earnings of their spouse for the last tax year. Parents and students must then project their earnings for the year in which the application for financial assistance is made.

Having done all this, applicants then code the form so that all the schools and programs to which they are applying receive copies of the determination of the family contribution. Applicants and their families automatically receive a copy of the report four to five weeks after the FAF or FFS is filed. They will then be able to estimate how much aid may be forthcoming from the colleges to which students have applied.

It is a good idea to keep track of all the pieces of an application for financial aid on a chart similar to the one for the admissions application shown in Chapter 5.

Evaluating the Financial Aid Award

When students are finally admitted to college and deemed eligible for financial aid, they receive a financial aid package in the mail along with their offer of admission. The financial aid statement normally presents two columns of figures, one on the left stating the student's expenses, and one on the right stating the resources from which those expenses will be met. The resources column is headed by the parents' contribution, then the student's contribution from savings and summer earnings. (The difference between the resource sum and the total expenses is explained later.) The key point to keep in mind when examining a financial aid package is the difference between *price* and *cost*. The *price* is what an institution charges the customer, plus expenses for books and incidentals. The *cost* is what the family will have to pay to send the student to a particular school.

There are three categories of aid possible: (1) *outright grants* or *scholarships* from the federal government, the college, or both (these will not have to be repaid); (2) *loans* that students and perhaps their families are expected to take out; and (3) *work-study,* the amount of money that students are expected to make at a job during the course of the academic year.

In cases of high need, the grant aid tends to be very high relative to the total cost of attending the institution; the loan component is generally large as well. High-need packages usually include funds from the Pell Grant program and sometimes include special funds that the college has set aside for disadvantaged students. When the family's financial need is relatively low, grant aid declines and loan aid rises proportionately. When family need is marginal, the only form of financial aid offered may be in the form of a College Work-Study job.

Students and their families should remember that the estimate of the family contribution they received earlier was just that, an estimate. Some colleges are able to decrease the expected parental/family contribution below that computed by the CSS or ACT's Student Need Analysis Service and thereby increase assistance. Others may not be able to do that. Some students and families may not receive as much aid as they expected, but they should understand that most colleges assume that applicants and their parents have a responsibility to pay as much as they can reasonably afford toward the cost of higher education. In fact, they should be prepared for college financial aid officers sometimes to view certain assets differently and suggest family contributions in excess of those arrived at by the CSS or ACT. These assets might be savings, stocks, bonds, rental property, Social Security benefits, merit scholarship awards, or the money a student can contribute from summer employment.

In the first year of college, moreover, students are usually expected to contribute 35 percent of their assets and $1200 from summer earnings. Generally, the amount of the student contribution from summer earnings increases over the course of four years. Financial aid applicants should try to develop a marketable skill so that they can increase their summer earnings as they move through college.

Amounts of scholarship aid will vary, and applicants should apply to their state university in order to ensure that they have a low-cost option to consider when they receive their various acceptances and financial aid packages in mid-April.

The chart on the following page displays the different ways in which colleges and universities "package" financial aid and the resulting cost to the family. Set up a similar chart to compare your financial aid awards this spring.

Once parents and students have digested the implications of their financial aid award, they may still have questions about the future. Some common ones are:

"What happens to my award after the freshman year?"

Each spring the financial aid office asks families to complete a new FAF or FFS on which an award will be based for the next academic year. If your family's circumstances have not changed appreciably, you can generally expect that the college will meet your need as in the past year. In all cases, the granting of financial aid is an annual process.

"If my family's situation changes, is there anything that can be done?"

Your family should write a letter explaining what has happened and, in cases of a decrease in income, appeal for more assistance. Colleges often maintain small contingency funds for this purpose.

"When my brother and sister enter college in two years, what happens?"

Your family's need will probably be greater then, and most colleges will try to meet it. If you did not qualify for aid when you entered college, perhaps, with your brother and sister enrolled, you will qualify. By all means complete an FAF or FFS and apply.

"I may get a local scholarship at graduation. What happens then?"

The college has met your need as you have described it. There are always other worthy students who cannot be helped; therefore, the financial aid office expects you to report the amount of the outside

	COLLEGE A (Small, selective private college)	COLLEGE B (State college, moderate size)	COLLEGE C (State university, large)	COLLEGE D (Large, selective private university)
Tuition and fees	$ 10,425	$ 2,500	$ 4,000	$ 13,000
Room & board	+3,190	+2,800	+2,900	+3,400
Price	**13,615**	**5,300**	**6,900**	**16,400**
Miscellaneous (books, supplies, etc.)	+1,050	+850	+1,000	+1,050
Total price of attendance	14,665	6,150	7,900	17,450
Cost (expected family contribution)	**–4,000**	**–4,000**	**–4,000**	**–4,000**
Eligibility for need-based aid	10,665	2,150	3,900	13,450
Financial aid packages (estimated)				
Grant (gift money)	6,665	–0–	475	8,825
Loan (to be repaid)	3,000	2,150	2,625	3,500
Work (student employment)	1,000	–0–	800	1,125
Total aid awarded	$ 10,665	$ 2,150	$ 3,900	$ 13,450

Source: Allegheny College, *Financing College: Price Versus Cost.* Meadville, Pa.: 1988.

scholarship and will subtract that amount from your financial aid. The funds your outside scholarship saved the college are then distributed to another candidate.

"What happens if I cannot procure a Stafford Loan at a local bank?"

If you cannot procure a Stafford Loan at a local bank, the college will help you find a lender near the university. But you must try to prevail on your local bank first.

"What is a dependent student? An independent student?"

Most financial aid is based on the premise that both students and their families have the primary responsibility to pay the educational bill. However, if you are truly independent of your parents, financial aid will be computed differently. To be considered independent, you have to have not lived with either of your parents, not received more than $750 per year from them, and not been claimed by them as an income tax exemption for three consecutive years prior to the academic year for which you are requesting aid.

"Do I have to accept the work-study job offered to me as a condition for my other scholarship and loan aid?"

Absolutely not. If you can make an equivalent amount during the summer, or your family can provide you with equivalent funds, that is satisfactory. Your other aid remains intact.

"What if I still need aid and am not awarded any?"

This is the point where PLUS loans and an array of college-sponsored loans can help. Colleges often have relationships with banks that will make long-term loans or offer monthly tuition-payment plans. Financial aid officers will also be able to advise parents on low-interest loans from the New England Education Loan Marketing Corporation (Nellie May) and The Educational Resources Institute (TERI). Consult the college's financial aid office.

Before comparing the financial aid offers of the colleges that accepted you, you and your parents may want to consider some general advice about financial aid awards. Consult the preceding chart again.

First, pay careful attention to the relative amounts of aid included in each offer, as well as to the bottom line, which is how much families are expected to contribute. Obviously, high grant and scholarship offers should command careful attention if the schools are of equal quality and cost. (Colleges A and D are examples.) However, if the school's tuition and fees are high to begin with, the high grant may have less net impact than a slightly lower grant at a much less expensive school. Or, when one school costs less than another overall, and both have made equal grant offers, you should consider attending the less expensive of the two, where your loan and work-study commitments would be smaller. (Note the differences between College C and College D.) When schools of roughly equal quality and cost offer different levels of support, you should strongly consider the school offering the larger financial aid package.

Second, you and your parents should examine the loan structure in detail. Federally supported loans are generally easier to carry than those from private banks or the university itself. The same holds true for state guaranteed loan programs. Students who are considering going on to graduate school will not want to incur a heavy loan burden for their undergraduate education and may therefore favor an undergraduate college that offers them a large scholarship grant and a loan program backed by federal or state money. (Colleges A and D may well do this.) On the other hand, families may be eligible for various parent loan programs offered by some private colleges and not available at public universities. These loans, normally carrying an interest rate of 10 to 12 percent, enable families to spread out the cost of educating their children over a period of up to fifteen years.

Third, you and your family should be wary of financial aid offers with an extensive work-study commitment. Some schools expect students to earn in excess of $3000 during the academic year. This is more easily said than done, especially when withholding taxes are taken out of earnings. The low skill level of some students may dictate that they work only at jobs paying the minimum wage and requiring long hours at the expense of study time and extracurricular interests.

As students and their families ponder financial aid awards, they will soon realize that not all of their financial need is necessarily going to be met by the college. There are some ways, however, to save money on the costs of books, supplies, room and board, entertainment, and travel. Shrewd students and their parents should consider the following:

1) Book costs can be reduced by buying used texts from the college bookstore. Get there early!

2) Supplies are likely to be a constant expense, particularly for students majoring in engineering, a lab science, fine arts, or the graphic arts; often the financial aid package does not provide adequately for such expenses. Resourceful students can reduce the cost of supplies somewhat by seeking used equipment, advertising their needs on index cards and posting them on department, dormitory, and student center bulletin boards. Often used equipment and supplies will serve very well for the beginner.

3) Scrutinize charges for board and room very carefully. Some colleges permit students to live off campus and to share apartments. Most colleges have meal plans that allow students to take some meals outside the dining hall. Students may be able to cook simple meals in

their rooms or apartments and eat only one meal a day in the dining hall. Some institutions also offer cooperative housing arrangements, so students on tight budgets can get together and rent a housing unit with kitchen facilities, cutting costs on room and board that way.

4) Miscellaneous personal expenses for entertainment, laundry, and the like can often be reduced. Consult the school newspaper for the free entertainment on campus each week. Use self-service laundries.

5) Normally financial aid officers base their computation of travel expenses on three round-trips home per year by the cheapest means of transportation. Sharing rides home or forgoing one trip will reduce expenses. Buying nonrefundable airline tickets will cut costs as well.

Actually, tuition and fees also can be reduced in a variety of ways:

1) Students can accelerate their course of study in college. This may be done by taking Advanced Placement examinations in various subjects in the last two years of high school. Many colleges and universities grant advanced standing on the basis of these tests, and qualified students are thus able to meet the requirements for graduation in three and a half years or less, thus saving a large chunk of tuition and fees.

2) Students may wish to consider schools with cooperative education programs, whereby they may attend college for one semester and then work in their field of interest for the next semester. Or work and study may be arranged on an equal-time basis while students go ahead with their college education. Naturally such programs prolong the span of undergraduate education, but they do make it affordable and often lead to direct job placement on graduation.

3) Students should investigate institutions that offer merit scholarships. (See previous discussion under "Terms and Their Abbreviations" in this chapter.)

Often students and their families consider establishing the student as an independent rather than a dependent person, in hopes that a greater financial aid offer may be received. Students and families embarking on this course should keep in mind three considerations: (1) such students should not plan to live with their families for more than six weeks during the entire calendar year, (2) the parents may not treat their children as dependents for tax purposes for the previous three tax years, and (3) families cannot contribute more than $750 to a child's welfare during any calendar year. State colleges and universities, which have been inundated with students seeking to attend because of low tuition, may add to these requirements. They may require proof of residence for six months of a given year and ask for a voter registration card or a local property tax receipt as proof of independent status. They may also require a state driver's license and/or a state income tax return (if applicable) from students who declare themselves independent. So it may not be advantageous to declare independence. Students may indeed receive more scholarship funds as independent candidates but still find that they are unable to meet the costs of going to college.

College Payment Plans

Planning for college should also take into account the form of payment to the colleges. Parents need to look at the entire four-year period of their child's education and weigh the various forms of payment colleges offer them.

If parents are well-off, they may want to take advantage of the tuition prepayment plan offered by many colleges. Under this plan, parents pay the whole four-year tuition (usually not room and board) at the beginning of the student's freshman year. Parents are assured of the fixed cost for the four years, while the college gains access to additional funds.

If families have to borrow money to pay tuition, most colleges insist that they secure a Stafford Loan and/or a PLUS loan first, then avail themselves of institutional loan funds. Particularly needy students may receive a Perkins Loan also. Normally any funds an institution sets aside for parental borrowing are administered by a private agency appointed by the college. Some parents choose to borrow a large amount over a long term in order to take advantage of the tuition prepayment program; others borrow by the year. Still others establish a schedule of payments that allows them to pay tuition charges over a twelve-month period rather than on two separate dates, or they may seek a schedule of payments over four, six, or even ten years, when such plans are available from the college.

Parents in many states also have state loan programs available to them; these are designed to buttress colleges that are without funds for elaborate loan and repayment plans. Your state department of education will know the address of the appropriate state agency. As an example, the state loan authority in Massachusetts offers loans at a 12.5 percent interest rate for 75 percent of the student's college costs, with payments extended for a fifteen-year term. To borrow $5000 would cost the borrower $535.59 the first year and result in monthly interest payments of $61.62.

Behind the state agencies lie the private agencies and banks that specialize in education financing. The Richard C. Knight Agency (53 Beacon Street, Boston, MA 02108) and the Tuition Plan, Inc. (Donovan Street Extension, Concord, NH 03303) are well known. Academic Management Service (110 Central Avenue, Pawtucket, RI 02867), the Girard Trust Bank (Second and Chestnut Streets, Philadelphia, PA 19101), and the Bank of Boston (Federal Street, Boston, MA 02110) have also entered the field. These institutions pay student charges as they come due in return for a fee, which is incorporated into the monthly charges that families pay to the agency.

The large number of payment plans available in the public sector should not obscure the fact that planning in advance for college expenses is better than planning during the college years to meet those expenses.

Planning Ahead for College Costs

The sharply rising costs of a college education have produced not only anxiety but a good deal of creativity among parents faced with tuition bills that may soar to $25,000 a year before the decade of the nineties is over. Most parents now realize that at least two axioms govern the financing of a college education: first, plan early, and second, keep it simple. Parents with young children should start saving immediately so that the savings habit becomes a part of the family's pattern of living from the present right through the college years. Keeping the planning simple will enable parents to remember what they did and when, in case a college or the Internal Revenue Service inquires.

The following arrangements are appropriate to families in differing financial situations:

— **Custodial accounts** One of the simplest methods of financing educational costs is to set up a custodial account in the child's name. The parent then purchases one of three investment vehicles: Series EE U.S. government bonds, a commercial zero-coupon bond, or a no-income growth stock. All three of these are vehicles for deferring income to the point of maturation or sale. With zero-coupon bonds, for instance, the farther away the date of maturity, the less the bonds cost. Assuming a lead time of fifteen years, parents can purchase $50,000 worth of bonds for $8350. The child or trustee who holds the bonds has to pay a tax on the "artificial" interest received each year, even though it is being compounded to build up the original investment. However, these interest taxes do not take effect until the child earns $500 and then are based on the child's lower tax rate until $1000 is reached. Some families may want to establish investments that do not "pay off" until a child turns 14, when the gains will be taxed at his or her lower tax rate. By investing $100 a month in Series EE bonds, parents will be able to create a college fund of about $50,000 by the time the child is ready to enter the freshman year. The toll-free number for information about government bonds is 800-US-BONDS.

— **Individual Retirement Account** Another relatively uncomplicated method of advance savings for college employs individual retirement account (IRA) funding. Even though IRAs are intended for retirement and carry a 10 percent penalty for early withdrawal of funds, the accrued tax-free interest operating in tandem with the tax reduction for every deposit to the account makes them an attractive option for some families. If a family is in a high tax bracket, for instance, and an IRA is earning them 10 percent interest, the break-even holding

141

period can be reached after approximately five years. After that time they enjoy the benefits of the interest rate, even though they plan to withdraw their funds before retirement. (Note: Some of the examples here are drawn from *Nearly Free Tuition* by Alexander A. Bove Jr. Bove is a lawyer and an estate planner with an interest in helping families navigate the murky waters of financial planning.)

— **Gift and lease-back** The following illustrates this arrangement and its benefits. Heidi is 18 and about to go off to college. Her father and her mother give her $10,000 each in December of her senior year of high school. They do the same in January, so Heidi now has $40,000. Her father then borrows the money back from Heidi, paying her 14 percent per year for four years. When the fall tuition bill comes due, Dad pays Heidi the $6400 interest payment for the first year, and she pays her own tuition. Dad actually is paying only $3840 in real dollars because he is in a high tax bracket. Heidi has to pay her own taxes on the interest payment because it is income to her, but in her low tax bracket the bill is only $600. So the family has saved $1960 for each of four years, or $7840. Two important caveats about gift and lease-back arrangements: (1) the gift to the child must be absolute and (2) the terms of repayment or lease must be at fair market rates.

— **Personal Investment Plan** Many parents will want to make personal investments of their own on the child's behalf. Some will prefer tax-free municipal bonds, others will invest in the stock market, and still others will opt for high-growth mutual funds. Here are some guidelines for parents to keep in mind when making these sorts of investment: (1) they can invest up to $14,000 before the child will earn more than $1000 a year and be subject to their higher tax rate; (2) it is sensible for them to fashion the investment so that the gains are not taxed until after the child turns 14 and is no longer subject to their higher tax rate; (3) they should begin investing for their child at the earliest age possible, but no later than 10 years old—at that point they should estimate how much they think college will cost when the child is 17 and put two thirds of that amount in a custodial account (even if the child does not elect to go to college, he or she could still elect to keep the money!); and (4) they should begin with stocks or growth investments, but switch when the child is within two years of starting college—at that point they should invest in money market funds or Certificates of Deposit calculated to pay off at six-month intervals so that tuition bills can be met (Randall Hedlund, "College Planning," *Money,* January 1988, p. 124).

The New Realism

No reader can be unaware of the tremendous controversy about financial aid raging in this country today. Ever since World War II and the G.I. bill, the federal government has extended its support of student financial aid. An initial commitment of $700-million a year has risen to an annual education budget of $16-billion a year. However, the energy crisis and the recession of the 1970s reduced the ability of the federal government to support higher education at the high level of the 1960s and the Great Society. In recent years Congress has substantially reduced funds for education in the face of the federal budget deficit. The watchword has become "cutback." The financial burden of college education now falls more squarely on families and students.

The reduction of federal aid and other economic factors have led to sharply rising college costs, which could drive the cost of a private education to $100,000 within the next few years. The education consumers— families and students—are caught in a vise and must plan carefully for the college years. In some cases students will have to attend public colleges instead of more costly private ones. In most cases students and their families will have to go into debt in order to sustain college costs. Nonetheless, there are a few encouraging signs.

First is the sincere commitment of the nation's private colleges to try to meet students' financial need. Through innovative loans, grants, support programs, and work-study arrangements, not to mention cost-cutting in areas such as new building and faculty salaries, many of the nation's private colleges have expanded their financial aid budgets to meet the increasing needs of their students.

State governments have also rallied round, assisting colleges through loan-funding programs and tuition-prepayment plans. Financial institutions are entering into the vital area of education financing as well. In addition, some novel approaches have been suggested. John Silber, president of Boston University, has proposed the Tuition Assistance Plan, which would make the government initially responsible for needy students. After the indebted student enters the work force, the burden would shift, in the form of a 2 percent income tax for a substantial number of years. In other less elaborate schemes, private industries have increased their efforts to donate surplus equipment to colleges. Other companies have developed scholarship programs of their own.

On a more general level, the financial stringency of the past decade has instilled in Americans a sense of resilience and an understanding of what tough decisions and trade-offs the business of attending college depends on. Americans are beginning to accept the fact that college costs are justifiably high and will remain that way for the indefinite future. They now realize that attending college means making sacrifices.

Unfortunately the "new realism" manifested among some college officials, teachers, and many government leaders, as well as the numerous families sacrificing so their children can go to college, has led to an alarming cultural myopia. This "realism" tends to overlook the families and students at the low end of the social and economic spectrum with virtually no resources for meeting college costs.

Somehow in the years ahead the national leadership will have to find a better balance between the need for the federal government to play a diminished role in financing higher education and our society's need to fulfill its promise to provide equal opportunity for all.

For More Information

Here is a list of publications families exploring financial aid may find useful:

American College Testing Program, *Applying for Financial Aid: A Guide for Students and Parents.* Iowa City, Iowa. Published annually.
From ACT's Student Need Analysis Service, describes the process of applying for financial aid and, specifically, how to fill out the FFS. It is the equivalent of CSS's descriptive materials for those using ACT's services, and it is available free from high school guidance offices.

American Legion, *Need a Lift?* Indianapolis, Ind. Published annually.
Useful brochure for children of veterans, particularly those who wish to pursue a technical or military career.

Robert L. Bailey, *How and Where to Get a Scholarship and Financial Aid for College.* New York: Arco, 1988.
Bailey is director of admissions at the University of California at Berkeley and has compiled a helpful list of all the scholarship monies available from colleges in each of the regions of the United States. Addresses and phone numbers are included.

Alexander A. Bove Jr., *Nearly Free Tuition.* New York: Viking Penguin, 1988.
Provocative survey of numerous ways in which families can cut their college tuition costs. Written from the point of view of a tax lawyer, the advantages and disadvantages of each method are spelled out. This volume is an especially useful guide as families try to navigate between the Scylla and Charybdis of tightening federal tax laws and declining federal aid to the college-age student. However, impending tax laws have to be kept in mind when reading Bove's book.

College Scholarship Service, *Meeting College Costs.* New York: The College Board. Published annually.
Pamphlet available free from high school guidance offices and particularly useful in advising students how to determine their eligibility for financial aid. Also explains the FAF and the role of CSS.

Coopers and Lybrand, *Early Planning for College Costs.* Available from P.O. Box 46, Rockville, Maryland 20850.
Coopers and Lybrand is a large accounting and consulting firm with vast experience in advising clients on planning for college costs.

Alan Deutschman, *Winning Money for College,* 2nd ed. Princeton, N.J.: Peterson's Guides, 1988.
First complete guide to competitions students can enter on their own. Contains facts, figures, and advice on how to win contests ranging from public speaking to essay writing to scientific experiments.

(continued)

Priscilla S. Goeller, *College Checkmate: Innovative Tuition Plans That Make You a Winner.* Alexandria, Va.: Octameron Press, 1988.
Practical document for families seeking information about "tuition futures," bonds offered for college tuition by some thirteen states. Also has easy-to-read charts listing all the types of aid, including loan plans, offered by each college in those states.

Elizabeth Hoffman, *Financial Aid for College Through Scholarships and Loans,* 4th ed. Wellesley Hills, Mass.: Richards House, 1985.
Complete explanation of terminology, with helpful worksheets for estimating college budgets and financial aid awards. Long and valuable listing of privately funded sources of scholarship aid, including churches, businesses, trade unions, veterans' groups, and minority and ethnic organizations.

Robert Leider and Anna Leider, *Don't Miss Out: The Ambitious Student's Guide to Financial Aid.* Alexandria, Va.: Octameron Press, 1988.
Listing of lesser-known sources of merit scholarship and need-based aid that is not tied to a particular university or college.

Peterson's Guides, *Peterson's College Money Handbook 1989.* Princeton, N.J.: Peterson's Guides, 1988.
A 591-page tome containing a wealth of information. One section is devoted to profiles of the nation's colleges: cost, percentage of students on aid, and no-need and specialized scholarships offered. Another section consists of directories of colleges offering athletic and merit scholarships and co-op and ROTC programs.

Peterson's Guides, Peterson's Financial Aid Service 1989. Princeton, N.J.: Peterson's Guides, 1988.
For a number of Apple and IBM PC models, this software parallels the popular *College Money Handbook* but has additional sections on estimating family contributions and calculating financial need. Another useful section enables the operator to group colleges by cost and type. There are also sections on federal and state aid programs, sources of private aid for college, and merit scholarships available from certain colleges.

U.S. Government, *Federal Benefits for Veterans and Dependents.* Washington, D.C.: GPO. Published annually.
Booklet providing a comprehensive summary of benefits available to veterans and their dependents. Especially precise when it comes to service-related disabilities and the benefits that pertain to them.

U.S. Government, *The Student Guide—Financial Aid from the U.S. Department of Education: Grants, Loans, and Work-Study 1989–90.* Washington, D.C.: GPO, 1989.
Detailed description of rules and regulations surrounding Pell Grants, PLUS loans, Stafford Loans, and the other federal aid programs for students. Guidance offices have this 81-page brochure.

8

For Parents Only: The Myth of College and Success

In late February of 1860, Abraham Lincoln packed an old carpetbag with several shirts and a black silk suit and boarded the eastbound train from Springfield, Illinois. The ostensible purpose of his trip was to make a visit to his son Robert, who was then a senior at the Phillips Exeter Academy in New Hampshire. Lincoln's hidden purpose, as in much of what he did, was to test the political winds in what was probably the most critical election year in American history. Only his first purpose need concern us here, for it demonstrates one of the fundamental myths about college choice that beguile parents to this day. Abraham Lincoln and his wife, Mary Todd, had sent their son east to school the previous fall so that he could gain admission to a prestigious college. They wanted their son Robert to gain much of what his father had been denied in life. Even though the elder Lincoln was now 51 years old, he still spoke with a midwestern twang. "Mr. Chairman" came out "Mr. Cheermun"; "are not" was still sometimes "ain't." Lincoln and his wife hoped that Robert would meet the "right" people at Exeter and acquire a social patina. They hoped that, through his own efforts and the network of friends that he would make at Exeter and later at Harvard, Robert would rise quickly to the top of American society. They were not to be disappointed. In the years that followed, Robert Lincoln rose to prominence as a Chicago lawyer, chairman of the board of the Pullman Palace Car Company, and later a cabinet officer for President Garfield.

The recurrence of this type of story over and over again in American history has led parents to believe the myth that college is the key to the future, to financial success, to social prominence, and to self-fulfillment.

Yet one wonders if college adequately prepared young Lincoln for the tragedy of his father's death and for a lifetime of being judged against the heroic standards his father exemplified. Did college prepare Robert Lincoln for the rampant and irresponsible capitalism that engulfed the country in his time, occasionally linking his own name with scandal and oppression? Did college give him the inner strength to deal with the death of his younger brothers and the increasing madness of his mother?

Yet the myth endures that college is the adolescent's karma, a fate that all young people must embrace in order to attain happiness in the life to come. Parents whose children are facing the decision of whether or not to attend college have a responsibility, to themselves and to their off-spring, to examine closely the premises behind their desire to see their children embark on a college education. First among suspect premises should be the one holding that college is the *only* key to a successful and profitable life. Parents who subscribe to this myth foist it on their children, who may then go off to college for the wrong reasons and end up bored or unhappy or worse. According to G. Gary Ripple, former dean of admissions at the College of William and Mary, ". . . far too many kids end up . . . doubly distressed because [they are] doing poorly in college and because [they have] failed to stand up to [their] parents" ("Gold Plating Our Kids," *Newsweek*, 4 Apr. 1988, p. 9).

College as Fulfillment of Parents' Aspirations

Parents who see their own fulfillment in terms of their child's applying to and being accepted by the right college are in the grip of a second familiar misapprehension. They often force their children to attend a specific college, particularly a prestigious one, because they believe it somehow reflects glory on themselves. One father, who insisted that his son apply to Harvard/Radcliffe—where the boy had no chance of being admitted—told me that he did so because he himself had not had the chance to go to a prestigious school. And this came from a psychologist! So the boy dutifully applied to Harvard/Radcliffe and several other prestigious colleges and was turned down by all of them. An unfortunate episode that didn't have to happen.

The sources of parental stress are as diverse as the stress itself is real. Nonetheless parents need to distinguish their child's needs from their own, lest both fall victim to confusion about whose needs are being fulfilled. Consider for a moment the untenable position in which the psychologist had placed his son. Children do not want to lose their parents' love, so they quickly learn to do the "right" thing to please their family. This young man, in an effort to please his father, suffered a significant loss of self-esteem when those prestigious schools all rejected his application. He had been encouraged to put himself forward, to strive toward the apparently unattainable, but not for his own reasons. The needs of the father had been substituted for those of the son, and it was these that prevailed. If the psychologist father had looked honestly at the discrepancy between his own needs and those of his son, the family might have made a better selection of colleges. The father should have considered the son's educational needs in guiding his choice of college: his areas of academic interest, his learning style, his extracurricular interests, and the kind of social environment in which he might prosper.

It was that father's job—and it is the job of every parent—to hold an honest conversation with his son to ascertain his real motives for wanting to go to college. Had he done so, he might have found out that *his* motives and *his* ego needs were controlling his son's decision to apply to Harvard/Radcliffe. The father should have tried to separate his own aspirations and needs from those of his son and so bring to the discussion an objectivity consistent with his training and years.

Parents who push their children toward college run great risks. Often it does not occur to them that they might be using the child to fulfill their own unrealized wishes. The dead giveaway that parents are subordinating their children's wishes to their own is the employment of the pronoun "we," as in "We are applying to Skidmore."

When parents hear themselves using this "we," they should be aware that they are controlling the process too much. Unconsciously they are treating their children as symbols. These "symbols free [them] from the energy-consuming task of knowing the child as a totality, a whole person," writes David Elkind, a noted child psychologist. He goes on to say: "Thus by treating children as symbols, parents conserve energy needed for coping with [their own] stress" (*The Hurried Child: Growing Up Too Fast Too Soon*. Reading, Mass.: Addison-Wesley, 1981, pp. 28–29).

Education as a Commodity

Another view that frequently overshadows objective parental decision making about college is the myth that education is something that can be purchased like a commodity. As with any consumer item, the argument runs, its price reflects its value; good schools are expensive and poor schools are not expensive. Recently a parent in a wealthy suburb was asked by her daughter's guidance counselor, "Why won't you let Jeannie apply to the state university?" The answer was "I am not spending $9000 a year for my daughter to go to the state university when she can get twice as good an education for only 50 percent more at one of the 'prestige' colleges!" There is an equally simplistic flip side to the commodity myth. It goes, "Why should I spend $15,000 a year to send my son to a so-called 'prestige' college when for half the price he can have a good time at the state university?"

People espousing the commodity point of view invariably know the price of things but not necessarily the value of them. They somehow equate the quality of the educational experience with the money being expended, rather than basing their approach on the question "What type of educational institution is best for my child?" Ironically, the parents who are most often conscious of price are frequently the least concerned about value, ignoring schools where, for a little more or a little less money, their children could get a fine education and spend a happy and productive four years. As long as parents are determined to "buy the best," whatever that may mean to a particular family, their children will experience enormous difficulty in making a rational college choice.

College as Utopia

Parents often advise their children to go to a particular college on the fallacious premise that it is "good" and "good" colleges ultimately lead to the "good" life. They view the chosen college as a kind of utopia. Some parents talk about these "good" colleges as if they actually know what that means or, for that matter, as if anyone knows what that means. In the face of their neat division of the world into good and bad, the rest of us can only wonder how they recognize their "good" college. Do they look at what other institutions say about it or how many applications come flooding in to its admissions office? Do they count how many of its students are accepted to graduate school, particularly to medical schools, or the number of scholarly treatises published by its faculty? Is it size, endowment per student, scholarship aid, the size of the library, or the number and quality of other facilities? Is there no middle ground?

Another variation on the utopia theme perceives college as a place where children can spend four more years of innocence before encountering the harsh realities of the everyday world. In such instances parents don't view the college years as inaugurating a new period of independence for their children but rather see college as temporarily taking over parental responsibility. They think that somehow the idyllic atmosphere of home can be transported magically to a bustling campus in a city a hundred miles away. Nothing could be further from reality, and this utopian view is frequently shattered abruptly when the student arrives on campus. Setting aside this myth of utopia, along with the others mentioned, will prepare parents to help their children make reasonable and healthy decisions about college life.

Preparation for Choosing

In order to make sensible college choices, parents have to know their children as individuals. What are their children's needs, both personal and academic? What are their talents, both expressed and still to be realized? What kinds of people do their children like or dislike? What is the nature of their children's relationship to them and to the community? The answers to these questions need to be formulated in discussions between parents and, where appropriate, between parents and their children.

Imagine the beneficial effect of such a discussion on an only son who is small, retiring, moderately able, and scientifically inclined. To send that young man to a large, prestigious liberal arts school, where he would likely be socially and academically out of his depth, would be a mistake. He would probably fare much better in a small liberal arts college with a strong program in the sciences. In a different way, a similar family talk could help focus the aspirations of a bright and versatile young woman who made the National Honor Society, captained the field hockey team, and was elected vice president of her class. She might be the type of person who would thrive in a large and cosmopolitan university. (One young woman like this, who had done very well at a small, demanding preparatory school where she was well known by most of the students and faculty, told her counselor that she wanted to attend a huge university that offered her "the luxury of anonymity.")

Parents should sit down and talk to their children about what they hope to achieve at college. Do they wish, for example, to continue their extracurricular and creative activities in college? Are they applying to a college where these interests will be overwhelmed by the talent of other students or one where their talents will sparkle unchallenged by those of others? The high school track star who has already set the New England record in his event should not apply to a school where he will be far better than everyone else on the track team. That will not be any fun for the others on the team during the next four years, nor will it provide much of an inducement to the young man to set even higher goals for himself.

Parents should also talk to their children about career plans, especially when these involve the professions, such as medicine or law. It may be a good idea for parents to encourage children to take some of the interest and skill inventory tests described in Chapter 1 and to discuss the results with their guidance counselor. If a child's mind is already too firmly made up, a little practical experience can help reduce a fixation on a particular career. Perhaps the fervent premed should spend a year working in an emergency room or a lab before embarking on her college career. If that is not possible, she might take some courses outside her field in order to broaden her perspective. To narrow career choices too soon is a costly mistake that often leads to disillusionment in college. Even professional schools are catching on to the significance of a broad liberal arts training. As an observer of the committee selecting candidates for the intensive six-year medical program at a major midwestern university commented, "The ones who get through are invariably the ones who have something other than sheer excellence in science to offer. They have dropped out for a year to work in a nursing home; they have managed to make the Olympic skating finals while getting Bs in organic chemistry; they have written and published poetry; they have done *something* that will give them a broad perspective as a doctor six years from now." When wise parents focus on their children's career interests, they help them to understand how a broad base of liberal arts courses and extracurricular experiences in college will enhance their credentials for the careers they eventually plan to pursue.

Sensible parents will also realize that beneath the educational and career questions their children face in making the decision to attend college lies an array of psychological forces that must be reckoned with. On the simplest level, the college admissions process brings young people and their families face to face with considerable stress. In some cases this is the first time students and their families have faced such a great challenge together.

At the end of a meeting with her counselor, a versatile and able high school senior may very well moan, "I don't know why, I am just terribly anxious about all this." Whether she knows it or not, part of the stress she feels stems from her sense that for the first time she is moving out of a world in which the competition had been essentially controlled—by teachers, coaches, and family—into the real world, where the forces that decide the outcome of events are much more uncertain. It is understandable that such a young woman might be terrified of not gaining admission to the prestigious college where her father studied. She has always achieved her goals until now—honors student, captain of one sport, star of another, handsome boyfriend. Now things are different, and even the best-laid plans—her own, her guidance counselor's, and her family's—might go awry. What she needs to hear from her family is how sensible planning can reduce the risks of failure to an acceptable level, along with the message "We love you, no matter what." By seriously investigating all the colleges recommended by her counselor and applying to colleges of varying difficulty, she will learn that a fine education can be found not only in the eight Ivies or the Little Three or the Big Ten. When this realization has been reached, the young woman and her family will be able to relax a little and bear gracefully the normal stresses of applying to colleges.

Would that uncertainty of outcome were the sole psychological variable in the college admissions landscape! Of course it is not; there are other developmental issues that attend the ceremony of college choice. In helping to plan their children's applications to college, parents need to understand that students are also learning to deal with shifting peer relationships. The admissions process itself often affects personal relationships. A Yale freshman has described his relationship with a young woman during the critical year of college application, when both were seeking their autonomy: "Our relationship was essentially backward-looking, setting up our senior year of high school as the norm against which all other times and challenges were to be measured." As the young man moved on toward college, his career interest shifted, and, partly as a result, he eventually dropped his relationship with the young woman in question. "My movement away from Barbara represented a movement away from medicine, and away from those colleges that offered strong premedical programs," he wrote (Herbert A. Sacks, *Hurdles: The Admissions Dilemma in Higher Education*. New York: Atheneum, 1978, p. 272).

Another variation on the theme of shifting peer relationships is less subtle. It has to do with the competitive process itself and the alienation it engenders. When one student contemplated the high admissions standards of the University of Chicago, a school that he and a number of his friends wished to attend, he said to his guidance counselor, "Perhaps I shouldn't say this, but after knowing Bob for four years, I really don't think that he has worked hard enough to deserve the University of Chicago." Needless to say, that relationship cooled considerably when Bob was admitted, and the speaker, who thought he had worked harder, was not.

Relationships between parents and their children are likewise altered by the college admissions process. As children struggle to assert their own identity they often put great distances—literal and figurative—between themselves and their parents. "I want to go to school in California," a girl from Connecticut insisted. "Out there I will be free from my parents' wanting to know what I am doing all the time." She then added, "Besides, my mother wants me to take a lot of prenursing courses, and I am not sure yet that that is what I want to do."

Parents have their own agenda and may use the geographical argument the other way. A parent who lives in a comfortable home and has a good job asserted to me, "I don't want Lucia studying communications at Northwestern; we simply cannot afford the transportation costs." However, as the discussion moved along toward schools offering programs in communications in the East, I could see that the father did not want to relinquish control over his vivacious and talented daughter. Money, in fact, had little to do with his college preference for her. He simply did not want to "lose" his daughter. Perhaps the father was having some misgivings about how good a job of parenting he and Lucia's mother had done. Perhaps the bond of affection was too strong for *him* to sever. Whatever the case, he should have looked first at the quality of education to which his daughter would be exposed, tried to explore the validity of her desire to go to the Midwest, and subordinated his own misgivings to her need for independence and freedom.

Invariably the college admissions process brings closer that day of final separation of parents and children. What the decision to select Northwestern should have brought to the forefront was Lucia's capacity to take final and full responsibility for her own decisions. Her father needed to learn how to support her while simultaneously letting her go. It is a delicate dance—support, advise, step back, give space and time for the child to decide, then begin again—support, advise, step back. . . .

The Campus Visit
Once a student and family have agreed on six to eight colleges to investigate seriously, they must make plans for visiting those campuses. Some parents will want to accompany their children on these visits; others will not. A family should do what is natural within its tradition of decision

making. If the child has always acted independently and responsibly, then he or she may prefer to go alone. If on the other hand the family tradition is one of democratic decision making in which the parents and children have decided things together, then at least one parent should accompany the child.

College visits can serve to alter a tradition, too. Consider the boy who has never ventured far from home on his own. College visits, his father decides, come at an important juncture, so he sends his son off to investigate colleges on his own. The boy makes all his appointments and finds his way, but he runs out of money by the time he reaches his last college. At that point the young man decides to approach the nearest father figure for a financial infusion. That person happens to be the director of admissions. The boy is a little embarrassed at having to request a loan, but he compensates for this by repaying it as soon as he returns home the next day. The swiftness of the repayment and the forthrightness of the young man impress the admissions director; when the boy's grades and school recommendation come through, he has little trouble gaining admission to the college. Without the independence thrust on him by a thoughtful father, this young man might never have had the chance to show himself as a person of sound character, a trait held in high esteem by many selective colleges.

When parents do decide to accompany a child on college visits, what do they do? Sit in the stuffy car and try to pay attention to a boring detective novel? Or go to the other extreme and try to make the visit count by going right in to the waiting room and attempting to have a word with the admissions officer, in hopes of getting some idea of their child's chances of admission? Obviously, neither.

Parents should remember these basic rules in the matter of college visits:

1) They must be sure to allow their child to make all the arrangements for the visit: estimating the travel time, setting up an appointment for the tour and the interview, and procuring printed information about the college before making the visit.

2) Campus visits should not be planned during a college's vacation or special event, such as winter carnival or homecoming. At such times the campus is likely to look like a ghost town or a big party, but it will not give an accurate picture of day-to-day college life.

3) Parents should conduct their own exploration of the college their child is visiting. While their child is being interviewed, they can take the campus tour run by the admissions office and then revisit the facilities that interest them later. Most families will want to visit colleges that are in session so that they can make it a point to talk to students in a frank and casual way. Students can be asked for their summary advice to a person who is considering applying to that college. Would they send a son or daughter to this college, and why?

Their answers can be passed along to the child.

4) They should attend a class, if possible, trying to pick a subject they know something about so that they can judge the sophistication and clarity of what is being communicated to the students. If they feel natural doing it, they can ask the instructor to comment on undergraduate education at the institution. This should be done at the end of the class. Questions could concern, for example, how often instructors see students individually and for how long, what type of papers students write, whether the students are serious and productive, and how many go on to graduate school.

5) Bulletin boards on campus are worth looking at. This particular rule of thumb (useful for the applicant, too) was given to me by a father who had taken each of his five children on the college tour. "Always look at bulletin boards," he said. "They tell you what is going on and what the issues are, and they give you some idea of the vibrancy of the place." If a bulletin board can't be found, parents can ask to be shown one.

6) Having a meal at the institution is also a good idea, if possible. This gives parents a chance to study how the students treat each other and how the faculty and students intermix. They can see whether there are cliques, as when all the members of a fraternity eat together.

7) In the course of their tour of the college, parents will probably want to see where students live. If the admissions tour does not include a dormitory room, they should ask to see one. They can ask about the variety of living options for students: are undergraduates guaranteed housing for every term or must they take their chances with private accommodations off campus for one, two, or more semesters?

8) Parents should find out what the nonacademic support system is. Where do students go if they have a problem? To whom do students turn? Is there a network of adults and older students who can help freshmen through the adjustment of leaving home and living on their own?

9) Having done all this, they should try to formulate an overall impression of the mood of the college or university they have been visiting. Does it project a particular feeling of community? Do students and faculty like each other and what they are doing together? If the answers are affirmative, parents can feel confident in supporting their son's or daughter's interest in the school.

After visiting a small New England school, one mother wrote, "I'm glad I came. There's a chemistry here you can't explain. . . . Whatever happens after this visit, my husband and I will feel that we were involved. We had our eyes and our ears opened, and consequently we know what our son is getting into."

Some parents may wonder whether they should seek a word with their child's interviewer at the conclusion of the interview. The best advice is to stay in the background. If for any reason the interviewer wants to speak to the parent—some schools have a protocol calling for this—he or she will be summoned. Whatever takes place in this brief conversation, parents should try not to be overzealous on behalf of their child. The declining population figures for the college-bound generation have produced an environment for admissions that is generally more favorable than five or six years ago. If their child is able, parents will encounter a receptive atmosphere on most college campuses.

When all the college visits have been completed, parents will want to discuss their impressions with their child, but they should take care to let him or her draw conclusions without their direction. The child's applications should cover a range of schools, from those that are sure to accept him or her, through various intermediate choices, to the one that represents his or her—not the parents'—highest aspirations. In the process of arriving at this final list, parents and child will have to adjust their criteria as they move from top to bottom. They should try to keep the quality of education constant throughout and alter the other criteria—size, location, cost, special programs—to suit the level of admission difficulty.

Applications and Assistance

When all the visiting is done, the child goes off to begin the fall term of the senior year in high school and to complete college applications. What is the parents' role at this stage of the process? They must walk a fine line between giving too much assistance and too little. If the child needs guidance in filling out applications, parents might help establish a schedule for completing each one so that they all reach the colleges at the proper time.

If a child comes to the parent with a question about what to write about for an essay question, it is acceptable to make a few suggestions. By all means parents can help with the cost of postage, photocopying, and the application fees. But they should not participate in the formulation and writing of responses on the application itself. And they should never communicate with the admissions office on behalf of their son or daughter, even about routine matters. A few years ago, I had just finished what I thought was a fairly eloquent speech on behalf of a candidate to the shrewd dean of admissions at a major eastern university. By way of response he picked up a letter from the candidate's file, held it between his thumb and forefinger, and waved it slowly back and forth in front of my face. "What's that say?" I asked. "It is not what it says—it merely thanks the boy's interviewer. It's *who* says it," he replied sardonically. "It was obviously produced by Daddy's secretary on the office word processor, and the boy just signed it." Sure enough, it even bore the father's business address. The dean continued, "We're considering the kid, not the old man, and we want to hear from the candidate, not Papa. That is why we ask that the application essay be filled out in the candidate's own handwriting." That boy's chances for admission were hurt severely by his father's intrusion into the admissions process. Parents should take seriously the colleges' desire to develop the fullest possible relationship with their candidates for admission. It is possible to expedite the application process without taking a direct hand in it. The parents' job is to make sure that their child gives his or her best effort to all college applications, and leave it at that.

Influence

Very often parents have questions about how to use their supposed influence, or that of relatives and colleagues, with a college admissions office.

> *"Should I write to the director of admissions and tell him that my child definitely wants to go to Coburn as I did?"*

The answer is no, the child should do that.

> *"The other day at lunch my old client Clint Jones begged me to let him put in a good word for my daughter Luanne at Siwash. Says he knows the president from graduate school days. Should I let him do it?"*

The answer? Probably not. It doesn't sound like Clint and the president have kept up their relationship over the years. Moreover, Clint hardly knows Luanne at all. What new perspective could he shed on her candidacy through this obvious attempt to capitalize on an old acquaintanceship? It might upset the applecart completely.

> *"My son came home the other night and said that out of the blue his boss on the construction site where he worked last summer offered to write him a letter to his colleges. Should I encourage him to have the letter sent?"*

The answer is yes, for it will cast a new perspective on the boy both as a person and as an employee—a perspective that the college would not be able to obtain from any other source.

> *"A good acquaintance of mine in college and in graduate school is now president of Hawthorne, where my daughter definitely wants to go to college. My friend and I have drifted apart over the years, since my husband Jack was transferred so much in the service. We only exchange cards at Christmas. But I really think she would want to know that Louise is applying. I would if I were in her position. What should I do?"*

This mother's instinct is correct! She should write a short, informative letter, so her friend at least knows that Louise is applying. After all, there isn't much either can do after the decision is made, so the time to act is now.

These common examples suggest a few guidelines for parents to follow in the matter of exercising their influence on the college admissions process. The following things should be taken into consideration before any letters are sent:

1) The person writing a letter should know the child well and be able to cast a different light on the candidacy from that available through any of the usual sources, such as school, teacher, or employer recommendations.

2) If recommenders are basing their influence on connection to a college, that connection should be strong. Being an enthusiastic supporter of the college's athletic teams and an annual contributor to the Dean's Fund is not usually strong enough. Being a trustee, a high administrative officer of the school, or a major donor is another matter.

3) Parents should not solicit letters. They can let people know their child is applying to a particular college but allow the conversation to end there. Many people with great influence maintain it by not involving themselves constantly in the internal workings of the school's admissions office. "They write occasionally and reasonably," according to one grateful admissions dean.

4) The integrity and intelligence of the college should be respected. Most colleges have an elaborate system for assessing the potential financial worth of their candidates and keep in mind the possibility that some of their future assets may eventually flow to the college. Most admissions deans and development officers confer about applicants who could prove financially or politically beneficial to the college. At a given school there might be six to a dozen candidates who are "must takes" in this regard, another twenty or more in the "highly desirable" category, and perhaps a longer list whom "it would be nice to have." The same categories apply for students who come recommended by university officials, politicians, or other prominent individuals.

By and large the admissions office establishes the categories in which these "special influence" applicants are placed, and its decisions are respected and upheld by college officials. Why? Because college presidents, development officers, and alumni chairpersons learned long ago that it is far more equitable to have an autonomous, thorough, and professional admissions staff making the final decisions than to meddle excessively themselves, even though they could do so if they chose. So parents must respect the autonomy of admissions officers, as well.

A Talk with the Guidance Counselor

At some point during the college choice process, parents should seek a conference with their child's guidance counselor. This visit probably should come after the child has had one or two meetings with the counselor and after both family and student have done some research on particular colleges and know something about the application process itself. This conference should include the child and focus on the division of responsibilities among student, family, and counselor.

Parents need to be aware that some counselors may misinterpret such a visit as a form of subtle pressure on them or the school to produce certain results in the admissions process. Such are the drawbacks of our consumer-oriented society and the sometimes excessive involvement of the public in the operation of some high schools today. Consequently, parents must ensure that the purpose of their visit is not viewed as intimidating, but rather as informational. Its true purpose should be to help the counselor get to know the family and to bring to light information and viewpoints that will in the end produce a positive outcome to the college application process.

The frustration parents may feel at not being able to communicate certain information to colleges can often be allayed in a conference with their child's guidance counselor. Conferences can sometimes lead to illumination, as in the following conversation, begun by a parent: "It is too bad that the colleges won't be able to learn how much Ginny has overcome. She is too proud to say anything herself." The counselor looked confused. "Would you tell me what you mean by that?" she asked the parent. Then she learned that Ginny had been born with a hip defect and could not walk until she was four. At that point the doctor had recommended that Ginny take up swimming to strengthen her lower body and legs. She did this, and, in her tenacious pursuit of the sport, she not only eliminated her limp, she became a champion intermediate freestyle swimmer as well. When the guidance counselor added this moving and significant information to Ginny's school recommendation, her candidacy, which was in every other way a modest one, took on another dimension. The admissions director at one selective college with a fine swimming program said of it, "We'd like to take a chance on Ginny; there are heartstrings in her folder."

Conversations with guidance counselors can clarify a whole range of topics that often puzzle parents and for some reason cannot be explained by their sons or daughters: how many times to take the SAT, how many colleges they should apply to, or how to present their extracurricular activities.

A talk with the counselor can also take a more analytical bent. If the proper atmosphere of trust and respect is established by the parents, counselors are usually more than willing to assess a child's chances for admission at certain colleges. The counselor can also give the parents a realistic view of their child in relation to other seniors with similar credentials who will be applying to some of the same colleges. It is important for the student and the family to hear what the reality of the admissions environment is.

A conversation with a counselor in the guidance office can be the beginning of a dialogue that will continue over the telephone as the application process rolls ahead. Rapport between parents and counselor can also give students a sense of emotional support. Young people will see that there are several adults ready and willing to support them and advance their cause.

As the application process takes its course, counselors are sometimes given tentative evaluations of candidates by the colleges, and their inferences from this information can be relayed to students and parents so that any strategic adjustments can be made. Even if no tangible feedback comes from the colleges, counselors are always there to answer the inevitable questions that surface at the last minute. Parents' questions about the use of influence, real or imagined, are best put to a counselor, who has an overall view of the student's chances at a particular college and of how that college responds to pressure of that type.

The visit to a counselor also makes the subtle statement that the family wants to understand the counselor's position and is appreciative of his or her efforts on behalf of the child. Parents should not underestimate what the little extra energy involved in making this visit may mean in the admissions process. Counselors can play an important role in the college admissions process and sometimes influence the decisions that colleges make. It makes sense to assume that a friendly visit to the child's counselor is in everyone's best interest.

On the other hand, parents should guard against overplaying their hands with counselors. Steadfastly refusing to take advice on such points as limiting the number of applications to "top" colleges, attempting to go over the counselor's head by talking to the principal or superintendent, secretly relying on an outside source such as a private counselor, or leaving the counselor in the dark about certain tactics being employed all serve to undercut the counselor's authority, eroding potential goodwill and, through lack of coordinated efforts, jeopardizing the child's chances of admission.

The increased pressures associated with college admissions today have impelled some parents to seek the services of a private counselor. Many of these individuals are well trained and know the vagaries of the system well enough to avoid making outlandish promises. In some instances they can provide much-needed assistance. For example, after a visit to the guidance counselor, a parent finds that the school's guidance department is not able to provide accurate and individualized college counseling. Their child needs special testing for values clarification and career preference, as well as academic tutoring and coaching for standardized tests, that the high school is simply unable to provide. In this case, a private counselor's services are called for.

When selecting a counselor, the parent needs to make sure that this person is registered with the Independent Educational Counselors Association or another professional group. This will ensure that he or she has proper counseling experience and/or training and adheres to professional guidelines when representing the child to colleges and universities and helping in the preparation of applications and other materials.

Counselors—public and private—aside, parents should recognize that they have a vital role to play in their child's quest for a college. This means engaging in dialogue with the child all the way along; aiding in making college visits; carrying out research on the colleges and the literature, both on their own and among their knowledgeable friends; and mostly just "being there" for the young person as he or she moves ahead.

Unusual Circumstances
Occasionally parents are called on to play an even more direct role. As the admissions process nears its end in March or in instances where a candidate has been put on a waiting list, parents sometimes write what is known in places as an IFL—an "impassioned family letter." The sample that follows was written by the father of a boy seeking admission to a prestigious university with very high admission standards. After checking with his son's counselor, he wrote this letter on plain stationery (that did not call attention to his status as a prominent diplomat):

14 rue Cardinal Richelieu
Paris, France

Mr. Dwight A. Twombley
Director of Admissions
Hanover University
Middlemarch, Connecticut 06590

Dear Mr. Twombley:

My son, Daniel A. Foss, is currently on the waiting list for admission to the class of 1991. Since his most fervent wish is to attend Hanover, I thought it might be helpful if I wrote a letter on his behalf.

From Dan's application you know that he has lived in Paris and attended French schools for the past five years. Last September he returned to the United States to spend his senior year at Saint James Academy. Saint James has been an ideal decompression chamber for Dan's reentry into the academic and social world of the United States. At Saint James, Dan achieved high honors for the first semester as well as for the current marking period. He has also been active in the theater there, and he has continued to play his beloved clarinet in the Saint James jazz band.

My plea for Dan is based mainly on the fact that Hanover magically combines all the standards that he set in selecting his ideal college. He

161

wanted an institution that had retained its academic integrity over the years and that still supports and respects individual accomplishment. Perhaps because of his European background, Dan has always insisted on an urban school, preferably one in the East. He also wants a school that is fairly large and able to attract a diversified student body. To Dan there is something in the Hanover ambience that appears more cosmopolitan, less homogeneous, and more individualized than that of other colleges of comparable standing. As Dan is very interested in international relations, he was hoping to be able to major in that field at Hanover. I simply cannot resist putting my case in the words of the recent *Times* article on the Hanover admissions office. Dan is "H for H—Hungry for Hanover."

I sincerely believe that Daniel would prove to be a responsible if not prominent person on the campus, both making a solid contribution to the community and deriving solid benefits from a Hanover education.

Moreover, Dan's classmates will find him a thoroughly enjoyable, warm, and kind young man. He is a mature and thoughtful 18-year-old, with a great deal of self-reliance and a sincere desire to learn. He is quite happy in himself and enjoys his moments of relaxation and solitude.

In the difficult days that lie ahead for you and the admissions committee, I earnestly hope that you will review Dan's case and deem him a worthy gamble. You will not be disappointed.

Yours sincerely,
George A. Foss Jr.

This letter has both style and substance. The tone is properly deferential, and Mr. Foss even sympathizes with the pressures that are heaped on the director of admissions after the letters of acceptance have been sent out. While he does not reiterate all of Dan's accomplishments and abilities, he reminds Mr. Twombley of his son's ability to contribute to the musical and theatrical life of Hanover. Further, Mr. Foss makes the point that Dan is a mature and thoughtful young man who knows what he wants to do once he gets to college. His letter also emphasizes, subtly, Dan's unusual educational training in Europe and in America. Finally, Mr. Foss shows his understanding of what kind of university Hanover is, what it stands for academically, and what kind of students it wants to attract.

The tone of the letter is reasonable, too. The case is forcefully made, but there are moments of humor. Dan is depicted not as a perfect candidate but as a human being who enjoys his moments of solitude and relaxation.

Also the letter is not too long!

Helping Out While Letting Go

There is absolutely no question that parents have an extremely difficult and delicate role to play in the college decision-making process. There is no routinely "right" way to handle all its challenges. There are only some simple words of advice that may help families find their own answers in the college admissions experience.

First, parents must try to separate their own aspirations from those of their children. Obviously parents want their sons and daughters to be the best that they can be, but at the same time they need to let their children make some if not all of the crucial decisions about college. Parents who say things like "We are applying to College X," are seriously mixing up their own lives and goals with those of their children. This should be avoided. We all want to live *for* our children, setting examples for them, supporting them, and counseling them. However, we don't want to live *through* our children, directing them, insulating them, and controlling them.

Second, parents need to remind themselves that the college search and application process should be a journey from adolescent dependence to adult independence. Many children may not see it this way, but the progression toward independence is part of the college admissions process. This means that parents have a dual responsibility: to educate their children about the realities of the admissions process and to inform them about the responsibilities that come with the immense freedom they will enjoy from the moment they step onto a college campus as freshmen.

Parents should also remember that, deep down, children do want to act on the advice of their mothers and fathers. They may stumble on occasion and not follow some piece of their parents' advice, but they want and need that advice all the same. The job of parents is to allow children to make their own judgments and to support them when errors are made. Guiding their children through the college admissions process is probably one of the most difficult challenges parents will face during these critical years of development.

The difficulty lies as much in parents' natural reluctance to let their children go as it does in identifying when to give them the freedom that will help them grow. Do parents say arbitrarily: "Well, you get to pick three schools on the list, and we, as your parents, get to choose two"? Of course not. Rather, they should try to create opportunities for their child to make his or her own decisions. Suggesting to a daughter that she visit one or two colleges near home on her own might be a good idea. Reacting favorably to a son's suggestion that he would like to consider a college that is far away from home and difficult to gain admission to might send him the message that his judgment can be trusted.

Third, parents should look on the college admissions process as one of their last major opportunities to educate their children. In the brief time between the summer before the senior year and the college decision time in April of the following year, parents have a chance once again to teach their children about the things they value most and the importance of education to a useful life. They can show how much they trust their child to fashion his or her own values and to act reasonably and humanely in the not-so-reasonable-or-humane outside world. Parents also have a valuable opportunity to instill in their children a crucial sense of self-worth as the family goes through the college search process. In advising them, in supporting them, in letting them make mistakes, and in letting them go, parents can give their children a healthy feeling of self-esteem as they make the journey from adolescence to adulthood. Parents, guidance counselors, teachers, and college admissions personnel all must strive to ensure that through communication, involvement, support, and love, we leave a legacy that not only is useful to our children but represents the best of what we claim to be.

9

It's Over:

Dealing with

the Decisions

When high school juniors embark on their college search in the spring, they think of the process as lasting one year, a year that closes somewhere near April 10, when the major colleges in the United States send out their letters of acceptance and rejection. Little do these students know that April 10 is only a milepost on a journey that is not complete until they have successfully adjusted to the freshman year. Too often high school seniors focus on admission rather than placement. If their application is accepted by the college of their choice, they rejoice; if it is rejected, they are tearful. Their emotions swirl around, often obscuring the major question before them: Which college is the best one for me to attend next fall?

Accepted candidates should feel a sense of relief that they have gained admission, but they should not take the position that admission has validated every feature of their scholastic record and their moral character. The admissions process is an imperfect one; it relies mainly on documents prepared by students, counselors, and teachers. Occasionally students look better on paper than they do in fact, and admission is granted. This is especially true for students who test well. College admissions officers are all too frequently influenced by high test scores and their own desire to impress their superiors with an ability to attract able students—those with high grade point averages and test scores—to the college. Social and geographical diversity also figure prominently in admissions decisions. Some candidates whose applications are in other ways marginal are, in fact, admitted for reasons of their social or geographic origin.

"The Ides of March" takes its modern meaning from the fact that students hear from the colleges at about this time, and the vast majority of their applications to the most selective colleges are rejected. Students who are successful should walk humbly and share their joy by extending a friendly hand to those who are not as fortunate. Accepted candidates should heed the words of Ecclesiastes: "I returned, and saw under the sun, that the race *is* not to the swift, nor the battle to the strong, neither yet bread to the wise, nor yet riches to men of understanding, nor yet favour to men of skill; but time and chance happeneth to them all."

Rejection

Time and chance do play a large role in the admissions process, and those whose applications are rejected have an important responsibility to themselves not to allow the colleges' decisions to serve as a definitive evaluation of their worth as people, or even as scholars. If only I had been a better athlete; if only my mother had gone to the college that I wanted to enter; if only I had studied harder, been born rich or, better yet, poor, or lived in Alaska: the litany of "if onlys" is both mournful and unproductive and imposes a false simplicity on the college admissions process.

High school seniors whose applications are rejected by their first-choice college should realize the dangers of too much sorrow and over-simplification. Both may come back to haunt them in later life. Excessive concern about the outcome of admissions decisions can undermine the confidence that others have worked to instill in them.

Families and guidance counselors frequently advise students to reach for a top college in the application process. They do so to ensure that candidates set a high goal and put in a maximum effort toward attaining it. Even if candidates do not actually achieve that objective, educational progress has still been made. In their striving, candidates may have found new reserves of skill and inner strength. This kind of immeasurable academic, emotional, and spiritual growth should not be forgotten just because a prestigious college has sent a rejection. The realization of heightened inner strength will remain, regardless of the decision made by any college. As we learn from Ecclesiastes, there is nothing better "than that a man should rejoice in his own works; for that is his portion."

So as high school seniors rush home to find out how colleges have decided their cases, they should ponder this ultimate truth: True education is not to be found in a particular college or university, nor in any combination of colleges and universities around the country. It is a process in which individuals pursue their own interests and perfect their own abilities under the discerning and compassionate eye of an interested and competent teacher. No educational institution has a monopoly on this process. Therefore acceptance and rejection per se are ultimately of little consequence in the education of the truly intelligent person who is able to make the most of the college experience. The intellectually curious person can learn in a variety of educational environments and become a thoughtful contributor to our society.

The Waiting List

Because students apply to many colleges and can go to only one, colleges have to compensate by accepting more applicants than they can actually accommodate. Since some admitted applicants may elect to go elswhere, institutional pride also impels colleges toward rather large waiting lists. Even at the prestigious schools with classes of 1,000 and with a 60 percent matriculation rate among accepted candidates, waiting lists of 700 to 1,000 are not uncommon.

Being placed on a waiting list is in some ways more agonizing for students than outright rejection of their application. College candidates must prepare themselves for this ambiguous response and react as quickly as possible. The meaning of the waiting list may vary from college to college. In some cases it is a polite way of refusing an application without offending the student's parents with an outright rejection.

In other cases colleges view the waiting list as a kind of holding pattern for applicants who are very near the margin of admission. In this instance the colleges wait until they have heard from all those to whom they have sent offers of admission and then begin to accept students from their waiting list.

Students who find themselves on a waiting list should therefore avoid getting their hopes up too high. Still, although the chances of eventual acceptance may not be great, there are some useful approaches that a student on a waiting list can employ.

In the first place, take a positive and assertive stance. You will have to campaign to change your waiting list status to an actual acceptance. This campaign has to be undertaken with a good deal of gusto and even humor. You have to show enthusiasm and commitment, for, as the saying goes, "Many are called, but few are chosen."

Second, ensure your place at one of the schools that did accept you. Send back the acceptance card and a deposit to the most appealing of those schools. This is standard practice. Colleges understand that some students who accept their offer will later withdraw to attend another school where they had been placed on a waiting list. Colleges can accurately predict what this number will be, so they overaccept accordingly.

Third, you will have to find out from the college that has placed you on the waiting list what that status means. Is yours a viable candidacy, one that could lead to acceptance if places develop? Or have you been placed on the waiting list for "political" reasons and therefore have no real chance of admission? Your guidance counselor is best suited to ask these questions tactfully of the admissions office. Ideally, this contact should be made with the director or dean of admissions, who probably has the final say. Only as a second recourse should parents become involved. One can easily imagine that a college would be reluctant to admit to a loyal alumnus that his daughter is really on the waiting list simply because it did not want to offend him by rejecting her application, thus jeopardizing its receipt of his financial support in the future. Likewise, the college admissions office will not want to tell a family or a student that the athletic coach who had earlier virtually promised the candidate admission was overruled in the final deliberations of the admissions committee, and that, to save face, the committee opted to place the applicant on the waiting list. The admissions director may be willing to admit this to a trustworthy guidance counselor, who can then avoid hurting feelings while advising the candidate to forget the waiting list at that college.

Inquiries to the admissions office may reveal more favorable information, too; your candidacy may still be viable. In this instance, your college guidance counselor should ask the college's admissions office to review your folder, so that the weaknesses that prevented your application from being accepted outright can be addressed and, perhaps, remedied. In some instances where the candidacy is still alive, you might call the admissions office to ask: "Where did I go wrong? Were my scores too low? If so, can these be offset by another teacher recommendation in math or English? Was the essay portion of the application weak? If so, may I write another?"

Then approach the same topic from a different vantage point by asking: "What new information would you like to see concerning me? I have additional and better sprint times from last Saturday's meet. May I submit them? Or the tape of a recent recital?" You should make it clear to the admissions officer that you are definitely interested in being accepted from the waiting list. If at all possible, you should say that you would definitely accept an offer of admission if tendered by the college. Remember that the one thing admissions officers don't want to do is accept people from the waiting list who then won't come!

Finally, you should ask about the projected schedule for admitting candidates from the waiting list. Very often colleges will admit in batches, taking the most critical (read "vociferous") cases first, then proceeding at intervals to accept groups of diminishing size until the class is filled. Normally the process takes a month to six weeks; sometimes it even extends into early summer. Whatever the case, you, your family, and your guidance counselor should make a fresh overture to the college each time the admissions committee meets to consider the next batch of candidates to be admitted.

Being placed on a waiting list allows you to take stock of your own feelings before moving on. If you are only marginally interested in a college that has wait-listed you and think it might be only a little better than others that accepted you, drop it and forget the whole waiting list campaign.

If this is not the case, and you want to proceed, fine. Move on to the next step—using influence. Here a few rules enunciated earlier need to be changed. "All prior bets are off" in regard to waiting lists. At this point, it becomes perfectly permissible to use alumni influence to bring maximum pressure on the college. Modesty may have caused you to decline your neighbor's offer to write a letter to her alma mater for you last winter. Now you should get in touch with her and ask if she would still be willing to write a few lines on your behalf. Chances are she will.

Second, you should consider involving your parents in this quest. If they are not too upset by the college's decision to wait-list you, they may want to contact the admissions office directly (with the advice and consent of your guidance counselor) or to write a letter of entreaty for you (see Chapter 8). Allow them to do this. Don't let false pride stand in the way. Occasionally wait-listed students and their parents visit a college again to reiterate the family's interest in the school. If the opportunity arises, take it.

Third, after consulting with your counselor, you should undertake direct negotiations with the college yourself. These negotiations should begin with a personal letter written to the director of admissions (by name). State that you want very much to attend the college and will come if accepted. This way you assure the director that if the college takes the trouble to admit you, its effort will not be wasted. Also bring the director up-to-date about your current courses and grades, and make known any additional honors that have come your way since you submitted your application in January. Conclude the note with a restatement of what you believe you can contribute to the college. This kind of letter can be very persuasive. At this anxious and busy time of year, directors of admissions certainly want to admit enthusiastic supporters of the college from the waiting list, so don't be lukewarm and don't hold back. Be sincere and give the admissions office lots of assurances about your interest in the college.

Fourth, risk "overkill." Enlist the support of your teachers. Get a letter of support from a teacher who knows you well but who did not write in support of your application in the course of the regular admissions process. If it happens that you would be bringing a special expertise such as athletic skill to the college, coaches should be mobilized to call or write on your behalf. Call the relevant coach or department head yourself. This will enable you to get a sense of the degree of support you will ultimately receive.

Fifth, ask your guidance counselor for additional advice and written support.

After letters are solicited and sent, you or your guidance counselor should telephone the college again to reiterate your interest. The call also can be made for the purpose of gathering information—to ask if the waiting list is beginning to move, for example. If you had an interview with a particular admissions officer at the college, then call that person to ask your questions.

Most colleges do not rank the people on their waiting lists because they know that they are going to have to respond to various pressures in selecting them. They realize that waiting lists are political in every sense of the term. Admissions directors are beset from every quarter: by coaches—their best-laid plans gone awry—who need two more divers or quarterbacks; by development officers who want them to accept a candidate whose father is on the education committee of the state legislature; and by influential guidance counselors who are asking, "How could you not have taken Jennie?"

In this somewhat chaotic situation, you should realize that your own chances may be slim because of various demands and institutional priorities that have to be met. Whether you like it or not, the swimming coach cannot present a team without any divers, and the guidance counselor who sends the college fifty good candidates each year has to be heard, and perhaps even accommodated. Nonetheless, the candidate who presents himself or herself vigorously and who is not afraid to take a few risks and overstep a few of the conventions often has a chance.

No Acceptances!
In the unhappy event that you are not accepted by any of the colleges to which you applied, an agonizing reappraisal is called for. Working directly with your guidance counselor or with one or more of the colleges that rejected your application, you must find out what the weaknesses in your application were. Once these are uncovered and addressed, you can move ahead with your efforts to gain admission to another college. If your scores on the Achievement Tests were weak, you should consider taking those tests on which you think you can do better on the May test date. If your academic average was insufficient from the colleges' point of view, you should make a last-minute effort to finish the year in the strongest fashion possible. Frankly informing teachers of your difficulty and taking on projects for extra credit will help produce better results for new colleges to consider.

Remedying the defects in your candidacy is only one part of a multipronged response to a complete lack of acceptances. A second and essential element is adherence to the advice of your guidance counselor. The counselor can also ask the colleges some of the embarrassing questions that have to be asked; e.g., "Didn't you think she worked up to her capacity? Did you think her parents played too large a role in her application? What was so bad about her essay?" Once you, your counselor, and your family have had a frank discussion of what went wrong, then you can try to remedy the situation. There are several routes that the counselor, or the student working alone, can follow.

First, initiate an application to a new college in late April. Try to find a school that has openings and academic standards that you can meet. College counselors usually keep a list of schools that are approachable in April. In fact, your counselor may be on the mailing list of the National Association of College Admission Counselors, which publishes a list of spaces available in more than 500 colleges across the nation. Once you have a list of schools with spaces, select *one* and, in conjunction with your counselor or, less preferably, your parents, call the director of admissions of that college.

After ascertaining that there may indeed be some openings this year, the person calling on your behalf should mention that, although you have not been accepted by the other colleges to which you applied, you definitely want to go to college in the fall and to that particular college if possible. The point should be made strongly that you have researched the school, are definitely interested in it, and would attend if accepted at this late date. Furthermore, you would very much appreciate being sent the necessary forms and being allowed the opportunity to apply for admission. The caller should summarize your high school record, both academic and extracurricular, and state that you are willing to come to the campus for an interview. Before the conversation is over, the caller should establish that this is the only school you want to consider and that you would not make any other applications if you received an indication that you might be accepted.

Such an approach plays on the college's natural desire at this late point to consider applicants who are actually going to attend the school.

Public Colleges

Candidates who find themselves without a college acceptance in late April should consider approaching one of two different types of school. The first is their state university. These institutions have, after all, a special obligation to the taxpayers who support them, and they are apt to be large enough to have room for just one more student in September. If candidates are willing to forgo student housing and financial aid, admissions officers at state universities can often find a place for them.

State universities frequently have some academic programs or schools that are underenrolled in April, and if students can adapt their plans to one of these their chances for admission are considerably increased. Often they will be able to transfer to the program or major they prefer at a later date.

Some state universities will also admit students late if they agree to begin in the summer. Ask about this option. In addition, most state universities have branch campuses where candidates can begin their work before transferring to the main campus later. Even though a state college might not have sounded attractive back in September, it may appeal to candidates with no acceptances who want to salvage some self-esteem and, more important, get on with their education. Beginning work at a branch campus and finding a job in order to help their families with tuition expenses may give them a sense of independence that they would have been denied had they been accepted at their first-choice school. It goes without saying that state or public universities are cheaper than private colleges, too. Furthermore, when the student

171

has established a fine record at the state school, he or she may want to contemplate transferring to a private college.

Private Liberal Arts Colleges

Alternatively, the candidate with no acceptances could approach some of the lesser-known private liberal arts colleges hard hit by the declining student population. These schools are seeking students and are more than willing to consider late applications. Your guidance counselor may be able to suggest some of these schools and advise which one would be best for you. Sometimes schools in this category send information to a large number of college applicants in the fall, so now is the time to look through any "fan mail" you may have received and reevaluate those colleges that wrote to you.

If, for some reason, both you and your counselor are stymied, you can both turn to the local or regional board of higher education. These institutions invariably publish on a monthly or biweekly basis the names of the colleges in the region that still have vacancies. The New England Board of Higher Education (68 Walnut Road, Wenham, Massachusetts 01984), for instance, lists the openings at member institutions—public and private, two-year and four-year. Then it lists vacancies in New England colleges according to boarding men, boarding women, and commuters. A telephone call to your regional board of higher education is definitely in order if you have no other way of obtaining information about local schools with vacancies.

In their quest for advice and counsel, disappointed applicants, their families, and their counselors should not overlook the colleges that rejected the student's application as a potential source of guidance. The line of inquiry could start simply with: "I wish I could have come here next year, but I understand why that is impossible. I wonder if you could give me some help. Could you advise me what to do next? What would you do if you were me?"

Later Admission

Another option for candidates who have received no acceptances is forgoing admission in September and striving for admission a year later—or even midyear admission—at one of the schools that rejected their application this year. The variations on this approach are so numerous they cannot be described adequately here. Applicants should have a particular college in mind, as they want to be in a position to say and mean: "I really like your college and I really want to come. If I wait six months or a year and follow your advice on how I should spend the intervening time, perhaps you would be willing to consider me again, because I will come if you accept me."

Whether candidates pursue the new-application option, the midyear option, or the next-year option, they should realize the importance of personal relationships in formulating their plans. The relationships they or their counselors have built up through phone conversations with college admissions officers in pursuit of an acceptance may eventually lead to a favorable outcome. So it is very important that both candidates and their representatives take a responsible attitude toward what admittedly is not a very happy predicament. The student should not be negative about himself or herself or make spiteful remarks about the inequities of the system; neither will elicit interest, much less assistance, from a college admissions officer. Both will defeat the ultimate purpose—gaining admission to the college.

On the other hand, applicants should not be timid. The admissions process is not perfect. The decisions are close; occasionally an injustice is done. Most admissions officers recognize this and consequently are more than willing to help students whose applications have been rejected in whatever way they can. If an applicant and counselor feel that a college has made a mistake, then the applicant can legitimately request a formal review of his or her application and a written response from the director of admissions. Occasionally this procedure does result in a change of decision. However, the process can be an enlightening one for both the candidate and the college, especially when the student and perhaps a member of the family arrange to visit the campus for a frank discussion with admissions officials.

Year Off

In some instances candidates whose applications are rejected at all the schools to which they apply may choose to take the year off and reapply for admission for September of the following year. These students should make it their first order of business to discover the deficiencies in their candidacy. They should make a journey to one or more of the colleges that rejected their application and find out just where it fell short. They should then seek specific suggestions from the colleges about what to do to remedy their deficiencies in the year ahead.

However, it is equally important for candidates to have some ideas of their own and not to rely on the colleges to do all the educational planning for them. Take the initiative. If your academic record was weak, for instance, then consider enrolling in your local junior college and taking two courses in your weak areas during the year. If your application lacked focus about potential career directions, then maybe you should take one of the variety of preference tests to see where your real strengths lie. You can then follow this up with course work in your area of strength and perhaps a work experience that will acquaint you with the practical side of a field in which you have an interest or latent skills.

Discussions with guidance counselors and college admissions officers may have revealed more subtle weaknesses than simple academic deficiency or career uncertainty. You may, for instance, have manifested certain unimpressive personal traits. Nonchalance about the admissions process itself, incomplete or frivolous responses to questions on the application, or lack of self-confidence displayed in the interview might have figured in the decision to reject your application. Naturally, these traits are harder to discern than academic or extracurricular weakness, and the college admissions officers may only allude to them in passing. If they do allude to something of this sort, try to deal with it honestly. Be open to criticism and try to develop a genuine desire to deal with your own imperfections.

In cases where immaturity, indifference, arrogance, or similar qualities have become problems, students should consider using their year off to participate in an activity that could sharpen their own sense of self-worth and appreciation for others. Participating in Outward Bound, which would require several weeks of wilderness living, may be too radical a solution for you, but some kind of voluntary social work that would bring you into contact with those less fortunate than you might be quite educational. It would broaden your perspective and might incline a college to look on you more favorably next year.

Candidates should use their lack of college acceptances to focus on their own imperfections and to correct them. They should combine the advice of college admissions officers, their families, and their guidance counselors with their own values and goals. Inevitably they will emerge from their adversity as stronger people. When they do secure college admission the following year, their acceptance will be a lot less important to them than the educational and personal growth they have gained in the interim.

Which College to Choose?
Most college applicants will be in the happy position of having multiple acceptances to ponder at decision time in April. If they have applied selectively—that is, to colleges of varying difficulty—they should have at least three acceptances to consider. The criteria for establishing the original range of choices—academic programs, location, size, extracurricular activities, and cost—are equally relevant now, but entrance difficulty no longer is. Once students have been accepted by a number of colleges, they should not automatically choose the one that was hardest to get into. They need to discover where they would be happiest, and that means a place where they are likely to succeed, not struggle.

By extending and revising the original criteria somewhat, accepted applicants will be able to make a careful decision about which college to attend in the fall. The revised criteria are: *curriculum and course requirements; student-faculty relationships* both inside and outside the classroom; *student life; special programs*—athletic, overseas, or extracurricular; and *cost.*

Before applying these criteria, successful applicants should consider how to gather information about the accepting schools. The first and most useful means is another campus visit. Return to the campuses of the schools that have accepted you and study them again at first hand.

Often the admissions offices will assist you by arranging for class visits, a night in a dormitory, and free meals while you are on campus. Some schools have special programs for admitted students. If a campus visit is impossible, call the admissions office and get the telephone numbers of students and faculty members to whom you can address your questions. Scholarship students and their families may have questions for the financial aid office. Find out that phone number, too. Several colleges currently lease toll-free telephone numbers for the month following the date on which acceptances are sent out so accepted candidates can pose questions directly to college administrators and students. Frequently colleges will offer to identify students who live close to a candidate's home so the candidate can contact them directly.

Guidance counselors can be extremely helpful as a second source of information. Remember their role is not just to "get you in" to college. It is to "place" you in a college that is suited to your individual needs. Counselors and teachers who have attended schools that have accepted you can provide special insight and raise questions for you to consider before making your final decision.

Peers—with all due respect—are the third and least valuable source of information. Consult friends who have been accepted at a college you are considering only after you have exhausted the resources of the faculty and of your counselor. Then listen to friends who, through visits or personal contacts, have had an opportunity to learn more about the school than you. The best sort of peer information comes from friends who actually attend a college you are considering. They should be heard.

However you go about garnering further and final information about the colleges that have accepted you, the criteria you use in evaluating them are of paramount importance. Information should be grouped under the headings curriculum and course requirements, student-faculty relationships, student life, special programs, and cost.

Curriculum and Course Requirements

Pick up the catalog of the school you are investigating and examine its curriculum. Does it still meet your specific needs with sufficient breadth? Let us say you wish to focus on computer engineering. Are there sufficient courses in this field to enable you to develop a specialty? Is computer engineering a department or just a major? What difference will that make to you?

Turn next to the distribution requirements. Here you face a real dilemma, because you want to have enough latitude both to take courses relevant to your major and to explore other areas in which you have a keen interest. At the same time, you do not want to be controlled by excessive distribution requirements. If, for instance, you have to take three courses in the humanities, three in the social sciences, and three in the physical sciences, will the requirements prevent you from keeping

175

up with your interests in Spanish and music while majoring in computer engineering?

The only way to determine whether a college will allow you enough latitude is to make a mock schedule of your four-year program. Do this for each college that has accepted you. Remember, a curriculum that has lots of distribution requirements may not be restrictive if the college runs on a trimester system and if it offers a good number of courses that satisfy those requirements. (See Chapter 10 for a detailed explanation of planning your course of study in college.) You also need to bear in mind that you want to emerge from your undergraduate experience well trained in a particular area *and* having had a healthy exposure to the liberal arts. In other words, your expertise has to be coupled with a capacity for independent thinking and broad awareness of other subjects if your education is to be truly valuable.

Apart from examining the catalog description of the courses you would have to take, as well as those you might want to take, you will need to find out about the quality of teaching in those courses. Statistics about class size can tell you something, but an actual campus visit to attend several classes can be very revealing. Ask the admissions office to arrange for you to talk to professors in your field of interest so that you can address specific queries to them. While making the campus visit, ask if there is a confidential guide to courses and teachers prepared by students. Its frank appraisals will tell you what to expect in terms of grades, work load, and individual assistance in a particular course.

There is also the question of prior preparation. You need to ask the colleges what credit, if any, is given for exceptional high school preparation or Advanced Placement study. If you have been enrolled in Advanced Placement courses in your high school, you should already have found out whether or not your college choices give credit for Advanced Placement before taking the relevant Advanced Placement tests in mid-May. Some colleges will grant no credit for Advanced Placement, so students are obliged to remain in college for the full four years. Other colleges grant placement but no credit, meaning they will allow students to move into advanced courses on the strength of their Advanced Placement test results. This may be appealing to some students with established career goals or fields of interest or to those who want to place out of requirements in order to explore the curriculum. Other colleges have their own tests for advanced standing, and you need to find out what your opportunities for such placement would be based on your current high school courses. These questions can all be answered by professors and department heads when you visit the campuses of the schools that have accepted you.

Student-Faculty Relationships
Accepted candidates should investigate this elusive subject carefully by consulting both faculty and students directly. Ask faculty members how

much time they spend with students outside the classroom and what their attitude is toward students who are taking courses just to meet distribution requirements. Do they have students over to their house? Are they advisers to any extracurricular activities on campus? In other words, do they take their out-of-class commitments seriously?

Because of a growing consumerism among students in recent years, many academic departments take the relationship between faculty members and students into consideration as a formal part of the tenure process. Ask faculty members if this is true of their department. Certainly responses indicating that professors begrudge students time outside the classroom or do not place much stock in student opinion of course content and teaching methodology may be reasons for considering another institution of higher learning.

Student Life

You will also want to investigate the quality of student life on the campuses you are considering. There are at least two elements to this question—the way students look on education at their particular college and the way they interact with one another. Perceptive candidates should interview students in order to make judgments about both these elements. Ask current students how well their college experience has lived up to the expectations they had when they arrived.

If you sense some disillusionment—and there probably will be some—try to find explanations for it. Does it originate with the undergraduates themselves? Were they unrealistic in their expectations of the college to begin with, or are there institutional problems? Think about how you might avoid similar pitfalls. For instance, if you should end up with an uninterested adviser, would there be a way to change advisers? Is there an unofficial advisory system through which students can get answers to questions they face? Are there resident advisers in dormitories, and how well does this work? Are there minority support groups? Is there a learning assistance center for help with study skills and writing problems? Is there a counseling system that can be turned to in times of need? Are there popular and accessible professors to whom students can turn in times of stress? How well does this "invisible" system of advising work?

Accepted candidates will also want to know just how serious most of the undergraduates at each college are about their education and personal and career development. "What are the first words that come to your mind when you are asked to think about your experiences here?" is one question that can be asked of students at each school. If certain answers keep coming up—"Too much work," "Great parties," "The teaching is great," "Girls have it tough," "The winters are awful"—then you know what to expect should you decide to matriculate there. Each of these responses should then be examined more carefully, measured against your own needs and preferences. As you go from college to college, your questions will become sharper, and your imagination will begin to suggest ways that you might cope with the challenges described to you. Bear in mind that no school is perfect, and no single response is universally true for all the students at a given institution. Talk to as many students as you can before making up your mind.

Another important part of your investigation should center on how students at a particular college treat each other. Do they respect each other's differences in personality and interests, or are they callous? Take an especially good look at the dormitory situation. Are there periods during the evening when people try to keep the noise down to a dull roar so that others can study or sleep? What is the accepted practice for entertaining visitors in rooms overnight? What happens to roommates who are not particularly social and like to have some private time? Are their rights honored? Try to spend a Saturday night in a campus dormitory to observe how the different personalities interact and whether students seem to enjoy themselves.

The library is another place to look at. Can students who have work to do find privacy there, or is there much talking and socializing going on? Quite apart from the seating capacity of the library and the size and availability of the reserve collection, are the rights of users respected there? When the noise level in the beautiful undergraduate library at the University of Chicago became unbearable, a group of students had buttons printed that read "SPQR: Save Peace and Quiet at Regenstein." Many college students have never been away from home before, and you may be shocked at how they interpret their freedom to do as they please, often at the expense of the rights and interests of others. Responsible students will want to find a school where relationships among undergraduates are not only harmonious but respectful and where an appreciation of individual differences, a sense of fun, and a serious attitude toward learning all coexist amicably.

Special Programs

Sensible candidates should also explore in greater depth any extracurricular programs that attracted them initially at the colleges where they have since gained admission. When, for example, promising swimmers visit a campus before making their final decision, they should talk to the swimming coach about their prospects for making the team in the fall. It may well be that many more swimmers than predicted have accepted the college's offer of admission, thus raising the level of competition for the team. Consequently, a student who swims may opt to look more closely at one of his or her alternative schools. Or fewer swimmers than predicted may be attending, in which case a candidate may be so superior to other freshman swimmers that he or she would not be challenged sufficiently by teammates over the coming four years.

The orchestra may be unexpectedly flooded with oboists this year, or the radio station with sports announcers. In order to be assured of a reasonable opportunity of applying his or her skills, an accepted candidate should assess the situation before signing up to attend a particular college. Coaches, advisers, deans, and even admissions officers can be of assistance here. They realize that college is not all studying, and they want their students to be happy and productive on the athletic fields, in the studios, in the entire variety of undergraduate activities that make a campus vibrant.

Now that you are trying to distinguish among the schools that have accepted you, one special service deserves particular attention, though it perhaps held only passing interest for you when you were applying—that offered by the career planning and job placement office. Many students enter college with a less than clear idea of what they want to study and an even dimmer notion of what they might wish to do with their lives when they complete their undergraduate education. An effective and interested career planning and job placement officer can be of inestimable help to such students as they seek to clarify their objectives and crystallize their plans over the four undergraduate years.

Make a special point of finding out whether this office has a testing program that enables students to discover the areas in which they have special interest and talent. Does the office offer a course, or informal advice, on decision making and career preparation? What sort of reference library does it maintain for undergraduates? Can a freshman drop by to receive some preliminary advice? Are speakers invited to the campus to describe particular fields of expertise? Are there field trips or educational media accessible to undergraduates who are surveying the world of work and trying to determine what area they want to enter?

In relation to graduate school and job placement, does the office offer a program of instruction in completing applications, attending interviews, and assessing the salary offers and provisions for further education of various companies? How well is this college's placement office regarded by its counterparts in other colleges and by the various companies and graduate schools that have contact with it? How do its instructional materials compare with similar materials at other colleges?

Cost

Finally, there is the question of financial aid and/or the cost of your education. (This has been discussed in Chapter 7 in some detail.) What you need to remember is that financial aid offices do not exist only for those students who are on scholarship. A majority of families find it hard to bear the high cost of a college education today. When it comes to distinguishing among the costs of several accepting institutions, candidates should ask financial aid officers for advice about the costs they and their families will face over the next four years. For example, what are the various methods of payment that can be used? Are there both short-term and long-term payment plans? Are there tuition prepayment options? How much is it reasonable to expect students to earn on their own during the college year? And over the summer? Nonscholarship students who have to monitor their expenses carefully may want to know what access they will have to campus jobs and loan programs administered by the school. In particular, will scholarship students be given preference in the assignment of on-campus jobs?

Perhaps accepted candidates and their families have not evaluated their own finances correctly or figured the costs of the rival institutions accurately. In this instance, the opinion of a college financial aid officer should be sought. This may seem like comparison shopping, but remember that college expenses are high. You and your family could conceivably be investing more than $80,000 over the next four years, and you will want to do it in the most sensible way possible.

Colleges do not want their students to fall on hard times either. You can help avoid that unhappy circumstance by having a detailed discussion of your resources with a member of the financial aid office at the outset. Colleges want to make sure families understand and appreciate all the opportunities available for financing the cost of a college education. So any visit to a college prior to deciding which school to attend probably ought to include a stop at the financial aid office.

Once you have visited the financial aid office, the career planning and placement office, and various classes; talked to students and faculty; and spent a night in a dormitory, you are ready to make your final judgment about a school. If the schools that you are considering seem to blur during this final analysis, you should not be alarmed. After all, your original choice of colleges was based on similarities in academic program, location, size, cost, and quality of student life. Your final decision *should* be a difficult one if you chose wisely in the first place!

As you ponder all your notes and reexamine your criteria, you should not be ashamed to fall back on your instincts, because, although you may not realize it, they really are informed instincts at this point. If you can see yourself happy at one particular school, then you probably should decide to attend that school. If one college seems to have a good sense of itself, an idea of what it does well and what it needs to do better, and if the students at the school are both happy and reasonably serious and respect one another's differences, then *your* chances of being happy and productive at that school are probably ensured. In the end, even if you think you are making a visceral judgment, you probably are not. If you feel that this school is where you really want to be, then go there and rejoice in the fact that you are doing the right thing. After all, there has to be some emotional element in your decision, some intangible dimension; otherwise you are not going to make a very enthusiastic alumnus or alumna, are you?

10

Making the Most of the Freshman Year

When Barbara Crowley decided to accept the offer of Hanover College, she knew that she had much planning to do. Selecting a college did not signal the end of the college admissions process for Barbara; instead, it marked the start of a new phase, one in which she would be required to make intelligent decisions about her freshman year.

Her first order of business was to select courses for the fall term and send in her registration card to the college. So Barbara sat down with the Hanover catalog one evening and began by surveying the requirements that she would need to meet in order to get her degree. Once she understood those, she would be on her way to making an intelligent selection of courses.

Charting the Academic Course

After perusing the catalog, Barbara decided to sketch out the big picture for herself. She decided to try to plan her freshman and sophomore years, considering both the summers and academic years. She began with three objectives. She knew that she wanted to major in economics so that she could enter the business world on graduation. She knew also that she wanted to take a broad range of courses while in college and avoid overspecialization—specializing could wait until graduate school. She also wanted her education to include a mix of practical experience and book learning.

The Hanover catalog stated that majoring in a given subject required taking at least eight courses within the department and at least four courses in a related field. In addition, each student had to take six other courses that represented a sampling of the three broad areas of knowledge: the social sciences, the humanities, and the sciences. Two courses were required in each of these areas, and no two could be taken in the same department. Thus a student, in meeting the distribution requirements, would be exposed to at least six different subject areas.

Barbara now made three shrewd practical decisions so that she could reach her broad educational objectives. First, she decided to begin work on her major right away so that she could attain an advanced level of study and qualify for special programs by her senior year.

Second, she decided to meet her distribution requirements as soon as possible so she could benefit from the breadth of the subject matter. Completing these requirements would also give her the freedom to take more courses of her own choosing in her junior and senior years. "Keeping your options open" is what her father called it.

Finally, Barbara decided to try to take courses that overlapped slightly, at least two per semester. Doing so made sound educational sense because it would cause Barbara to learn and compare the modes of inquiry of different disciplines, say, economics and political science. It would also provide Barbara with knowledge that could transfer from one subject area to another. By electing to take the introductory course in economic theory (Economics 11) and a course in the basic history of ideas (History 11) in the fall of her freshman year, Barbara hoped to capitalize on the fact that both courses focused attention on Karl Marx and Adam Smith.

Barbara also decided that she would try to concentrate on the economic dimension of the courses she took outside her department and thus inform herself about the relationships of economics and literature, economics and philosophy, economics and social history, and so on.

Before putting pen to paper and projecting her course during the next four years at college, Barbara made a telephone call to a Hanover undergraduate, Ron Barrow, who lived in the next town. Ron was studying economics at the college and was just completing his junior year. The office of the freshman dean had suggested that she talk to him before deciding whether or not to attend Hanover. Barbara found Ron's comments very helpful. Ron suggested that she take the course in research and methods in economics (Economics 90), even though it was not required by the department. In his opinion, Economics 90 should be a required course for economics majors and would be of inestimable value to Barbara when it came time to write her senior thesis. Ron also suggested that she study the economy of one particular region intensively, and since this advice coincided with that of her father, who was a corporate executive of some experience, Barbara decided to follow it.

Ron told Barbara more about the "Confidential Guide to Courses and Instructors at Hanover," a pamphlet that Barbara had seen on the desk of the admissions officer who interviewed her. She called the college bookstore the next day and had a copy sent to her.

The Hanover guide was similar to those prepared by resourceful students at other colleges around the country. It listed each course in the catalog, giving its number, instructor, informal title, number of pages of reading required per week, number of papers assigned, and relative difficulty. An explanatory paragraph told what students ought to expect in regard to grading procedures, assistance from the instructor, exam questions, and student participation in classroom discussions.

The guide's analysis of Political Science 35, Political Economy of the U.S., went like this:

> **Political Science 35,** Political Economy of the U.S.: Money and Power. Prof. Peter Fowles. Two lectures and one seminar per week.
>
> Although this is one of the toughest courses at Hanover, it is a must. Fowles is inimitable as a lecturer, with a broad command of his subject gained from eleven years of perfecting this course, a real compassion for students, and service on several government committees. (He is currently helping the President draft a new set of guidelines for Washington lobbyists.) You will have to do virtually all of the 200 pages of reading each week, because Fowles has a way of referring to it on exams. Fortunately, most of it is in inexpensive paperbacks, so extensive note-taking is not necessary.
>
> Fowles and his two assistants expect you to ask questions in the seminars. And if you don't, they will, so do the reading on schedule and don't leave it until the end of the course. Fowles is not above stopping his lecture from time to time and asking a student if he has understood what has just been said. Who else would bother?
>
> There are two short papers—one a description of how a particular institution operates, the other an analysis of a policy question, e.g., "The Proper Role of the Federal Reserve Bank Today." There is also a stiffly graded hour exam and a final. However, the range of questions on the final invariably enables students to bring in what they have learned, and it is a valuable learning experience, not just another test. Fowles is going on leave next year, so this is the year to take this course. It is one of Hanover's crown jewels.

After Barbara had digested the contents of the guide, she made an additional decision about her program at Hanover. She decided to make full use of the January term. The catalog described the January term as either a period in which students could study a particular topic in depth, working in a small group under the direct guidance of a faculty member, or as a period during which they could take some time away from the college to enrich their life in any way they saw fit.

At this point, Barbara drew up a "course of study" sheet (see page 186). She made a series of columns: one for the fall semester, one for the January term, one for the spring semester. Then she added three columns in which she could keep both a running total of the concentration and distribution requirements she had met and an overall total of the credits she had accumulated at the end of each year. A final column was for summer activities.

Barbara then entered the courses she had decided to take for the fall and winter—based on her study of the catalog and the confidential guide and on her conversation with Barrow. She next wrote down her projected summer work experience and her thoughts about how she would utilize the first two January terms at Hanover. Since she wanted eventually to enter the world of business, Barbara decided that for her first summer vacation she would seek a job that would acquaint her with the inside of a major business operation. Realizing that her credentials would not be all that strong for a high-level job, she thought tentatively of applying to her local bank for a job as a teller, messenger, or credit coordinator of some sort. In case anything more advanced opened up, Barbara decided a good dose of mathematics in her freshman year would be a good idea. She would go on with calculus in the fall and then take the probability and statistics course in the spring term. The calculus course (Math 35) would meet a concentration requirement for a course related to economics, and the probability and statistics course (Math 37) would satisfy a distribution requirement. After writing these courses down on her course sheet, she indicated the requirements they met, recording "C" for concentration requirement and "D" for distribution requirement; then she entered her totals for concentration and distribution in the appropriate columns.

Barbara saw that the principle of overlap had led her to choose History 11 to go with her introductory course in economic theory, and that her practical sense had led her to add calculus (Math 35). What about the fourth and final course for the fall semester? At this point Barbara decided to take the plunge into the broad lake of the liberal arts and elect a course in music theory and harmony (Music 30). She had always felt deprived of music in her home. Music was not of interest to her older brother or to her parents. On the other hand, some of her more interesting friends had a musical background of some sort. Barbara decided to investigate this unknown territory. The confidential guide said that Music 30 was a very popular course for nonmusic majors at Hanover and that the instructors, a wonderful German couple named Kelberg, were famous for being as interested in students who were just passing through to meet a humanities requirement as they were in avowed music majors. Barbara also learned from the guide that most students enjoyed the research paper that required them to discuss a musician of their choosing in relation to his times. Barbara's decision to take Music 30 also gave her course of study the breadth that all liberal arts students should strive for.

Barbara did not take long to make up her mind about the January term of her freshman year. She decided to go skiing. She would then return to campus refreshed from her break. Her spring semester schedule would include a course in applied economics (Economics 12)—the second course of the introductory sequence in economics—and Professor Fowles's political science course. Barbara hoped that the overlapping study of economic and political systems (Political Science 35) would enhance her perspective in both areas. She also chose probability and statistics (Math 37), a course that she hoped would help in her quest for summer employment.

Lastly Barbara chose an art history course, The Art of the United States (Art History 10), which would meet her third distribution requirement for this year and, more important, satisfy her long-standing craving for some knowledge about the work of American painters. Barbara traced her interest in American art back to a visit she had made to the U.S. Customhouse in New York; she had been only a little girl at the time, but she vividly recalled her sense of wonder at the beautiful murals there. One of the reasons she decided to attend Hanover was the strong reputation of its art history department.

As Barbara thought about her second year at Hanover, she reaffirmed her decision to focus on her major early on in her career at college. Thus she decided to take the course in corporate management (Economics 41), described by the confidential guide as "a heavy course, for majors only." She then elected to take a course in imperialism in the nineteenth and twentieth centuries (History 33), which would introduce her to the interplay of history and economics on the international level. Barbara hoped for some overlap between Economics 41 and History 33. There ought to be some relationship between the way in which corporations manage their international affairs today and the experience gained from the imperialism of an earlier age, she speculated. If not, Barbara knew that the interface of literature and imperialism in the nineteenth century would be an interesting one, so she opted to take English 29, a literary analysis of the prominent Victorian writers of England.

Barbara also decided to complete her foray into mathematics by taking an intensive course in computer programming (Math 41). She knew this would provide valuable training for the kind of job she would be seeking two years later. Under the January term of her sophomore year Barbara wrote down a course called The Ethics of Investment. A course taught jointly by a member of the economics department and a member of the philosophy department, it provided a case study of South Africa and had received good reports from Ron Barrow.

In the spring of her sophomore year she would capitalize on her study of both imperialism and the ethics of investment and attempt a course in corporate finance (Economics 42). She also thought it would make good sense to enroll in Organizational Behavior (Psychology 15), since it was a distant cousin of Corporate Management (Economics 41), which she planned to have taken in the fall. She then picked up on Ron Barrow's suggestion that she take the course in research methods in economics (Economics 90). She would complete her distribution requirements with Ecology and Progress (Biology 37). This course had been designed for nonmajors and was reputed not to be too hard. Barbara had three tough courses already and did not want to risk pulling down her grade point average with another. Furthermore, she hoped that some of the practice research projects for Economics 90 might also be developed for her Biology 37 papers, of which there would be three. Fortunately, however, there were no hour exams in the biology course.

Barbara Crowley's Course of Study Sheet

	Fall Semester	January Term	Spring Semester	Fall	Jan.	Spring	Total Concentration (C)	Total Distribution (D)	Summer
Freshman Year	Economics 11. Foundations of Economic Theory (C); History 11. Western Tradition: The Greeks to the Enlightenment; Math 35. Calculus (C); Music 30. Theory and Harmony (D); Freshman Writing Course (no credit)	Ski break at Christmas; Work in department store	Economics 12. Applied Economics: Money and Banking (C); Political Science 35. Political Economy of the U.S. (C); Math 37. Probability and Statistics (D); Art History 10. The Art of the U.S. (D)	4		4	4	3	Bank teller, messenger, credit coordinator (work experience within the business world)
						8	4	3	
Sophomore Year	Economics 41. Corporate Management (C); History 33. Imperialism in the Nineteenth and Twentieth Centuries (C); Math 41. Computer Programming (C); English 29. The Literature of the Victorians (D)	Ethics of Investment: U.S. and South Africa—A Case Study	Economics 42. Corporate Finance (C); Economics 90. Research Methods in Economics (C); Biology 37. Ecology and Progress (D); Psychology 15. Organizational Behavior (D)	4	1	4	5	3	Camp counselor, social service job; National Forest Service (work experience outside the business world)
						9	5	3	
						17	9	6	

C = A course required for concentration. At Hanover College the requirement for concentration in economics is eight courses within the economics department plus four from related departments. Total: twelve courses minimum.

D = Distribution courses. Each student must take six courses to meet this requirement: two in different departments of the social sciences, two in different departments of the humanities, and two in different departments of the sciences.

186

Bearing in mind her idea of gaining a broad perspective on her chosen field, Barbara decided to seek a summer experience outside the field of business during the summer after her sophomore year. She thought she might try for summer work with the National Forest Service or, failing that, a camp counselor's position or a job with a social service agency in her hometown. So she noted those possibilities in the appropriate space.

Barbara had thus planned a sensible course of study for her first two years—one that enabled her to sample a broad range of subjects while getting a good start on her major. She realized that some changes might be made if her interests shifted, or if her academic adviser convinced her of the wisdom of following other paths. However, her careful planning would allow her quite a bit of flexibility in her final two years.

She thought she would probably want to study a foreign language, perhaps Spanish, and pursue a special concentration in Latin American studies within her major, since she felt a second language and knowledge of other cultures was very important in a global economy. She also might want to study abroad or pursue an internship. She would also continue to take courses outside the social sciences in such areas as music, art, and literature. These areas of knowledge would always be accessible to her and enable her to communicate with and learn from others who shared an interest in them. Equally important, Barbara would have been broadened as a human being by her exposure to the humanities and the sciences. She would be more aware of the world beyond her chosen specialty than others who chose a narrower and safer route. This breadth of knowledge, especially if she continued to expand it on her own, would inevitably help Barbara to put her own life and work in their proper perspective and at the same time inform and enlighten the decisions she would have to make within her own field.

Having carefully considered both the liberal arts and the practical dimensions of her education, Barbara Crowley was ready to make optimum use of her opportunity to attend Hanover, educating herself so that she could eventually play a useful role in the complex world beyond college.

As Barbara put the finishing touches on her plan of study, her mind naturally raced ahead to the social relationships she hoped to form on the Hanover campus in the next four years. Would she be radicalized by her involvement in the politics on campus? Would she fall in love? Would she feel lonely and lost and miss her family? "Probably all of the above," she thought.

Roommates

"But first things first. How about my roommate?" she wondered. "How can I make sure that I get along with her?" Barbara considered this question for a day or two, then decided that this was one dimension of her college experience she could control. She would write the office of the freshman dean and request a particular kind of roommate. It certainly could not hurt. She resolved not to be fussy; she would simply ask for someone who was quiet and serious about pursuing her academic studies and had an interest in the arts, and leave it at that. In making a request for one roommate, and therefore a double room, Barbara hoped to reduce her chances of having to live with more than one roommate, a situation that would be harder for her to control. It was not customary to request roommates at Hanover; the school had sent a form asking only whether she preferred a smoker or nonsmoker. Barbara hoped by taking the initiative to put herself among the small group of students who would make similar requests and would probably be able to get along reasonably well because of their mutual interest in a stable living situation.

When the dean's office acceded to Barbara's request a few weeks later and sent her the name of her roommate for the fall, Barbara wrote the young woman a cheerful letter of introduction. This overture led to an exchange of letters, and by the time that fall term opened, Barbara and her roommate were actually friends. They had divided the responsibilities for furnishing the room, thus saving a good deal of duplication of wall hangings, appliances, and even some general reference books. More important, they had established a tradition of discussing their needs and aspirations, and this would help them deal with any controversies that might arise later. On a larger scale, Barbara and her roommate had confronted one of the biggest anxieties facing college freshmen—the loss of high school friends whom they may have known all their lives—and eliminated the fear that it would be impossible to make lasting friendships in college.

Barbara and her roommate had succeeded in placing their relationship on a solid basis from the outset and maximizing the chances that a strong friendship might grow from it. In so doing, they had prepared themselves to handle some of the usual challenges that college undergraduates face: how to divide their time in their room between socializing and study, how to respect an individual's right to privacy, how to share their possessions equitably. They were thus able to avoid the sort of shock experienced by one undergraduate woman at an Ivy League school who, in the first week of school, returned to her room to find that her roommate was entertaining a young man. Because the young woman had to study, she sought refuge in the bathroom until 2 a.m., then returned to her room to find her colleague and the young man in bed together. This became a nightly practice, forcing the serious and motivated young woman to retreat to the common-room couch with her sleeping bag. Eventually she became so exhausted by the routine that her grades plummeted, and she had to go to the infirmary for a decent night's sleep.

Barbara Crowley would probably not have to experience such a difficulty, because she and her roommate made it a principle of their relationship that they would discuss any points of friction once a week, on Mondays, and that they would seek compromise and mutual accommodation in their relationship.

Deans and Advisers

When Barbara arrived at Hanover, she discovered that the college had advisory and counseling services to which she and her roommate would have access whenever they encountered academic or social difficulties. The first line of defense was the resident adviser system, under which upperclass students living in the dormitory were assigned to advise students in lower classes and help to arrange dormitory social functions. This system worked only sporadically, Barbara found. Some resident advisers were concerned and careful counselors who could keep their relationships with advisees confidential. Others were less discreet and less skilled. Some flatly avoided involvement with students in need of advice. They had taken the job merely for the money and often put their own careers and interests ahead of those of the undergraduates they were obliged to have in their charge.

Beyond the resident adviser system lay the dean's office with its clutch of tireless and concerned deans. Barbara found that at Hanover one could turn to the counselors in the dean's office on any matter, from parking or laundry to a relationship that threatened to become overwhelming.

Students at many schools seem unaware of the capability of the dean's office to counsel undergraduates in need of guidance and its interest in doing so. Some schools have spent thousands of dollars to make their counseling services first-rate. At the University of Chicago, twenty counselors operating from the dean's office, most of them full-time, oversee the relatively small undergraduate population of some 2,700. These counselors frequently give both academic and personal advice and follow the progress of their advisees throughout their four-year stay at the university.

At some schools, student health centers operate effective counseling programs. At still others, members of the religion or psychology departments enjoy special status as counselors. Whatever the particular structure may be, it is every freshman's duty to locate this resource and utilize it whenever necessary. Here is a good rule of thumb: if you are thinking about whether to seek advice and counseling, then the chances are that you should.

As Barbara Crowley drove with her family to Hanover that fall, she was only dimly aware of how much her educational experience in the next four years would hinge on her own self-awareness and the development of personal relationships with others. But she had studied the college's pamphlet for freshmen and familiarized herself with the various ways in which she could use the counseling system as she cleared the path to her own educational and personal objectives. She also resolved to extend herself to other people and to try to forge new relationships. Such an effort would offset the loneliness of being away from her home and friends. This openness to new relationships would ensure her an education in the broadest sense and reduce the vulnerability that most college freshmen experience.

Understanding Yourself
If one were to visit any college campus during the beautiful days of September and October and ask passing freshmen to describe in a word the experience of their first few weeks, the response would undoubtedly be "freedom." It is only natural that the student's first reaction to college life is to laud the freedom from home, from family, from day-to-day assignments, from required sports, from required group activities, from a code of behavior dictated by others. Freedom, to ecstatic college freshmen in their first few weeks on campus, usually means freedom *from* rather than freedom *to.* That feeling obscures what may be a confusing and even depressing experience for them.

Psychologists know that the transition that a freshman has to make in the first few weeks of college is extremely difficult. In many cases, going to college involves a complete break with the past and hence a real discontinuity in a student's life. The structure and routine of family life are left behind, the numerous ties to community groups and peer groups are severed, and, most important, the regular nourishment of self-esteem that came from family members and from the prestige and respect earned in high school is interrupted and lost. A new life has to be started in college, new challenges discovered, and new relationships kindled. New outlets for talents have to be found. It isn't easy. A book like this can only scratch the surface of the freshman year experience and offer some kind words of counsel. It can set the prospective freshman a sort of informal agenda to consider during the summer before the freshman year and in the early weeks of the fall. (There are also books, such as Peterson's *College 101,* just about the freshman year and how to make the most of it.)

Big Fish in the Big Pond
The Big Fish in the Big Pond syndrome refers to a freshman's first exposure to a mass of other students who are as able, as resourceful, as funny, as good looking, as athletically or musically gifted as he or she is, and to the problem of dealing with that experience. Often students become depressed when they realize that they are no longer the big fish in a little pond, but rather the same fish among similar fish in a *big* pond. The fish is still big, but may appear smaller when grouped with so many others of the same size.

The challenge of dealing with the realization that there are others as good as we are is compounded by the times in which we live. In the economy of abundance of the late 1960s, when college campuses were aglow with discussion and dissent, students and their teachers assumed that if certain alterations were made in American institutions of higher education and in the society at large, productive change could take place, and society could move forward. It was also generally assumed that there were choices to make, and that desirable change would flow from those choices. Now that those days are gone and the economy of diminishing resources and indebtedness surrounds us, many college students believe that there are fewer choices to make, and that their freedom is limited. As they experience these limits during their first weeks of college—not being able to make the friends they want to or finding out that certain courses are full—they often become depressed. They either decide that they will focus their energies on career preparation and making money, or they talk about taking the extreme action of leaving college. They often seek to avoid making choices of courses, friends, or activities by resorting to inactivity, by not studying, by taking drugs, or by indiscriminate socializing. While maintaining a bold outward face and talking about their glorious freedom, they wrestle with their inner sense of loss of home, family, community, and self-esteem.

In his book *The Hurried Child,* David Elkind relates that many of the nation's brightest youngsters have been propelled by their parents into too fast a rate of intellectual and social growth, and he argues that they haven't had sufficient time to experience frustration and evolve ways of coping with it.

The anxiety that students face during their first weeks in college gathers strength from the culture around them. As products of the television generation, all Americans, but particularly the young, fall victim to the assumptions of the media: that although problems are everywhere, speedy solutions are possible for all of them. To grasp this point, think of the immense popularity of the television program "60 Minutes." The average segment on the program is fourteen minutes, and, as one former producer of the program lamented recently, "A whole generation will grow up thinking that any major issue can be dealt with in fourteen minutes."

Aside from television, the speed of communication and transportation lends a pace to our lives that we often mistake for a capacity to anticipate, to meet, and to solve the complex problems that confront us. The speed and excitement of the first days of the freshman year themselves tend to create the impression that all will be well and that the newfound freedom will indeed be emancipating. Alas, it is not so.

Some general advice to consider when confronting the challenge of the Big Fish in the Big Pond syndrome:

1) Acknowledge the legitimacy of your own feelings of loss. After all, stability, security, and success such as you have left behind cannot be permanent fixtures in our lives. Feelings of loss are a natural part of the process. It is important to accept these feelings, so you can continue to choose and move on.

2) Communicate your feelings of frustration and loss—and of elation and joy—to others, be they roommates, resident advisers, deans, professors, or chaplains. When seeking advice, remember to search for questions rather than answers. Each person's solution is different, but the kinds of questions we ask ourselves are similar.

3) Try to make your college your new home, with its own routine, relationships, activities, and support system. Avoid cultivating a fierce independence or separateness.

4) Redefine your conception of success. Lower those standards you simply cannot meet, and set new standards that you can meet. Move around the limits imposed by grades or social relationships or athletic competition, and look for new areas of interest and challenge. In doing so, try to avoid the feeling that you are betraying yourself. You may discover that there are myriad ways of proving yourself.

5) Remember, finally, that frustration and a sense of loss are cyclical phenomena for most people, and that excitement and progress follow periods of despondency. If you encounter a low point, keep in mind that it has probably been brought on by a shift of responsibility: from high school counselor, friends, and family telling you what to do to *you* telling yourself what to do.

On a practical level, the following rules can help you orient yourself and find direction amidst all the freedom of the first few weeks of college. Here is how to make your college community work for you:

1) Stay loose. Do not seek out a single small group of friends and cling only to them. Social groups of various sorts will coalesce during the first few weeks, and you will naturally want to be a part of one of them. Fine, but try to avoid loyalty to just one group, for it may eventually fall apart and leave you stranded. By definition, a group has to exclude someone, and that excluded person may interest you. If you find that you are going to the dining hall with only one group of friends, one that you are doing all your socializing with, then break away somewhat. Try to go to the dining hall with someone new, or even alone, once or twice a week, so that you will create the opportunity to meet different people from different backgrounds.

2) Join at least one, preferably two, extracurricular activities during the first week of your freshman year. Too often college students defer this type of decision. They say to themselves, "First, I've got to get my courses squared away, then get to know the people in my dorm, and then I will go out for the orchestra." Avoid this kind of thinking; enter extracurricular activities right away. One Harvard/Radcliffe freshman told a professor, "You know, when I came here from high school, the first thing I did was join the orchestra, and suddenly I found a bunch of friends." This may sound calculated, but a little planning of this sort will ensure that you develop different bases of friendship in

college—your classes, your dormitory, your extracurricular activities, and so on.

3) Avoid adopting a particular personal style lest you become known only as a campus character or a member of a particular group. This is particularly hard for minority and international students, whose culture shock on coming to college is sometimes greater than that of other students.

4) Try to get acquainted with one person or family that has no ties to the academic life of the college. Often an older family will be anxious to meet students—you might meet such a family by doing odd jobs through the student employment office. In the course of casual conversation, such people can render helpful advice and support to a young person facing the challenges of adjusting to a new community.

5) Try to locate an older student, preferably a senior, during the first weeks of school, and get to know this person. These elder statesmen can give all sorts of practical advice on where to shop, which courses to take and to avoid, and, in particular, how to sort out some of the turmoil of the early weeks of your freshman year.

6) Read a newspaper unconnected with the college at least twice a week. You may want to buy the local newspaper to find out what the relations of the college with the broader community are. A local paper will also tell you what events are occurring outside the college and what the major concerns of the community are. Reading it will help you relate to the townspeople you meet.

   Or you may wish to subscribe to your hometown newspaper, acknowledging that your home continues to have meaning and interest for you. Whichever you choose, read a *noncollege* newspaper. Keep yourself aware of the world beyond college. In so doing, you will develop a perspective on the challenges you face from day to day.

7) If you are a member of a church or synagogue in your home community, by all means continue your involvement while at college. Quite apart from the spiritual sustenance that religion provides, the opportunity to meet people outside the college and to have contact with the lives and concerns of others helps to put your own life in perspective.

8) Get to know your adviser. This person could be the resident adviser in your dormitory, who is apt to be an upperclass student, or the faculty adviser assigned by the dean of the college to monitor your academic progress. Contact with both advisers will be built into your program of the first few days. Afterward, try to establish a close relationship with one of them so that you can discuss your problems and your enthusiasms and solicit advice.

9) Write up a schedule. The most important task to accomplish is to prepare a schedule, by the week, of your classes, study times, sports,

and social activities. This task will introduce you to the need for reasonable time management. If you can set your priorities down on a schedule, then you can avert the disaster of frittering away your time. If there is one big difference between high school and college, it is the enormous blocks of free time you have in college. Learning to discipline yourself so you can manage that time effectively will help ensure the success of your freshman year.

In addition to keeping these bits of advice in mind, try to keep your sense of humor. Remember, everyone else is new too, and everyone else, to some degree, feels that he or she is no longer the big fish, but rather an infinitesimal minnow. What students need to do in their own ways is to build a structure for their lives that makes college their new home. That structure consists of multiple ties to various members of the college community—groups of friends, individual friends, counselors, and advisers. It includes affiliations to institutions within the college community, such as clubs, teams, church, and academic departments. Beyond these lie ties to the world at large: to the town and its people, through friendships you initiate yourself; to your home, through newspapers and contact with your family and friends; and to the more distant world, through newspapers, magazines, and contact with dignitaries visiting the campus. By taking the initiative to establish these ties and by making use of the second structural device—a schedule that helps you manage your time—you can create a college life that has meaning, continuity, and joy.

Saturday Night
In the 1940s, there was a song entitled "Saturday Night Is the Loneliest Night of the Week." College students do not have much worry about the message of that song today. There are many diversions for them on Saturday night, and on other nights as well. However, some of the more harmful diversions need to be considered before freshman week. Decisions about sex, drugs, and alcohol are challenges that freshmen face in their first weeks of college life. Some of these decisions will not be easy to make, for the peer pressure in these three areas can be extremely strong. Most freshmen will quite naturally want to belong and will find it hard to take a moral stand on sex or drugs or liquor. They fear that their reluctance to get along by going along might ostracize them from their newfound friends. What you need to realize is that feeling lonely makes you vulnerable, and when you are vulnerable you can be forced into behavior that often hurts others as well as yourself. So respect yourself and your values. Combat the pressures of loneliness with self-esteem and adopt a reasonable position toward the differing attitudes of others.

Sexual pressures
One of the pressures and unreasonable attitudes students encounter will certainly be sexual. With the restraints of parental presence and community awareness removed, the opportunity for full sexual relations

between a young man and a young woman perplexes and upsets many college freshmen. It often paralyzes their efforts to excel academically and athletically, and it sometimes fractures already tenuous relations with families back home. Social scientists believe that the high divorce rate among the parents of students has produced considerable instability in the lives of some college freshmen. Many students form strong bonds with another young person as a means of compensating for difficulties at home, not to mention those at college itself.

Still others feel terribly ostracized and isolated by the sexual intimacy between their college classmates. Strong religious feelings, common sense, and just plain fear of the unknown make a sizable proportion of college freshmen reluctant to engage in what may seem to be the thing to do.

The sexual freedom on most college campuses today derives support from contemporary culture. The value placed on individual freedom to choose a partner combines with that placed on the privacy of interpersonal relationships to produce a new sexual morality, quite different from that we might have read about in the last century, or even in the 1940s. The new morality holds that sex is nobody's business but that of the two people involved. It is a natural act between consenting adults, it is said, and should be free from any institutional restrictions and any moral objection by outsiders. So it is that deans of freshmen and writers of books such as this are cautious when broaching this sensitive subject. Still, a few simple words of advice may prove helpful:

1) Consult the medical staff when you have questions about your sexual activity. Do not try to work out your problems alone. The student health center staff is committed to complete confidentiality in its dealings with you. You may also wish to seek out a member of the counseling staff or a member of the chaplain's staff. Make sure that the adviser you turn to is an adult who is trained to discuss your situation with you in a professional and helpful way.

2) Attend any seminars offered on date rape and AIDS. College students are not immune from either.

3) Consider sex as a part of a relationship, not as a game. In contemporary culture, sex is often considered a function of achievement rather than an attribute of intimacy. If sex becomes a part of your life, let it be the result of a relationship incorporating genuine intimacy rather than a passing fancy. The watchword here is *object*. If you feel that you are being made an object in a sexual relationship, then that relationship is undoubtedly an unhealthy one. For instance, if you approach a relationship with sex in the forefront of your mind and measure that relationship by the amount of sex it provides, then the chances are you are treating your sexual partner as an object—someone from whom you obtain gratification. (Until very recently, women were the primary victims of such "objectification," but college deans and

health center personnel have reported recently that young men are experiencing a similar sort of treatment.)

The chances are that victims of such treatment will realize their predicament soon enough. At that point the basis of the relationship should definitely be discussed by the two people involved, and perhaps with a counselor. Often the treatment of one partner as an object results in the failure of the couple to enjoy the sexual experience itself.

Another sign that a relationship is too heavily sexual and exploitative is a lack of intimacy and spontaneity. If sex becomes routine and emotionally flat, then it is a sign for the couple to seriously consider the basis of the relationship.

4) Promiscuity invariably signals sexual difficulty and the inability to establish normal social relationships. Be aware of this danger sign. Observers of freshman classes can often identify a small group of men and women who seek to define their social roles in terms of their sexual activity. They sleep around randomly, often hurting themselves and others in the process. Occasionally their partners take the relationship seriously and suffer when they are left behind. These promiscuous people, too, reach the end of their "tour" at some point in the year and begin to look back at the trail of broken relationships left behind. As they contemplate their behavior, guilt wells up, along with the realization that they have had no serious and caring relationships. When the burden of guilt becomes intolerable, these unhappy students find their way to a counselor or chaplain.

College freshmen should consider their sexual behavior as an adjunct to developing serious and caring adult relationships. If they find themselves unable to sympathize with other people in relationships or to care about what happens to them—in short, if they are able to think only about themselves and their own gratification—they should consider seeking advice from a counselor.

One final fact reflects the complexity and frustrating challenges of sexual relationships among college undergraduates. Observers of colleges around the country have noticed that in small coeducational dormitories, students prefer to live together as brothers and sisters rather than as sexual partners. This pattern results from conscious and voluntary decisions by the students themselves and suggests that many have learned through hard experience that the intimacy and privacy required by a sexual affair are best separated from the place where they live and study.

One last suggestion: if you feel that you are not ready for sexual intimacy and all that it entails, do not be afraid to assert your independence and your point of view. Remember that a lot of sexual behavior exists primarily in the imaginations of outside observers and braggarts. Lots of people are not as sexually active as they say they are. Yet their exaggerated tales of conquest and ecstasy obscure the many quiet and sensible decisions of college students who limit their sexual activity, preferring serious, sensitive, and enduring relationships instead.

Drugs on Campus

Most college freshmen will have confronted the drug issue before entering college. They will already know that drug use permeates our society, from the playground to the Super Bowl, from the classroom to the boardroom, from the back alley to the penthouse. Drugs are a part of everyday American life.

College students need to realize that however innocent drugs may appear, even if used in moderation, they ultimately have a profound effect, altering personality and impairing motivation and performance.

Undergraduates today have to live with the drug question on a daily basis. Like it or not, drugs are always there. Students cannot withdraw from the issue as they could in high school. There is frequently no sanctuary in a college dormitory, no place to hide when the joints come out. And, too, the peer pressure to engage in casual drug use will probably be greater than it was in high school, since everyone is new and anxious to be accepted and to form social relationships in the strange and novel college environment. A few general comments may prove helpful:

1) In the first week of college life, avoid drifting toward groups that are obviously engaged in heavy drug use. These people may well be upperclass students who are undoubtedly unhappy. Their heavy involvement will tend to isolate you and them from the community at large, and this isolation runs exactly counter to what you want to achieve in the first few weeks—exposure to various people, groups, and activities.

2) If you find that your own drug use is confining you to one particular group, that you are not meeting new people, and that you are avoiding "straight" people, then you know that you have to make some rapid changes in your drug use and in your friends.

3) If you have questions about drug use or how to handle roommates or hallmates who are involved with drugs, seek counseling. Trust someone to advise you about how to proceed. Do not try to handle drug-related problems yourself. If there is heavy use or dealing on your hall, consult with a member of the dean's office. Your discussion will be totally confidential and supportive. Furthermore, the deans or the counseling staff in the health center will not normally initiate punitive measures against any students you mention. Their method of helping those students will also be private and confidential. They will endeavor to give counsel and help the students to reduce their use of drugs. At the same time they will honor the privacy of their relationship with you, so that the rights of all are protected.

College deans and counselors realize that drug use is a part of college life, and normally they do not take a narrow moral stand on it. They do, however, react strongly to students who push drugs.

Many schools have specific counseling programs or clinics for students who become involved with drug use, and they are justly proud of their ability to influence students to look beneath their drug consumption to discover the problems that may be causing it. The heightened personal awareness that many students gain from talking about drugs with counselors invariably translates into a greater awareness of how their college education can help them to cope with the challenges of living in our complex and competitive society.

Drinking on Campus

Our consideration of Saturday night cannot end without a discussion of liquor. Astute observers of the college scene today may disagree on many matters, but they tend to come together on the subject of alcohol abuse. Alcohol poses a serious problem for many students, and college officials are concerned. Many colleges, such as Stanford and Cornell, have specific programs to make students aware of the perils of alcoholism. Boston University has taken steps to limit the amount of alcohol a student may bring into a dormitory on a given night. Other colleges do not yet have complete programs. (One book to consult is *Peterson's Drug and Alcohol Programs and Policies at Four-Year Colleges.*)

For most students, the problem of alcohol begins with an erroneous assumption: you drink to get drunk, or close to it. Students may see their parents drink in moderation at home, yet they themselves do not always adopt similar restraint. Released from the restrictions of family, concerned about the awesome academic and social challenges of college, and under pressure from peers, many college students learn through bitter experience that alcohol is a real liability and that alcoholism is not a disease confined solely to middle-aged advertising executives and bored housewives.

College freshmen should realize that alcohol is a depressant. The morning after is not just a headache; it may also be a time for sorrow. Damaged property can be repaired but damaged friendships cannot, nor is it possible to calculate the missed opportunities for friendship—that is, the friends you might have made if you had been able to communicate. The following advice may help reasonable college freshmen handle the difficult question of alcohol use during the critical early weeks of college:

1) It is all right to say no. You should avoid situations in which you drink solely to conform. If you are not comfortable with alcohol, say so and stick with soft drinks. Both your weight and your peace of mind will benefit.

2) If you do elect to drink, remember that alcohol is a drug and a depressant. The temporary "high" you feel after the first one or two drinks

will ultimately be replaced by a "low" later on in the evening or the next day.

3) Keep count of the number of drinks you are having. Remember that it takes the body at least one hour to eliminate 1.5 ounces of whiskey or 12 ounces of beer or 4 ounces of wine. Pace yourself accordingly.

4) Avoid falling victim to the popular misconceptions that surround alcohol use, such as that eating a big meal will curtail the effects of drinking. A large amount of food in the stomach merely delays the absorption of the alcohol; it is not a defense against the effects. Another misconception is that beer and wine are less harmful or intoxicating than whiskey or gin. Similarly, fresh air and/or coffee will do little to reduce the effects of excessive alcohol consumption. The best solution is moderation or abstention.

5) Discuss any incidence of alcoholism in your family with a member of the health center staff. Studies have shown that the children of alcoholic parents are particularly prone to psychological difficulties themselves. Their sense of reality is frequently affected by their experience, their self-esteem is impaired, and they sometimes are more impulsive and crave more attention than their peers. Because they fear abandonment, they often drink in order to belong and so fall heir to their parents' alcoholic legacy (Janet Geringer Woititz, *Adult Children of Alcoholics*. Health Communications, Inc., 1983). Trained counselors can help you explore the implications of family alcoholism and avoid harming yourself.

Our society respects those who can hold their liquor, not those who get drunk and make fools of themselves. Holding your liquor means having less than you might like to have, less than you might be able to tolerate, and less than your peers. It also means that you can emerge from a party in pretty good shape, able to make your own way home, to think clearly, to drive safely, and to converse rationally and happily with others. It may mean having less alcohol, but it does not mean having a less happy time than everyone else. Quite the reverse. Controlling your alcoholic intake allows you to focus on the social life at a party or dance or concert, to enjoy the humor, the artistry, and the companionship of an occasion, and so to expand the circle of your college friends and enrich your education. It will ensure that you have a good time, too.

Parents

The pressures of Saturday night, of the Big Fish in the Big Pond syndrome, and of the enormous amount of free time have an impact on the parents of students, as well as on the students themselves. College freshmen should realize that "freshmanitis" is a communicable disease, and parents may become upset by their child's confusion and complaints. Often the frustrations of the freshman year lead students to talk about leaving college in November and December. This meets with strong

199

disapproval from parents, who argue that their children ought to get on with their education. The result is that a valuable support system, the family, may fail to function, and unhappiness can follow for all parties.

A few guidelines for communication between students and their parents will help the family play a positive and even crucial role in helping students adjust to college life:

1) Keep the lines of communication open. Being away from home, perhaps for the first time, should not mean that you drop all contact with your family, feigning independence. A weekly call or letter will keep your parents informed of your activities and your concerns. Show that you still care about your parents and other family members at home.

   Also, plan to show your parents some examples of your college work and discuss how you are performing, so that they know what is going on and can offer their advice occasionally.

2) Parents should realize that colleges are shifting the burden of education from the institution to the individual and that this is a totally new experience for the child. Young people who have been used to parental direction (and protection!) up to this point in their lives are now somewhat exposed and frightened at having to make decisions for themselves. Parents should empathize with this fear and try to help their children formulate the questions they should be asking of professors, advisers, and peers so they can begin to find answers for themselves.

   Parents should also understand that constantly exhorting their children to get to work will probably not achieve the desired result. Rather they should adopt the position of a sympathetic listener who can help the child discover the sources of assistance that are available and the options that present themselves.

3) Finally, both parents and students should realize that the trials and tribulations of the freshman year are short-lived. They should temper their reactions to problems with the knowledge that most crises are probably transitory. Matriculation statistics show that over 90 percent of freshmen graduate with their class four years later, and an even higher percentage of students obtain degrees five or six years after entering college.

4) In their attempts to help their children achieve independence, parents should not forget to show their ongoing love and concern. Care packages full of favorite things express this nicely.

More About Roommates

Some words of advice have already been offered on the question of selecting, and making initial overtures of friendship to, roommates. Now, in the first days of the freshman year, comes the next stage in that crucial relationship:

1) Sit down with your roommate or roommates during the first day that

you are together. Take time to get to know each other. Then turn to the important issues that you as a group must resolve. Begin by deciding where everyone will sleep, where people will study, and where they will socialize. Discuss the need for individual privacy as it applies to the activities of the other people living in the room(s). Try to agree on certain nights for social occasions and other nights for privacy and study. Make up a calendar and note down what has been agreed. For example, Sunday, Monday, and Tuesday nights from 7 p.m. until bedtime might be designated as study nights, and Wednesday and Saturday nights as social nights. During study nights, stereos are not to be played if other roommates are present. Come to some agreement on the noise level of stereos, and assign periods of quiet time when stereos are not to be played at all. Earphones, of course, are fine. Next, discuss items of personal property that can be shared by roommates and those that are not to be borrowed. Don't try to be a good sport and share all your possessions. Retain for your own use those things that mean a lot to you. If you don't respect your own property enough to designate it as off-limits, then it will probably become the property of everyone in the room and even the dormitory before long. Be candid, so that each person in the room can know, and let others know, where he or she stands. This will be important later on. If there are cleaning responsibilities that go with your housing arrangement, make a roster indicating who cleans what when, incorporate the roster with the overall schedule, and post it in a prominent place.

2) Institute some kind of decision-making procedure for activities that will occur in the room or for problems that may arise. Do nights designated for study mean that roommates may bring in friends who claim that they want to study? Or are study hours private—just for the inhabitants of the room? What will be the policy for overnight guests? Of the same sex? Of the opposite sex? You need to resolve as many of these matters as possible now; you also need to agree on how to resolve similar questions that will come up later.

3) Act quickly when there is a minor infraction of the agreed-upon rules of the room. Don't let the incident go by. Discuss it with your roommate the next day, seeking a clear understanding for the future. Tolerance is a virtue, but personal initiative may sometimes necessitate speaking out when unexpected problems arise.

For students who do not wish to engage in a long dialogue with their potential roommates but who do want some order in their lives, most colleges offer alternative living arrangements on request. Freshmen who want to accomplish a fair amount of studying in a reasonably quiet environment should consider making an inquiry to the dean's office during the summer. Most colleges have single-sex dormitories or dorms with certain rules of behavior that are enforced by a dorm committee and a house counselor. Some colleges allow students to have their own apartments off campus.

On the other hand, students who plan to live in a regular dormitory situation should try to work out their arrangements with their roommates in the first day or so of school. They should not plan to play it by ear, hoping that if the unexpected or the outrageous happens they can get solutions from the dean's office. When roommates are getting on each other's nerves in October and hour exams loom ahead, deans cannot simply push magic buttons and make the world right again. It is the responsibility of the occupants of each room to construct a series of sensible compromises so that they can live together reasonably and happily, in both fair weather and foul.

4) Find a quiet and secure place to study so that you do not have to depend on your roommates for peace and quiet. This alternate location can be the library, a dorm known to be quiet, a classroom, a department library or laboratory, or a quiet place where you work part-time.

If all these suggestions fail to provide you with a stable and productive rooming situation, remember that the college has a support structure to which you can turn for advice. Your resident adviser can help significantly if he or she is sensitive and interested in the spirit of the dormitory. Chaplains and deans of freshmen can also cast light on complex and unhappy relationships between roommates. Sometimes members of the student health staff can assist. Don't be afraid to take the first step; use your intelligence and keep your sense of humor, and you will survive and prosper.

Race Relations

"Race relations" is a term used here to describe relationships between the majority community of white students and the minority communities of black, Hispanic, Native American, and Asian students in a collegiate setting. There are also a variety of other minority groups in any broadly representative college community—women, athletes, musicians, gays, not to mention the various groups of ethnic Americans—but here we are concerned with minority as defined by race and the tensions that exist between the white majority and the minority racial groups.

Since the late 1960s, colleges and universities around the country have striven to increase the representation of the important racial minorities in their student populations. In response to growing social awareness, governmental encouragement, and a genuine concern for a democratic society, colleges and universities have made enormous progress in attracting, retaining, and educating members of racial groups that had previously been excluded from the mainstream of American education. Although tensions still exist and much needs to be done to improve the quality of race relations at many schools, few other countries have come so far in so short a time.

Because of this progress, minority freshmen will probably not encounter any outright situations of deliberate discrimination at most American colleges today. These students will, however, have to be mindful that residual prejudice may still exist in spite of the good intentions of students, teachers, and administrators. They will have to face the fact that inequities still linger and will have to work with leaders of the majority population to change them. Minority students may find that their college curriculum contains few courses about their group's history and development. They may find only a few members of their own race represented on the faculty or the administration of the college. Black students, the largest of the minority groups, may find no department of black studies overseeing the exploration of their cultural past. What they will find, however, is an openness to their ideas and interests on the part of college administrators and teachers.

Whites will find that their previous experience with minorities in high school may not translate readily to the collegiate situation. Most white students will have attended high schools where they were in an overwhelming majority. In college they may find 10 to 20 percent of their class composed of people of black, Asian, Hispanic, and Native American descent. Moreover, both minority and majority groups will now have to live together on a 24-hour-a-day basis. In high school, different groups lived in different neighborhoods, but that no longer applies. Students who formerly may have had no contact with those outside their group will necessarily have to develop relationships now. All freshmen will need to examine their own feelings about race and make their own exploration of race relations an integral part of their education.

Members of minority and majority communities approach the question of race relations from different vantage points. On questions of social relations, whites may wonder at the need for the exclusive, racially based membership of, say, a black students league or a Native American club. They may take exception to their exclusion from some social affairs put on by minority groups. Minority students may counter that they often congregate at meals and form their own clubs to kindle relationships with other members of their group and to support each other. They say they have no antipathy for the white community, with whom they have daily and frequent contact in classes, in sports, and around campus. Some Asian students may tend to internalize their feelings and stick to compatriots who share the same code, arguing that public behavior should be restrained and reasonable. No particular group response is "right." Tensions are bound to exist.

As they cope with these tensions, college freshmen of every race should consider the following bits of advice:

1) Avoid thinking in stereotypes about members of your own racial community or about members of communities other than your own. Take people on their own merits, as you find them. Avoid plugging people into preconceived categories. To think someone said or did some-

thing *because* of his or her racial background is to rely on a mental stereotype. To do so is unkind, simplistic, and, in the end, anti-intellectual. As such, it runs counter to the purpose of the education for which you have come to college.

2) Avoid assuming a pose, just because you think it will help you win friends and simplify the complex questions of racial interaction for the moment. Assuming the pose of a ghetto Chicano when you are in fact the well-educated daughter of a Mexican-American dentist merely obscures the challenge of meeting your brothers and sisters honestly and helping them to relate to members of the white middle-class community, with which you may be more familiar.

3) Avoid separatism; it only reinforces prejudice and eliminates communication. If you are moving only with members of your own racial group—to classes, to meals, and to various social activities—then you are succumbing to peer pressure and accepting social barriers that someone else has erected to imprison you.

   Observers have noticed that separatism along racial lines is occasionally a subtle way in which minority college students force others of their race to submit to their will. The ultimate test of separatism involves your friends: if all your friends are from one particular racial group, then you have failed to realize an important goal of your college education.

4) Avoid humorous attempts to harmonize race relations. These can be taken the wrong way and can perpetuate stereotyping. Leave such humor to the professionals, lest it unintentionally fracture the delicate bond among the races at your college.

5) Acquaint yourself with the grievance procedure for racial incidents at your college. If you have a question about the suitability of a paper's topic, a possibly prejudiced remark made by a professor, or a college policy such as separate orientation for minority freshmen, then ask the appropriate authority about it. You owe this to yourself. You will probably be satisfied with the answer you receive, but if you are not, then use the grievance procedure. Do not harbor your personal grievance, feeding your own prejudice. Trust in the good intentions and real commitment of university officials, who want to see inequities, however slight, corrected and justice done.

6) Seriously consider taking in your first two years of college at least one course that has to do with intercultural relations. If the goal of a college education is to gain a greater understanding of oneself in relation to the world at large, then it is both logical and necessary to take a course that probes the ways in which persons of different racial groups relate to each other. If a person completing a college education in America today has managed to do so without seriously contemplating racial and ethnic relationships within our society, then that

person is not adequately prepared to assume a position of leadership in this society.

Security

Except for the small rural colleges, most institutions of higher education today have what are politely called security problems. For the most part, these problems center on theft of personal belongings and occasional acts of vandalism to university property. Yet there are more insidious crimes, too. Students coming to a collegiate environment for the first time should take precautions for their personal safety as well as for the protection of their personal property.

As far as personal safety is concerned, most schools issue pamphlets containing easy-to-follow advice. Some simple, common-sense rules:

1) Acquaint yourself with security mechanisms in your dormitory and in the areas you travel frequently. These may include ordinary telephones, special phones, and alarms. It is a good idea to familiarize yourself with shuttle bus routes and their hours of operation. Some schools offer an escort service for journeys that students might have to make late at night. Use all the security systems available to you.

2) When you decide to explore some unfamiliar area, do so with a friend, especially if it is at night. Find a friend to make a late-evening excursion for a pizza with. Don't go alone. If circumstances oblige you to cross unfamiliar territory and you are frightened, call the university police and ask for a ride to your destination. If you are embarrassed by this, don't be. Remember that the university police want to help you, and, besides, the university police force is really one of the many services for which you pay.

As far as personal property goes, you should operate on the principle that you will not take to college more than you can afford to lose. If you have a treasured ten-speed bike or a fancy stereo or a personal computer, leave them at home. Buy second-hand equipment, and perhaps when it is worn out in a few years you will be in a secure living situation where you can bring your more expensive equipment from home. Consider leasing equipment on which the lessor pays the insurance. Again some simple rules:

1) Insure your personal belongings. They can often be added to your family's homeowner's policy.

2) Mark your personal belongings with your driver's license number. Special pens and marking tools are easily procured from the university police. Some dormitories have them as standard equipment.

3) Register your stereos, bikes, computers, typewriters, and other equipment with the appropriate authority at the college. Make a list of the items you value, briefly describing each item—color, model number, and serial number. Keep a copy of the list for yourself. Make sure that

your college address and phone number, as well as your home address and phone number, are on the list.

4) Lock the door to your room, even when you are away for only a few minutes. If this gets to be bothersome, at least observe the practice on weekends and before vacation breaks. Would-be thieves invariably descend when students are leaving the campus and when they can take advantage of confusion in a dormitory.

5) If you see unfamiliar people in the dormitory, especially alone in another student's room, ask to see their identification. This may sound obnoxious, but unless students take some responsibility for their own security, the whole system is jeopardized.

6) Bicycles present a special problem for college students. Always lock your bicycle to an immovable object, such as a rack, tree, or fence. Put the lock through at least one wheel and the frame. If you are using a padlock and can lock it through the sprocket, that is even better, as it will make it impossible for a thief to ride the bike off, even after the chain is cut. Leave your bicycle in well-lighted and well-traveled areas. If space permits, keep the bike in your room.

As much as college officials hate to admit it, a considerable amount of theft on campus is committed by students, some say up to 40 percent. Therefore if students abide by these simple suggestions and maintain an atmosphere of security consciousness, those who would otherwise steal will probably be deterred. Remember that a little common sense exercised in the interest of personal safety and the protection of personal property does not connote cowardice or total distrust of one's fellow man. It merely acknowledges that there are enormous advantages to living in a cosmopolitan and open environment, and security precautions are a small price to pay for these benefits.

Grade Frenzy

One does not have to be a college freshman to know that in American colleges today there is intense concern about career preparation. This has led to a virtual fixation on making good grades in order to gain admission to graduate and professional schools. Grade frenzy touches every college freshman in one form or another, yet it is to be avoided if at all possible. You should arrange to discuss course preparation for your chosen career with your adviser. Find out what the potential role of grades is in your admission to graduate school or the world of work. Try to give breadth to your course of study. For some of your course selections, choose fields you know nothing about but are nonetheless intrigued by. Don't avoid academic challenges just because you fear failure and the harsh judgment of a graduate school admissions committee. Many courses can be taken on a pass-fail basis, and the further such courses lie from the path of your major, the more appropriate it is to opt for pass-fail. Medical school committees are not going to be alarmed that you took music theory as a pass-fail course, or that you got a C in art history. Do your experimenting in the first two years of college so that if you happen to do less than well, your record for the last two years will clearly demonstrate your ability in your chosen field.

To avoid becoming a victim of grade frenzy yourself, watch for the following danger signs:

1) If you find yourself working on successive Saturday nights, it probably means either that you are too concerned about grades or that you are not planning your work efficiently. Discuss the situation with your adviser.

2) If you are beginning to lose your friends because you say you have to study and cannot join them for meals or socializing, then it is time to reassess your situation. Making friends and socializing are integral parts of your college education. You are crippling yourself if you can't keep old friends and make new ones and still get your work done.

3) If you are tempted to do something that you know is academically dishonest—such as copying another student's results, lifting an idea for a paper without crediting the source, or, worse, cheating on an exam—then you are already in the clutches of grade frenzy. You need to take a break. Discuss your situation with an adviser or friend. Try to relax.

4) If you reach the point where you are unable to carry on a major outside activity because of the urgency of academic studies, then you have also arrived at the edge of grade frenzy. Pull back. Maintain your outside activity. Remember that one of the main reasons for pursuing an extracurricular activity is that it provides perspective. If you find that you can no longer maintain your activity, then it has probably been serving that express purpose, i.e., acting as a check on overcommitment to your studies.

Finally, ponder the system of grading itself. Excessive emphasis on grades by students, faculty, and graduate admissions committees often reduces the whole educational process to this one standard of measurement. Too great an emphasis here teaches students that the whole process of graduate school admissions is a game of high grades and that creativity and experimentation have only a minor role to play. Be assured that discerning graduate schools recognize the breadth of your course selection, the variety of your extracurricular activities, and the value of your summer jobs and travel, not to mention other indications of the vitality and maturity of your personality. But even if they didn't, you should recognize and respect exploration for its own sake and not succumb to the frantic quest for grades.

A thoughtful and popular Dartmouth physics professor, Elisha R. Huggins, addressed the problem of grade frenzy at the end of his fall 1976 final exam:

Normally at this time in the course I pass out a questionnaire to see how students feel about various parts of the course. This time I am going to reverse the process and instead explain my feelings about the Physics 3–4 students.

Academically this was an outstanding class. In about eight years teaching these courses I have not seen such consistently good performance on tests and such a high level of quality on projects. And on an individual basis there were a number of students who showed considerable originality and enthusiasm and were extremely enjoyable to work with.

My main comments, however, are reserved for the majority (but not all) of the premedical students in the class who are sacrificing too much of their own personality and life toward the goal of admission to medical school. You know what kind of a distortion this has caused in your attitude toward courses and other opportunities here at Dartmouth.

I am aware of the pressures that medical school admissions policies cause, their overemphasis on and distorted use of grades and lack of appreciation of human understanding. However, this is not the first time you will face a screwed-up system, and life is too short to take it as seriously as you have done this year. It is possible to get into a habit of taking everything so seriously that you can never break away and see why it is worth living.

My comment is to let up a bit, look around at the opportunities that you have now and in the next couple of years at Dartmouth, and if you do not break through the med school barricade, to hell with them. I can tell you that there are a lot better things in life than being an overly serious, uptight doctor.

Afterword

An anonymous author once remarked that "history is the moral compass that must guide us in the future." The same could be said of college education. Your four years in college will be critical to the life that follows, and you should look on them with respect and excitement. You are going to college to train your mind. You are going to learn to communicate with others, orally and in writing, which requires listening to them as well. You are also going to college to hone your sense of what is right and good for the society you will enter. Douglas Heath, the widely known psychology professor at Haverford College, has suggested that most of the crucial decisions we face in life are based on subjective value judgments. They involve balancing what our training may show us is practical and feasible against what our sense of morality shows us is desirable for the people who will be affected by our decisions. In his study of a highly successful group of alumni, as rated by their professional colleagues, Heath found that their outstanding quality was ethical integrity.

It is important for all college freshmen to consider how they will sharpen their moral values and develop their strengths as human beings so that, as adults and operating members of society, they will be able to persuade others of the rightness of their decisions.

The college experience embraces both self-discovery and academic training. It is essential that freshmen put aside both the myth that college days are filled with freedom and joy, and the worry that they merely consist of one trauma after another. The college experience is, rather, one of exploration, of growth, of change, and of success, mixed with brief periods of frustration, unhappiness, and even pain. Students must be sure that they confront those frustrations and try to "own the pain" as well as the joy, for if they do, they will discover themselves in the process. Put another way, they need to relate what is learned to their own values to make education serve them in the way it should.

Many years ago, William Lyon Phelps, the eminent professor at Yale, put it this way:

> I know of no greater fallacy, nor one more widely believed in, than the statement that youth is the happiest time of life. As we advance in years, we grow happier [only] if we live intelligently. The universe is spectacular, and it is a free show. Difficulties and responsibilities strengthen and enrich the mind. To live abundantly is like climbing

a mountain or a tower. To say that youth is happier than maturity is like saying that the view from the bottom of the tower is better than the view from the top. As we ascend, the range of our view widens. The horizon is pushed farther away. Finally, as we reach the summit, it is as if we had the world at our feet.

With the tribulations and the joys of this ascent firmly in mind, you are ready to begin your college education.